CHRISTIANITY
IN
EVOLUTION

CHRISTIANITY
IN
EVOLUTION

Discovering the Harmony of Science and Faith

RALPH H.
ARMSTRONG

With a foreword by
THE RIGHT REVEREND
J. JON BRUNO
Episcopal Bishop of Los Angeles

CATHEDRAL CENTER PRESS
LOS ANGELES

ALSO BY
RALPH ARMSTRONG

CHRISTIANITY AND CHANGE:
STEPS TO GROWTH AND HEALING IN CHRISTIAN COUNSELING
1990 Sheed and Ward, Kansas City, Missouri

BT
712
.A76
2011

ISBN: 978-0-9827584-1-0

Cathedral Center Press
An imprint of the Episcopal Diocese of Los Angeles
840 Echo Park Avenue
Los Angeles, CA 90026
www.ladiocese.org

Linda Gray, copy editor
Molly Ruttan-Moffat, book design & production
Regal Printing Ltd., Hong Kong

www.christianityinevolution.com

TO MY WIFE, KAY,
AND TO LUKE, YVONNE, JESSE, AND DANNY

TO ALL FAMILIES
EVERYWHERE

TO ALL OF EARTH'S PEOPLES,
THAT THEY MAY KNOW THE FAMILY OF ALL OF LIFE

CONTENTS

PART ONE

**An Interpretation of the Science of Life's Complexity,
Agency, Evolution, and Conflict**

PART TWO

Evolving Christianity and the Redemption of Life in Conflict

ACKNOWLEDGMENTS

This work stems from the myriad teachers and writers from whom I have learned, both in my journey of faith and in my medical and writing careers. But personal mentors deserve special mention. When I was a second-year medical student at UCLA, I was blessed to meet the Rev. S. Dunham Wilson, an Episcopal priest. A skilled pastoral counselor, he was a student of W. Earl Biddle, a devout Catholic Christian psychiatrist who thought and wrote originally at a time when Sigmund Freud's Oedipus complex was the party line to which most psychiatrists adhered. After Fr. Wilson's counsel had set me on firmer footing, we spent literally hundreds of hours poring over my cases, considering each from scriptural, pastoral, and psychiatric perspectives. The whole seven-year period was a profoundly in-depth theological education.

In the realms of schools of psychiatry and psychotherapy, I first thank the hypnotist-psychiatrist Milton Erickson and then Paul Wazslawick and other members of the Mental Research Institute in Palo Alto, who taught me the importance and dynamics of community and human communication. I learned from the psychoanalyst James Masterson the intricacies of personality, including forgiveness. From Anthony Bateman and Peter Fonagy, I picked up the idea of the agentive self and, later, the critical importance of mentalization in human discourse. Last, I consider personal psychotherapies with Milton Erickson, gestalt therapist Jerry Greenwald, and psychoanalyst Ronald Blanchette formative theological experiences of the first order and critical to my own evolution.

In the realms of biology and evolution, Darrel Falk, geneticist and professor of biology at Point Loma Nazarene University focused me and kept me from straying into fruitless avenues. Richard Colling, professor of biology at Olivet Nazarene University, critiqued and refined my thinking. The Dutch biochemist and Anglican priest Sjoerd Bonting; Larry Myers, M.D., professor of neurology at UCLA; and Richard Deonier, professor of computational biology at USC, offered priceless opinion. The Very Reverend Jerome Kahler, rector of St. Paul's Episcopal Church, Ventura, California, and Michael Rhodes, Hollywood director, executive producer of *Romero* and winner of five Emmys, gave detailed theological and artistic guidance.

Finally, many thanks to Linda Gray, whose editorial expertise and advice regarding content rendered the manuscript immeasurably more readable. The Rt. Rev J. Jon Bruno, bishop of the Episcopal Diocese of Los Angeles, and Bob Williams and graphic designer Molly Ruttan-Moffat of Cathedral Center Press gave invaluable support throughout the publishing process. My daughter Yvonne Könneker, a former editor for Sage Publications, was always helpful. Stephanie Ivans, Bill Knutson, Diane Rhodes, and Roxanne Vettese read the manuscript and offered valuable input. Last but not least, I thank my wife Kay, who has been my constant companion throughout this journey.

Ultimately, I thank the Most High for the Presence and incessant dialogue that underlie all learning, understanding, and creativity, including mine.

— *Ralph H. Armstrong,*
March 2011

FOREWORD

by the Right Reverend J.Jon Bruno,
Episcopal Bishop of Los Angeles

Knowing the right questions is sometimes better than knowing the right answers. This dynamic comes to mind as I read this new book written by my longtime friend, the distinguished psychiatrist Ralph Armstrong.

Having known Ralph for some 40 years, going back to our days as parishioners in the same congregation, I well know the faithfulness with which he approaches his relationship with God, his family, his friends, his patients, his practice of medicine, and his field of study. This book is an extension of that faithfulness, attesting, as well, to the value Ralph places on life experienced in community.

That Ralph works so diligently to find the nexus of science, compassion, creation, and faith is very much part of his own DNA. The space he allows for mystery—and, indeed, for the questions—is a reminder to us, his readers, to do likewise. Similar advice comes from the poet Rainer Maria Rilke: "Live your questions now, and perhaps even without knowing it, you will live along some distant day into your answers."

In this same spirit, it is so important for each of us to ask and to discover who we are and to Whom we belong. Ralph is an exemplar on this path as he calls us to dig deeply not only into science but also into the presence of the Holy—finding God's own Breath, *Ruach*, as a creative force in our lives.

Again, it is Ralph's faithfulness to life's questions that makes me most glad for his partnership with Cathedral Center Press in publishing this book; would that all of us demonstrate such a commitment to finding the Holy in our midst. Some scientists, and perhaps some theologians too, may not agree with the hypotheses that Ralph offers in these pages. Be that as it may, the bottom line is that Ralph's work does much to engage age-old topics of inquiry and to help us, his friends and readers, live more fully not only the questions but also the holy lives to which God calls us.

I close here with a recent communication I received from Ralph:

Christianity in Evolution derives from a close reading of evolution a worldview that Life has participated in its own adaptations through its agency, its exercise of intelligence, and learning. Life proves to strategize and through its educated guesses is able to build, albeit over eons of time, its intelligences and the nervous systems from which intelligence emerges. Intelligence, however, is not just a property of individual creatures but emerges from the collective actions of hierarchies of cells, networks, and populations. Life is community. The resulting worldview is that of a biosphere unimaginably diverse, complex, and beautiful.

Life has created myriad creatures who successfully occupy one niche or another, but it is in humankind that Life has perfected intelligence. In fact, *Homo sapiens* has perhaps dozens of intelligences, but the apogee is the one that enables us to live in community. That is, we, of all the animals, are best able to love. The intelligence underlying love is called mentalization. That is, we have evolved the capability to read each other, to relate mind to mind, to see ourselves from the outside and others from the inside, to grasp the needs of others, and the capacity to meet those needs out of compassion for the other. This capacity, undeveloped in each of us, is an enormous potential.

Does all this beauty, complexity, and intelligence stem from living forms that are basically mechanical, or is there something more to Life? Could it be that it is the *Ruach*, the Breath of the Mighty God, that ultimately animates us? Could it be that the *Ruach* is the source of all Life, intelligence, and our ability to read each other and hence to love one another? Life is either utterly material and mechanical or it is animated by the Breath of God. To hold an opinion about this statement is to make an assumption, a leap of faith. Unfortunately, for many there is only one answer, and in their opinion to think otherwise is delusion. A conflict.

In fact, the elephant in the room is conflict. The community of all Life is shattered by conflict, war, predator, and prey and in humankind shows up as indifference, resentment, revenge, and malevolence. The beautiful capacity to mentalize, to listen to each other, to understand each other, and to act compassionately is overwhelmed and buried. All this is self-evident. The Life that God has lent to us is under siege. And this conflict is not skin-deep; it extends down to Life's very molecules.

God is not about to sit back and watch indifferently as Life struggles with itself. He has intervened by coming down and walking among us, living and dying as one of us. In doing so, he declares that this conflict-ridden Life is lovable and sacred. Jesus furthermore is the ultimate mentalizer. Adam and Eve, Life's counterparts in Heaven, moved against God, and Life has

followed suit. But Jesus as the new Adam rolls with
our resistance, and in doing so initiates the restoration of
community. Following his example of devotion to the Father
and his understanding and meeting the needs of others,
inspired by his Spirit, we build on that restoration.

At St. Paul's in Ventura, we have had a priest who for 22
years has consistently preserved the integrity of our parish
community. As a result, we have gradually come to love
each other, to respect and accept each other—die-hard
Republicans and liberal Democrats and all the other
potential factions one can think of that could quite quickly
lead to schism. Instead there is a palpable joy, a sense of
Heaven on Earth. The inevitable conflicts of life are
manageable by the grace of God among and within us.

✝ J. JON BRUNO
LOS ANGELES, CALIFORNIA
MARCH 1, 2011

CHRISTIANITY IN EVOLUTION

"What's very dangerous is not to evolve." [1]
—Jeff Bezos, Amazon founder and CEO

She was only 21 years old when I was assigned to take care of her. I was a third-year medical student on the internal medicine ward at UCLA, and this was my first clinical rotation. She was very pretty with an engaging smile and round brown eyes that didn't blink as I fumblingly drew blood from her overpunctured veins. She suffered from a chronic kidney disease, and with end-stage uremia she drifted in and out of delirium. At that time, before kidney transplants or dialysis, such renal disease led inevitably to death. As we gathered around her bed during rounds, even the usually ebullient attending physician was subdued. About three weeks into the rotation, I arrived one morning to find her bed empty and neatly made. She had died during the night.

I wasn't about to weep in front of my classmates, so I ducked into a broom closet and cried. But there was more. I was a new Christian, and death was new to me as well. Her passing confronted me suddenly and forcefully with the age-old question of God's relationship to suffering and death. I raged at God in that closet; it seemed a contradiction—the mighty God and the unjust demise of one of his creations.

Another set of contradictions has surfaced in the last 200 years, as a burgeoning literature in genetics, biology, and evolution has called into question the accuracy of the creation accounts in Genesis. Does a creation from the top-down versus evolution via biological processes pose a contradiction for you or have an impact on your faith? And does the related differing view, the Genesis account of the special creation of humankind, in the face of scientific evidence of our interrelatedness with all creatures, including chimpanzees, trouble you? Do you wonder at just how Christianity can make sense of and relate to the astonishing scientific discoveries of recent times? Do they contradict and falsify Christianity, or do they afford the Faith opportunity for growth? And last, what of the conundrum of an omnipotent, omnicompetent, and holy God and a creation that seems at war with itself?

Two questions run like a contrapuntal Bach fugue through all of these discrepancies. Is God the hands-on creator, the prime mover behind everything, or do the facts of evolution and the imperfections, sufferings, and conflicts of the creation suggest that he works much more subtly and indirectly? God's role in suffering hinges on the answers to these questions. The mystery of the beneficent God and his suffering and conflicted creation as well as the discrepancies between contemporary science and our 2,000-year-old religion have challenged my faith. This has led me to this study, one that embodies close readings of both the Scriptures and the various disciplines that undergird science's illumination of creation—evolution.

Positive and negative interest in evolution among American Christians runs very high. The website religioustolerance.org summarized six Gallup polls conducted from 1982 to 2004, concluding that on average, 45% of Americans believe that God created humankind in its present form within the last 10,000 years. Thirty-eight percent subscribe to a theistic evolution developing over millions of years. The remainder believe in a naturalistic evolution, with God having no part in the process. Some Christians see their daily lives unaffected by whether our existence is the result of evolution or creation, but for many believers (and nonbelievers), the subject of evolution has life or death significance.

As an undergraduate at the Colorado School of Mines, the geology courses, particularly Historical Geology, left me with no doubts about the accuracy of evolution. I am an Episcopalian; as a denomination, we have, for the most part, no problem with evolution, and we approve of the spirit of critical inquiry that so epitomized Charles Darwin. I gave it little thought until much later in life. Through training in medicine, psychiatry, neurology, and addiction medicine, I have been steeped in biological and neuroscience. The exciting scientific breakthroughs in genetics and evolutionary developmental biology have newly challenged Christians to seek a rapprochement, and I have also sensed in these sciences the possibility of resolving the question of God and suffering.

To begin reconciling Christianity, suffering, and evolution, let us look at five major schools that attempt to explain the mysteries of Life's history on Earth: Fowler and Kuebler, in *The Evolution Controversy: A Survey of Competing Theories,* list them as *Creationism, Theistic Evolution, Intelligent Design (ID), Neo-Darwinism,* and *Meta-Darwinism.*[2] Of the five, we will focus on ID and Neo- and Meta-Darwinism, inquiring about how faithful they are to the overall essences of science, the Scriptures, and Christianity.

CREATIONISM AND THEISTIC EVOLUTION

Briefly, *Creationism*, the first school, holds to a literal interpretation of the creation stories in Genesis and deals with the biological and evolutionary sciences by systematically discrediting and denying them. *Theistic Evolution*, the second school, encompasses a heterogeneous group of Christians who are comfortable with both Christianity and evolutionary science, without taking stances on just how the two disciplines relate. Two scientist Christians, Francis Collins[3] and Darrel Falk,[4] are at the vanguard of Theistic Evolution.

INTELLIGENT DESIGN

ID, the third theory of evolution, might be called "Neo-Creationism;" its proponents accept much of the science of evolution but argue that natural forces, particularly natural selection (NS), are unable to account for the creation of much of Life's dazzling complexity. Hence, they claim that certain "irreducibly complex objects" had to be created. The movement argues for the presence of design in the universe by positing that complex organs and systems such as cilia and the blood-clotting system are irreducibly complex. That is, because their unassembled component parts could not function independently, such systems must have been created whole cloth.

ID has focused on the bacterial flagellum (fig. 0.1) as a prime example, arguing that individual protein components would have no function unless most or all were in place. Hence, irreducibly complex and therefore created. However, recent research shows that nearly all the proteins present in the flagellum perform important functions elsewhere in the cell. For example, 10 of the proteins are present in a structure quite similar to the flagellum, the Type III secretion system (shown in fig. 0.1). This structure is a device to inject poison into other cells, making the bacterium virulent.[5] It is evident that diverse bacteria, in the course of their evolution, have built more elaborate flagella through such mechanisms as self-assembly of simple repeating subunits, gene duplication with subsequent modifications, recruitment of elements from other systems, and recombination of genes.[6] A wide variety of bacteria have appropriated old components and assembled them in novel combinations to produce new structures. *Such Lego Block-like rearrangements, or "tinkerings," underlie the remarkable plasticity of living tissue and appear over and over in the genesis of ever more complex living things.*

ID, like Creationism, has tried to defend Christianity from the attacks of a small number of scientists and commentators who insist that Neo-Darwinism (discussed below) invalidates the idea of God as Creator. ID has claimed to be science so that it can be taught in U.S. public schools. However, the courts have ruled against ID's claims. For example, Judge John Jones, a conservative Christian and George W. Bush appointee, ruled in the Dover trial[7] that ID was religion and not science and therefore could not be taught in public schools.[8] In addition, ID and debates about irreducible complexity are "god-of-the-gaps"

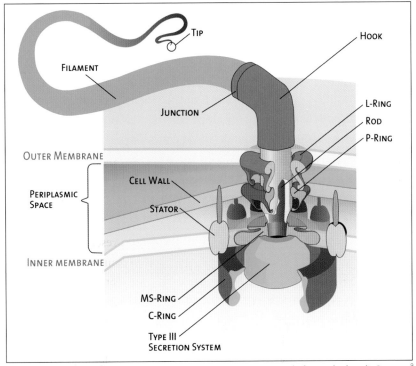

FILAMENT

TIP

HOOK

JUNCTION

L-RING
ROD
P-RING

OUTER MEMBRANE

CELL WALL

PERIPLASMIC
SPACE

STATOR

INNER MEMBRANE

MS-RING
C-RING

TYPE III
SECRETION SYSTEM

Courtesy LadyofHats and Wikimedia Commons[9]

FIGURE 0.1

A bacterial flagellum. Found in a variety of bacteria, including *E. coli*, it rotates like a propeller when the bacterium swims. Each component is composed of complicated proteins, which are in turn derived from specific genes. The Type III secretion system proteins form the base and core of the flagellum complex.

arguments. It is common for persons to attribute to the Almighty or the supernatural that which they do not understand. The term *explanatory gap* expresses the inadequacy of existing data or our knowledge of it to explain an observable fact or happening. People then will often fill the gap by crediting the power of some extraordinary force, be it astrology, fate, vital forces, or the hand of God. For example, Kandel notes that before the mechanisms of nerve impulses and their translation into muscle contraction were worked out, people assumed that an immaterial vital force was between one's will to move a finger and its subsequent motion.[10] Scientific inquiry has proven adept at filling in explanatory gaps, thereby falsifying many god-of-the-gaps arguments.

In contrast to ID, Creationism, and Theistic Evolution, I am suggesting a rapprochement of orthodox Christianity and evolution with a specific and detailed model that does not claim to be science but is nonetheless based on accurate descriptions and interpretations of the best that present-day science offers and a close reading of the Scriptures. Although the persevering nonscience reader will learn a lot about the sciences undergirding evolution, the goal of the book is to propose a model of how Christianity relates to these sciences and can learn from them.

NEO-DARWINISM

The fourth theory of evolution, and the paradigm endorsed by a majority of life scientists, is *Neo-Darwinism*. The brainchild of Charles Darwin, it has become almost synonymous with the word *evolution* itself. The theory states that Life evolved gradually from perhaps a single form roughly 3.5 billion years ago, branching out over time to produce numerous diverse species through (mostly) the mechanism of natural selection.[11] Jerry Coyne writes that this summary contains six components: evolution, gradualism, speciation, common ancestry, natural selection (NS), and nonselective mechanisms of evolutionary change. The essential idea is that over time creatures undergo random changes in their genetic makeup (mutations), and those varieties or variations that reproduce the best over geologic time (those that are the "fittest") are selected for, resulting in new species that are best adapted to, or suited for, the existing environment.

For example, how did the stick insect in Figure 0.2 come to be? Both creationism and ID insist that God has created the organism whole cloth. Neo-Darwinism offers a naturalistic explanation: The creature descended gradually from ancestors via random mutations to its genome,

FIGURE 0.2

Courtesy Firooo2 and Wikimedia Commons[12]

The stick insect *Ctenomorpha chronus.*

with those variations of form that produced the present shape selected for their adaptability to a changing environment.

Neo-Darwinists state that in effect the constant sieving action of NS, acting over geologic time, has enabled the genes underlying *Ctenomorpha* to become fixed in its population because it reproduced the most prolifically.

So what are the mutations, or variations in genomes, that led to such changes? Carroll points out that there are many different kinds of DNA mutations, including substitutions of single letters or blocks of letters, deletions, duplications of groups or blocks of letters, duplications of entire genes, rearrangements of blocks of letters, and the breakage and rejoining of segments of genes.[13] He notes that in humans there are an estimated 175 new mutations among the 7 billion DNA letters in every individual. There are in all this variation abundant opportunities for the modification of existing forms. How should we view this potential for change? Are we at the mercy of random forces ranging from mutations to earthquakes and tsunamis? Or could it be that random change in genomes is an *ability or strategy* that Life employs to deal with challenges and changing circumstances?

Richard Colling, former chairman of the Department of Biology at Olivet Nazarene University,[14] argues in his book *Random Designer* that random variation followed by NS is indeed the design strategy granted to Life[15] by the Creator to generate the diversities of living things that culminate in *Homo sapiens*, an organism capable of connecting with the Creator. He defines random design as "*a powerful method for creating higher order, particularly in living beings. It functions by first generating large arrays of potential building blocks from which the most suitable candidates are sequentially incorporated into an ever-advancing architectural design*"[16] [italics mine]. Note that while Coyne sees evolution as accidental and by chance, Colling sees random variation followed by NS to be God's grand strategy in creation. Colling would be the first to agree that his model is not science but rather a religious interpretation of his best understandings of science; as such, it is, to my knowledge, the first reconcilement of Christianity and Neo-Darwinism.

It seems far-fetched to posit that exquisite and harmonious complexity can emerge from random processes. But if you think of Life deploying randomness as a *strategy*, you suddenly have a different and exciting paradigm. For example, "directed evolution" is a widely used biotechnology method that exploits Life's strategic use of random genetic variation to evolve novelty. Bioengineers have resorted to directed evolution to improve "the stabilities or biochemical functions of proteins by repeated rounds of mutation and selection."[17] Experimenters begin with the protein they wish to improve upon, followed by isolation of the organism's gene that has generated the protein. In the next step, mutants of the gene are produced by causing it to replicate using error-prone polymerases (enzymes that facilitate the building of new copies of genes, in this case with errors—that is, mutations). The resulting replicating genes have one or two random mutations, and they produce an array of protein gene products with varying configurations. These products are then screened (NS), and improved, useful, and often novel and unexpected proteins are harvested, and the nonworkable proteins are rejected. A hypothetical application might be to take bacteria with a taste for crude oil and bioengineer it to more rapidly eat and digest petroleum products floating in the water following an oil spill. "Thus directed evolution can be used to discover mutations that fine-tune circuits and pathways and optimize their performance, all without requiring a detailed understanding of the mechanisms by which those improvements are achieved."[18] Now, compare this account of directed evolution with Colling's definition above of *random design*.

META-DARWINISM

I want to emphasize the central importance of *strategy*. Just as directed evolution is a strategy of human beings, so Neo-Darwinian evolution is, in Colling's and our religious framework, one of Life's strategies to cope with environmental changes and other challenges to its survival. But there are other paths to evolutionary change: This brings us to the fifth school of evolutionary thought, *Meta-Darwinism*. Fowler and Kuebler apply the term to a heterogeneous group of scientists who think that Neo-Darwinism does not include and/or adequately explain phenomena such as the following:

(1) Punctuated equilibrium, the rapid appearance of a variety of new species in the fossil record, as opposed to Darwin's idea that evolutionary change is very gradual.
(2) The utilization of old structures to produce something novel or new.
(3) Morphogenetic fields, where, in embryonic development, cells interact in the genesis of structures.
(4) Self-organization and complexity, where molecules and cells by themselves create highly ordered networks.

(5) Endosymbiosis, where organisms can merge or integrate to produce new forms.

(6) Epigenesis, where organisms can alter their form with heritable changes outside the genome.[19]

In my opinion, these six items have in common a dynamic quality; words like *rapid, produce, interact, create, merge,* and *alter* don't connote passivity. Throughout this work, I shall refer especially to seven scientists and authors whose work suggests the Meta-Darwinist view: Franklin Harold,[20] Eva Jablonka and Marion Lamb,[21] Lynn Caporale,[22] Lynn Margulis and Dorion Sagan,[23] and Anthony Trewavas.[24] I shall interpret their works and opinions and the findings of a number of other scientists as intimating a *worldview* of Life as agentive (i.e., Life having agency). This implies that Life's plasticity, its ability to transform itself to cope with changing circumstances, is an *active* capacity. Life has more going for it than just the strategy of random variation. That is, Life possesses intelligence, the ability to learn, and the capacity to modify itself.[25] It has at hand the strategy of random variation, but it also has numerous other means of self-modification.

For example, Lynn Caporale notes that the assumption that evolution "depends upon random mutation for the generation of new variations" has made it hard for many to accept the theory. But there is research that "leads to the conclusion that mutations are not all accidents and that mutations are not always random." The genomes of life forms, including ours, "have evolved mechanisms that *create* different kinds of mutations in their DNA, and they reuse and adapt useful pieces of DNA, even to the point that there are genomic 'interchangeable parts.'"

Randomness fades in a world that rewards each step of getting better at finding food, avoiding predators, or adapting to recurring challenges. . . . Over time, there emerged something that, viewing the effects now, we might call strategies—

such as the ability to actively generate diversity . . . [making] genomes more efficient at adapting and evolving. . . .

. . . Natural selection acts not only on fins and wings, but also on the mechanisms that change a genome. . . . "Successful" genomes—the ones that survive—are the genomes that evolve what here I will call mutation strategies. . . . the molecular mechanisms I will describe . . . have the effect of anticipating and responding to challenges and opportunities that continue to emerge in the environment.[26]

Note the agency implicit in Caporale's choice of words and phrases: *create, the ability to actively generate diversity, strategies that have the effect of anticipating and responding to challenges. It is in the thoughts of Meta-Darwinist thinkers that I find ideas truly useful to Christianity, and vice versa.*

THE HARMONY OF THE BIOLOGICAL AND EVOLUTIONARY SCIENCES AND CHRISTIANITY

The book is divided into two parts. Part One, the first six chapters of the book, is titled "An Interpretation of the Science of Life's Complexity, Agency, Evolution, and Conflict." In these six chapters, I offer evidence and argument that Life's agency—its intelligence, capacity for learning, and abilities to alter itself to meet changing circumstances—is the driving force of evolution. Neo-Darwinism, Creationism, and ID have one thing in common: None include the organism, or Life itself, as having any say in its evolution. All three regard Life as clay: In Creationism and ID, God is the potter, while in Neo-Darwinism, natural selection (NS) is the creator. I argue, however, that Life has the power to act. According to dictionary.com, an agent is an active or efficient cause. It is agentive; it can act and exert power. An agent is authorized to act on another's behalf. Agents are, within limits, *free* to act; they *choose*.

I do not mean to imply that Life's agency is similar to the conscious, self-reflective choices that we make. Animal's actions, on the scale of populations or individuals, can be directional and purposive, but on geologic timescales they are not teleological, in the sense of having in mind a future destination or purpose. Humankind has evolved to such a point, but the paths leading to our self-reflective consciousness have stretched out over billions of years, as organisms and their molecular networks ventured forth, experimented, learned, and remembered what worked. *This idea of Life as agent will allow for a very complete harmonizing of Life's material and mystical aspects and hence of the science of evolution, the Scriptures, and Christianity.*

I do want the reader to understand that the conclusions I draw from the work and opinions of various scientists and religious writers are my interpretations and may go beyond what was intended by the authors of the text. The first six chapters are devoted to some of the science of biology and evolution. I hope the reader will enjoy this discussion of the science of Life, about its stunning complexity and dazzling beauty and will not be intimidated by difficult passages. To assist the nonscientist reader, I have placed below each chapter subheading a short summary of the section. In addition, illustrations are carefully annotated. If at any point you find yourself getting bogged down, simply read the summary after each subheading, study the illustrations, and read the italicized conclusions at the end of each section.

In the first chapter, I address the question "What Is Life?" Indeed, how many of us ever stop to consider what exactly has been given to us? I introduce a synopsis of the fossil record and the commentary of several investigators about the cellular and molecular basis of Life and its animation; the chapter closes with a discussion of present efforts of scientists to create life in the laboratory. In Chapters 2 through 4, I provide evidence and commentary to support the idea of Life as agentive. Chapter 5 explores aspects of Life as community, for nothing in Life stands alone. The integrity of community is indispensable for Life's smooth functioning. Especially interesting is the idea of endosymbiosis. We are in part mosaics of remnants of viruses and bacteria that we captured and recruited in ancient infections. At the end of Chapter 5, I review some of the work of Anthony Trewavas on plant intelligence. Yes, plants are also intelligent and agentive.

Chapter 6 addresses the distressing reality that Life is full of conflict. We have all seen nature films that show the brutal side of evolution, with animals regularly and violently killing each other, even their own kind. Much less is said of the genetic and molecular conflicts that take place within the genomes of all living. Viruses in particular constantly attack us, and within our genomes, *transposons* (viruslike cut-and-paste genes) can move about and act against the broader interests of our genomes. This has real consequences for us in the present, for self-conflict is very much a part of the human condition. *We will see that the subject of self-conflict is intrinsic to understanding evolution and Christianity's relationship to it.* With the establishment of the scientific worldview of Life as an intelligent, creative, but conflicted agent in its evolution, we are ready for its rapprochement with orthodox Christianity.

Part Two of the book is titled "Evolving Christianity and the Redemption of Life in Conflict." The religious interpretation of Life as agent is developed in Chapter 7. Agentive Life exists because God has breathed his breath, the *Ruach*, into the dust that biological science has so elegantly described, making us, along with all of life animated, living beings. By his word, breath, and hands he creates, *albeit indirectly!* But the breath is the key! *God's breath is itself intelligent and the ultimate source of animation, mind, consciousness, agency, and Life's plasticity.*[27] It is with and through the breath that God enables and allows the creation to create. He has lent to all Life and every creature his breath and has granted Life the radical freedom to develop in all directions to cope with the many exigencies of life. This freedom is drastic; after imparting his breath to Life, God has allowed animated Life to play out its hand. Life is free to conflict within itself and among its selves, even down to the molecules, and it does so with a vengeance, leaving it tragically broken. Also, Life is free to make mistakes! But just because God has licensed Life to re-create itself to meet changing circumstances, this does not mean that Life is left alone; God is intimately concerned with the creation, loves and guides the creation, and incessantly dialogues with all his creatures on every level of their being.

Parenthetically, I bring a different angle to the discussion of self-conflict. As a physician specializing in psychiatry and addiction medicine, I have a feel for biological and behavioral sciences, the subtle intentions of persons, the critical importance of learning in their formation, and the intricacies of community and communication. It stands to reason that a psychiatrist might consider mind, intelligence, and cognition central to the understanding of Life and its evolution. Conflict is a salient feature of Life and must be considered in any theory of Christianity and evolution. The study and resolution of conflict, both within persons and between them, has been my bread and butter for 40 years. I am no stranger to my own conflicts and sufferings, as I will make clear as we go along.

If you think I am leading up to the Christian idea of Sin,[28] you are right. It is clear on biological and psychological levels that Life is in intense conflict with itself. Christianity informs the study of biological and psychological conflict, and vice versa. Christianity tells us that Sin entered when Life's prototypes, Adam and Eve, moved against God and that shame (the epitome of self-conflict) and Abel's murder (the ultimate in interpersonal conflict) quickly followed. Biology and evolutionary science tell us that selfishness is not really the issue in Sin or in self-conflict, for all of Life, from viruses to *Homo sapiens*, has self-interests that compel it to make a living. As a hedge against selfishness, Christianity prescribes the tithe, the giving of 10% of one's income. *Psychiatry, psychology, and the social sciences, on the other hand, tell us that self-conflicts such as shame and self-hate fuel the violence plaguing the planet.* It follows that moral failures are a downstream occurrence of self-conflict, much as fever and chills are a symptom of an underlying infection. In these areas, the sciences, the Scriptures, and Christianity will be found to complement and inform one another.

Recall what I noted earlier about the contradictions in the Book of Genesis—biblical cosmology versus modern cosmology—that is, a biblical versus a scientific view of the nature of the universe, creation top-down versus evolution from within, and the special creation of humankind versus descent from common ancestors? In Chapter 7, titled "Christianity and a Plausible Genesis: The Old Testament," I suggest a plausible rapprochement. I then proceed in Chapters 7 and 8 to discuss the primary aim of Genesis and indeed all Scripture, that of leading humankind and all Life out of alienation from God and resulting self-conflict to reconciliation with him and subsequent safety. Prayer is an essential part of resolving self-conflict and connecting with the Most High, so I address it in Chapter 9.

With the data and concepts of Life as agentive, evolving, and conflicted, a fresh and novel theodicy—a defense of God's justice and righteousness in the face of our suffering—is introduced. This I offer in Chapter 10, titled "God on Trial." The good news is that God is innocent of inflicting pain on us and has joined us in our struggles and pain. He is not part of the problem; he is, rather, the prime mover of the solution! We are not alone.

In Chapter 11, titled "The Future of Christianity," I propose a synthesis of the *mind* of Jesus as described in the New Testament Gospels, the idea of Life and us as intelligent agents, and some very new psychiatric research about human attachments that sheds fresh light onto *nothing less than the nature and process of love*. The implications and practical outgrowths of this are enormous. The result of this combination is the discovery of a capacity, or a way of thinking about old capacities, that can propel all Christians toward the future that God has intended for us all along.

Christianity in Evolution is a work in progress. To foster dialog, accommodate the inevitable future discoveries of science, and make some new friends, the website **www.christianityinevolution.com** welcomes you.

Science and theology enlighten each other.

PART ONE

AN

INTERPRETATION

OF THE SCIENCE

OF LIFE'S

COMPLEXITY, AGENCY,

EVOLUTION,

AND CONFLICT

CHAPTER ONE

WHAT IS LIFE?

A particularly awesome moment in life, for me, is the instant of death. To be present at an unsuccessful CPR, or with a terminally ill person who quietly slips away, holds up a frame to Life. Without the reminder of the tenuousness and evanescence of Life, it is easy to take it for granted and not grasp it as the utterly unlikely miracle it is. We get caught up in the pursuit of Life and chained to its details—busy making a living, taking care of the children, pursuing pleasures, or simply trying to survive—and fail to wonder, indeed, what Life is in the first place.

On the other hand, some physicists and biologists have seriously taken up the question. Erwin Schrödinger (fig. 1.1), one of the fathers of quantum mechanics, in 1944 wrote *What Is Life?*[1] from lectures delivered

FIGURE 1.1

Erwin Schrödinger (1887–1961), Austrian physicist, disliked Nazi anti-Semitism and left for Oxford in 1933. He won a Nobel Prize for the "Schrödinger Equation." He and Albert Einstein were personal friends.

Courtesy Wikimedia and Wikimedia Commons[2]

at Trinity College, Dublin. In it, Schrödinger predicts that the basis of heredity is a molecule that can encode an almost infinite number of possibilities with a small number of atoms. His work strongly influenced Francis Crick, one of the discoverers of the structure of DNA, to pursue his research.[3] The question was taken up specifically by Franklin Harold, professor emeritus of biochemistry at Colorado State University, in his book *The Way of the Cell*[4] and by Lynn Margulis, professor of botany and geosciences at the University of Massachusetts, in her book also titled *What Is Life?*[5] Both books are sources of inspiration and guidance for this present work. Finally, scientists currently researching the origins of Life are plumbing the question, with the ultimate goal of synthesizing Life in the laboratory. More on this at the end of this chapter.

Modern paleontology, biology, genetics, neuroscience, psychology, psychiatry, and studies of evolution (the history of Life) illuminate a number of aspects of Life; examining these facets can tell us a lot about what Life *is*. In this chapter, I examine briefly science's characterization of the physical aspects of Life. Different sections address Life and the

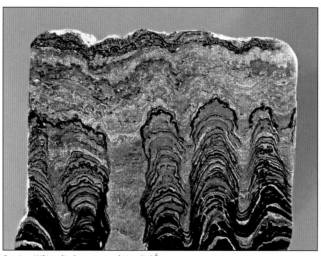

FIGURE 1.2
Proterozoic stromatolites, from the eastern Andes, Bolivia, dating back 2.3 billion years ago.

Courtesy Wikimedia Commons and User SNP [6]

fossil record, the cellular basis of Life, the molecular basis of Life, the genetic code, the genetic system, proteins and receptors, how organisms grow, the creation and fabrication of form, and how Life regulates itself. The chapter concludes with a discussion of origin of Life experiments. I suggest that the reader focus on this section, which summarizes the chapter. Those with the energy to read the chapter closely will gain a valuable overview of the science of Life. However, as I said in the Introduction, the goal of the book is not to impart a science education but to propose a model of how Christianity relates to evolutionary biology and can learn from it.

LIFE AND THE FOSSIL RECORD

The oldest visible fossils date back 2.7 billion years. Ancient bacteria supplied the earth's atmospheric oxygen. Life forms called *Ediacaria* suddenly burgeoned 575 million years ago. Prehuman hominids appeared about 4 million years ago. A variety of genus *Homo* with differing DNA and biology existed at the same time—for example, humans and Neanderthals.

The oldest fossils visible to the naked eye are stromatolites, formed by layers of bacterial films covered over by sediments in warm shallow seas.[7] They date as far back as 2.7 billion years (fig. 1.2). Scientists know a lot about these bacterial films, for they continue to exist today. These films and the stromatolites they produce are bacterial organisms (*prokaryotes*, to be discussed below) that produce oxygen through photosynthesis; such organisms over billions of years supplied the oxygen for the earth's atmosphere. Older still are the tiny hydrocarbon residues found in metamorphosed rocks dating back 3.85 billion years. Assuming that there were ancestors to even these organisms, it is estimated that Life began on earth about 4 billion years ago.[8]

The next life forms to figure prominently in the fossil record, the Ediacarans, appear in rocks roughly 575 to 542 million years ago.[9] About 100 species of these soft-bodied creatures have been identified; some resemble jellyfish, others worms; some have a curiously quilted form, others show some bilateral symmetry, and others even have a head region. They were definitely multicellular and have been found worldwide.[10] Life in its iterations had evolved from single to multicellular forms. As evidenced in the fossil record, life suddenly exploded again in the Cambrian period, around 543 million years ago. Numerous animal body plans, many of living phyla, appeared between 530 and 520 million years ago, in a limited time period making up only 1.7% of the duration of the fossil record of animals.[11] In other words, a great variety of animals appeared in a brief geologic time. These animals were much more complex than the preceding Ediacaran creatures. Finding two relatively brief periods in geologic time that produced bursts of organisms gives scientists reason to believe that macroevolution can proceed by "Big Bangs" as well as by gradual change, as Darwin originally postulated.[12]

In the interest of brevity, let us skip over about 500 million years, past the age of the dinosaurs and their extinction, past the age of an array of primitive mammals, to an example of fossils "only" 23 million years old and much closer to home. I found these fossil oyster shells (fig. 1.3) and sand dollars (fig. 1.4) in the 5,000-foot-high Pine Mountain region of Los Padres National Forest, about an hour north of my home at the beach in Ventura County, California. How did the fossils of inhabitants of an ancient sea come to rest near a 5,000-foot mountain? Through plate tectonics—specifically, the collision of the Pacific Plate and the North American Plates.

Let us move on to the fossil record pertaining to humankind. The present consensus is that the evolutionary tree of humans is more like a bush than a single linear trunk.[13] Two of the earliest of genus *Homo* (fig. 1.5) likely descended from a common ancestor somewhere between 2 and 3 million years ago.

FIGURE 1.3

Fossil oysters, Miocene, Pine Mountain, Ventura County, California.

FIGURE 1.4

Sand dollar, Miocene, Pine Mountain, Ventura County, California.

Photos by Don Anderson

Not shown on Figure 1.5 is *Ardipithecus ramidus*, a recently discovered upright walking creature dating back 4.4 million years. This human forebear looked nothing like a chimpanzee or other large primate, suggesting that the last common ancestor of primates, which existed 2 million years earlier, was dissimilar to both modern humans, and primates.[14] *Homo ergaster* is the oldest representative of the genus *Homo*, had short stature and very long arms, was least similar to humans and dates from around 2.5 million years ago. *Homo erectus*, dating from about 1.8 million years ago, was strikingly similar to humans, but the brain was about one-quarter smaller. *Homo sapiens* started in Africa about 200,000 years ago and have a larger brain. *Homo heidelbergensis* and *Homo neanderthalsis* were evolutionary dead ends. Neanderthal man, who lived 250,000 to 29,000 years ago, was a separate evolutionary lineage from *Homo sapiens*, having branched from a common ancestor at least 500,000 years ago.

The evidence holds up the idea that a variety of unrelated genus *Homo* appeared simultaneously instead of there being a single linear trunk.

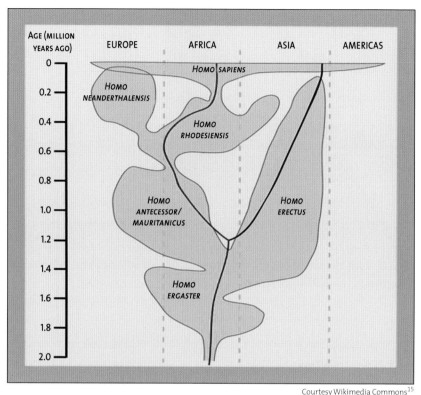

Courtesy Wikimedia Commons[15]

FIGURE 1.5

Temporal and geographical distribution of hominid populations.

Rather than a linear sequential view of brain evolution in which the human brain incorporates components resembling the brains of modern fish, amphibians, reptiles, and birds, all the evidence suggests that substantial cognitive abilities have *independently* evolved multiple times from differing neural substrates, giving a new view of divergent branches of brain and mind evolution.[16] This strongly supports the idea of *convergence*, in which intelligences of unrelated creatures such as cephalopods (octopus, squid, cuttlefish), birds, and mammals have separately emerged, with each having markedly different nervous systems.[17]

CELLULAR BASIS OF LIFE

Cells, fundamental to life, come in two forms: prokaryotes and eukaryotes.
The former, usually bacteria, lack a nucleus. The latter has a volume
up to 1,000 times larger, has a nucleus, and is the building block of complex
organisms. Bacteria are extremely widespread and can adapt to extreme
conditions. There are many single-celled eukaryotes. There is evidence that
eukaryotes resulted from the merger of differing prokaryotes.

All of Life's self-modification and multiplication begin with the cell. All the features of the phenomenon of life can be seen in a single cell, and all living tissues are aggregates of cells. Harold notes, "Each cell is an organism, endowed with the essential attributes of life."[18] There are two fundamental types of cells, prokaryotes and eukaryotes.

PROKARYOTES

Microbes are prokaryotes—that is, cells that are smaller, simpler, and lack a true nucleus. The workhorse of biochemical research is *E. coli*, a prokaryote that lives in our gut (fig. 1.6). This cell is not a bag of enzymes; rather, its proteins dynamically cooperate to create what is basically an "enzoskeleton." The plasma membrane, its outer coat, is a mosaic of small domains, with chemical-sensing proteins localized at the poles. In other words, *E. coli* has a nose. Harold writes that these bacteria detect foodstuffs and swim in the direction of gradients by moving and tumbling with their flagella.[19] The "nose" continuously measures concentrations of attractants and computes their gradients, responding in milliseconds to local changes. Under optimal conditions, it can detect a gradient as shallow as 1 part in 1,000 over the length of the cell. This is an example of *E. coli's* molecules interacting over multiple planes to exquisitely regulate its functions.[20]

Scientists have identified the fossil remains of bacteria in sedimentary rocks in Africa and Australia dating 3.4 billion years ago and the

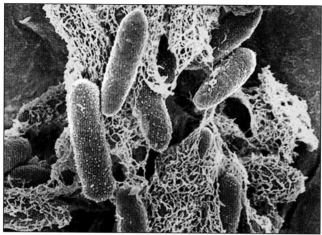

Courtesy Jengod and Wikimedia Commons[21]

FIGURE 1.6
E. coli.

remains of microbial mat communities that had flourished 3.5 billion years ago in cherts (a rock resembling flint) in southern Africa. The early Earth was hot and anoxic. It is thought that the earliest bacteria were similar to bacteria *currently* found in extreme conditions, such as around hot springs, thermal vents, and in places where there is no oxygen, such as in the gut of a cow. These archeabacteria learned to use sunlight to break down carbon dioxide to synthesize DNA, proteins, sugars, and other cell components.[22] In the process, they released vast amounts of oxygen. Earth's present atmosphere owes its existence to the metabolism of evolving bacteria. "Only through the workings of the most innovative bacteria of all time did the originally anoxic Earth gain an oxygen-rich atmosphere. . . . *It was bacteria that removed the carbon dioxide and produced the oxygen"*[23] [italics mine].

As much as 70% of the microbes alive on Earth reside on and below the ocean floor. The deep water in a spot along the East Pacific Rise, a mid-ocean ridge segment that lies off the northwestern coast of South America, contains between 8,000 and 90,000 microorganisms per cc, but the seafloor basalt holds, in its pore spaces, between 3 million and 1 billion microbes per gram.[24] In another study, core samples drilled off the shore of Newfoundland, at depths between 860 and 1,626 meters below the seafloor, held around 1.5 million microorganisms per cc. Of these, about 60% were alive and could reproduce. The temperatures of rocks at these depths range from 60 degrees Celsius to less than 100 degrees Celsius. If these figures can be generalized, seafloor sediments could house about 70% of the microbes now alive on Earth.[25]

Craig Venter, one of the principal investigators with the Human Genome Project, describes microorganisms that live in extremely strong acid or base solutions and microbes that withstand 3 million rads of radiation without being killed (their chromosomes get blown apart, but they stitch everything back together and just start replicating again). There are thermophilic microbes, which can withstand temperatures of 238 degrees Farenheit; they have stiffening agents in their membranes to keep them from melting away, and they build their cell proteins with a different assortment of amino acids than our cells do, allowing the construction of strongly bonded protein chains that won't collapse in the heat. Then there are microbes that live at 20,000 feet, in subzero conditions; their membranes are very loose and fluid and so resist stiffening and freezing. Venter states, "Nature over 4 billion years of evolutionary tinkering has created a wealth of biological and metabolic templates."[26]

Two issues come to mind as we study the complexity, resilience, and ingenuity of these humblest of life forms: their present morphology and how they arrived at their present states. First, they have existed for billions of years and have literally provided us with the oxygen we breathe. They have multiplied and filled the earth, and we would not be here without them. What is it within them that enables them to stitch back together exploded parts? And what about their computational ability, which can detect miniscule changes in the environment? Does their quickness to process information and comprehend it, their exercise of molecular logic, their repair–ability, and their tinkering to create a wealth of templates suggest a kind of intelligence? Second, what is their evolutionary dynamic?

Is their adaptability the result only of chance? Is Life merely a series of complicated material mechanisms, or is there in Life's utterly astounding harmony something else at work? Read on: Single-celled organisms, even with all their unexpected beauty, are just the beginning.

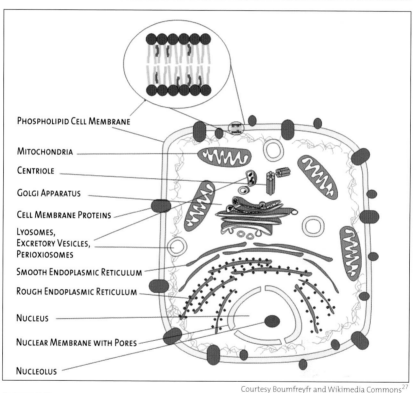

PHOSPHOLIPID CELL MEMBRANE

MITOCHONDRIA

CENTRIOLE

GOLGI APPARATUS

CELL MEMBRANE PROTEINS

LYOSOMES,
EXCRETORY VESICLES,
PERIOXIOSOMES

SMOOTH ENDOPLASMIC RETICULUM

ROUGH ENDOPLASMIC RETICULUM

NUCLEUS

NUCLEAR MEMBRANE WITH PORES

NUCLEOLUS

Courtesy Boumfreyfr and Wikimedia Commons[27]

FIGURE 1.7

Eukaryote. Mitochondrion produces the cell's chemical energy. Centriole assists in cell division. Golgi apparatus processes proteins and lipids. Lysosomes contain digestive enzymes to break down junk. Smooth endoplasmic reticulum metabolizes various cell chemicals. Rough endoplasmic reticulum is a network of sac-like structures to transport cell components. Ribosomes are where proteins are built. Nucleus contains the genes. Nucleolus transcribes ribosomal RNA.

EUKARYOTES

Eukaryotes are cells that have a discrete nucleus bounded by a special membrane, containing chromosomes that become visible during cell division. They are the cells of higher plants and animals, fungi, and many protists (defined below). They have intracellular organelles, a cytoskeleton, and an elaborate network of internal membranes.[28] Figure 1.7 depicts a eukaryote cell.

Protists (fig. 1.8) are a group of eukaryotes that include slime molds, amoeba, giardia, and marine plankton. One might wonder at the lowly slime mold, but we shall see in Chapter 2 evidence that this humblest of creatures possesses extraordinary networking capabilities. These basic life forms have in common a variety of biochemical, physiological, and structural themes, and they all evolved from a common ancestor.[29]

Eukaryotic cells are much more elaborate than prokaryotes. As can be seen in Figure 1.7, the eukaryotic cell has a discrete nucleus with its own membrane enclosing the chromosomes, a cytoplasm with tiny organs for

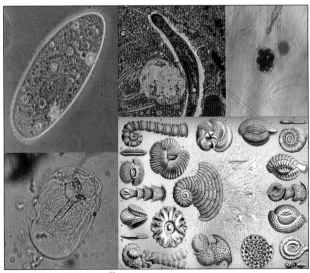

FIGURE 1.8
Protist collage.

Courtesy Wikimedia Commons[30]

creating chemical energy, a labyrinth of membranes, and a cytoskeleton. The much smaller bacterial cells are able to put all their genes on a single string and let diffusion distribute the metabolites and gene products. Eukaryotic cells generally have 10 times as many genes and types of proteins per cell and up to 1,000 times the volume of prokaryote cells. Their outer membrane, the plasma membrane, is geared to communicate with the outside, while internal organelles generate energy. The cytoskeleton is a scaffold of girders, cables, tracks, and tubes that ties all cellular operations into a coherent unit. This is an astounding progression in function, complexity, and utility. "Eukaryotes . . . represent an enormous evolutionary advance, 'surely the most drastic change in the history of the organic world.'"[31] *How in the world did this invention come about?* Accumulating evidence suggests that eukaryotic cells resulted stepwise from the merger of differing prokaryotes or from the eventual assimilation and cooperation of predator and prey prokaryotes.[32] I deal more with the phenomenon of endosymbiosis, the integration of one organism into another to form a new whole, in Chapter 5 "Life Is Community."

MOLECULAR BASIS OF LIFE

DNA is a very long helical molecule containing four letters, A, T, C, and G, connected in four combinations, AT, TA, GC, and CG. In groups of three, these base pairs code for 20 amino acids. The possible combinations are invariant and are collectively called the genetic code. By this code, DNA is transcribed by RNA to make multitudinous proteins. Figure 1.10 nicely summarizes this section.

The three most basic molecules of Life are DNA (deoxyribonucleic acid), RNA (ribonucleic acid), and their multitudinous offspring, proteins. The simplified equation "DNA makes RNA makes protein" is the molecular dynamic of Life (fig. 1.9). Think of a toolmaker (RNA) who copies written instructions or a die (DNA) to make a lock (a protein). I use commentary from several authors to give a glimpse of the intricacies and complexities of operations such as the assembly of proteins according to the "genetic code," the processes of DNA duplication and

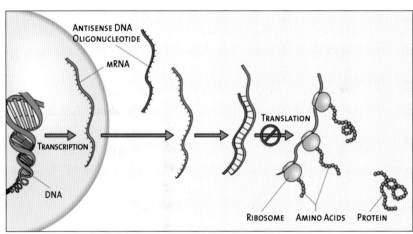

Courtesy author "not me," and Wikimedia Commons[33]

FIGURE 1.9

This very oversimplified schematic illustrates the sequence of DNA → RNA → Protein, as it carries out various functions, including interacting with the environment, dividing, maintaining metabolism, self-regulating, and building structures. The genome replicates itself through transcription, using enzymes (proteins that enable chemical reactions) such as DNA polymerase (breaks apart DNA into its two strands to prepare it for copying). It requires a supply of basic materials (nucleotides) and receives feedback from the environment, proteins, and ribozymes (RNA molecules that act as enzymes). DNA's information is converted to its RNA equivalent through transcription, facilitated by the enzyme RNA polymerase. One of the RNAs produced is messenger RNA (mRNA), which carries genomic orders via proteins to the rest of the cell. Proteins are built per orders from the genome. There are four basic roles of proteins: enzymes (such as RNA and DNA polymerase), regulatory, structural, and transport (carrying molecules across membranes or around the body). Amino acids are required for the fabrication of proteins, which takes place in ribosomes.[34]

repair, the system's vulnerability to error and damage, the operations of the genome, how the final protein products fold and act as signals, and last, how cells divide. These commentaries are meant to convey a flavor for the magnificent mystery of biological complexity and organization.

All of Life uses these same molecules. Caporale points out the similarities of all living matter. One in 10 of humankind's proteins resembles proteins in yeast, insects, worms, and mammals, with the most fundamental ancient protein designs pertaining to Life's most basic processes, such as metabolism and the copying and repairing of DNA. She states,

> More than 90 percent of the functional protein pieces, called *domains,* that can be identified in humans are also found in fruit flies and worms. . . .
>   . . . [Of] 1278 families of genes [found in the human genome], only 70 of our gene families and only 24 of our domain families are unique to vertebrates.

She goes on to say,

> These vertebrate-only domains and proteins are mostly involved in our vertebrate defenses and unique immune system, and in our nervous systems and brains. . . .
>   . . . As yet, I do not know of a single human-only gene family, and, indeed, I would be surprised to find one.[35]

As I said earlier, we are all cut from the same cloth.

The following paragraphs and images will expand on the DNA→ RNA→protein system. It starts with the molecule du jour, DNA, the carrier of all genetic information of all organisms, except viruses (which often use RNA). Consisting of two strands twisted into a double helix, DNA (fig. 1.10) transmits its information via four nitrogenous bases named adenine (A), guanine (G), thymine (T), and cytosine (C).

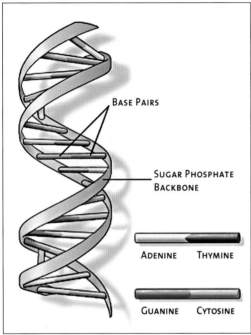

BASE PAIRS

SUGAR PHOSPHATE
BACKBONE

ADENINE   THYMINE

GUANINE   CYTOSINE

Courtesy US National Library of Medicine[36]

FIGURE 1.10

The structure of DNA. The double helix, composed of the sugar phosphate backbone, the nitrogenous purine and pyrimidine bases, and the hydrogen bonds that hold the two helices together. A, adenine; G, guanine; C, cytosine; T, thymine. Note the four combinations: AT, TA, GC, and CG. All of Life's information originates in how these four combinations are strung together.

Through the double helix, A always pairs with T, and G with C. So there are four possible combinations: AT, TA, GC, and CG. Like a computer code, how these are strung together, their sequences, determines the instructions they give to their transcriber RNA.

RNA will substitute the amino acid uracil (U) for T. Like any faithful transcriptionist, RNA[37] carries the DNA's genetic instructions to assemble combinations of 20 amino acids (Table 1.1) to make specific proteins, which in turn act to implement multitudinous cell operations. Phenylalanine (Phe), leucine (Leu), serine (Ser), and so on are the 20 amino acids. Any combination of three A, G, C, and U nucleotides (called a triplet) will specify a particular amino acid; this array of combinations is called the *genetic code* (Table 1.1). *This code is universal to almost all of Life; there are only a few exceptions.*

THE GENETIC CODE

Much of life is composed of proteins made from 20 amino acids whose sequences are specified by strict rules called the genetic code. The code is extremely optimized and hence minimizes damage done by mutations.

The genetic code is remarkably efficient, in the sense that it minimizes the damage done by inevitable mutations. Freeland and Hurst write that life on earth, with some minor exceptions, is made up of proteins that are in turn composed of various combinations of the same 20 amino acids. There are many more amino acids around, but only these 20 make

		1ST BASE				
		U	C	A	G	
2ND BASE	U	UUU Phenylalanine UUC Phenylalanine UUA Leucine UUG Leucine	UCU Serine UCC Serine UCA Serine UCG Serine	UAU Tyrosine UAC Tyrosine UAA Stop UAG Stop	UGU Cysteine UGC Cysteine UGA Stop UGG Tryptophan	U C A G
	C	CUU Leucine CUC Leucine CUA Leucine CUG Leucine	CCU Proline CCC Proline CCA Proline CCG Proline	CAU Histidine CAC Histidine CAA Glutamine CAG Glutamine	CGU Arginine CGC Arginine CGA Arginine CGG Arginine	U C A G
	A	AUU Isoleucine AUC Isoleucine AUA Isoleucine AUG Methionine (Start)	ACU Threonine ACC Threonine ACA Threonine ACG Threonine	AAU Asparagine AAC Asparagine AAA Lysine AAG Lysine	AGU Serine AGC Serine AGA Arginine AGG Arginine	U C A G
	G	GUU Valine GUC Valine GUA Valine GUG Valine	GCU Alanine GCC Alanine GCA Alanine GCG Alanine	GAU Aspartic Acid GAC Aspartic Acid GAA Aspartic Acid GAG Aspartic Acid	GGU Glycine GGC Glycine GGA Glycine GGG Glycine	U C A G

NONPOLAR, ALIPHATIC POLAR, UNCHARGED AROMATIC POSITIVELY CHARGED NEGATIVELY CHARGED

Courtesy Dave1501 and Wikimedia Commons[38]

TABLE 1.1

The genetic code. For example, the amino acid cysteine is specified by either of two codons, UGU or UGC. Note that there is considerable redundancy (arginine is specified by six codons), but there is no ambiguity.

up life's proteins. Proteins are fabricated by messenger RNA (mRNA) which is composed of combinations of the four bases. During fabrication, known as translation, the bases of mRNA are read in groups of three; these are known as codons. There are 64 possible codons, and these make up the genetic code. Each codon, except for those that dictate "start" or "stop," codes for a specific amino acid. For example, GUA (guanine-uracil-adenine) codes for the amino acid valine. If this code is randomized, there are 10^{18} combinations available. Using statistics to evaluate the relative efficiency (invulnerability to genetic errors) of these randomized codes, the authors found that "only 1 in every million random alternative codes generated is more efficient than the natural code." They go on to say, "The natural genetic code shows startling evidence of optimization. . . . our genetic code is quite literally '1 in a million.'"[39] In another paper, Freeland, Knight, and Landweber note, "Nature's choice might indeed be the best possible code."[40] Simon Conway Morris, wondering about how the code's refinement could have taken place in what he calculates to be a geologically brief 200-million year period, adds, "It is difficult to believe that the genetic code is not the product of selection, but to arrive at the best of all possible codes, selection has to be more than powerful, it has to be overwhelmingly effective." He somewhat incredulously concedes that "the evidence suggests that rapidly and with extraordinary effectiveness a very good, perhaps even the best, code is arrived at."[41]

So how did Life arrive at these 20 amino acids? Freeland and Hurst postulate that those amino acids that minimized the negative effects of mutations performed the best. In other words, these 20 won out because mutations among them produced the least damage to the proteins they fabricated. What amino acids did they win out over? The implication is that preceding them were other amino acid/codon combinations that were less efficient.[42] *The genetic code was undoubtedly refined not by natural selection acting on amino acids, but by selection acting on the populations of organisms choosing amino acids. Is there any evidence that Life contributed to the variation that selection acted upon, to produce the code's incredible optimization in the time frame that Morris calculates? I shall in the following chapters show opinions and findings suggesting that possibility in the present.*

THE GENETIC SYSTEM

For life to grow, cells must divide. DNA must be separated and meticulously copied. Mistakes must be repaired. These processes are extremely efficient, but errors are made and can add up.

Here are some details that illustrate the genetic system's complexity. Every cell in the human body contains 3 billion base pairs of DNA packaged in humankind's 46 chromosomes. These chromosomes make up the instructions for making the proteins that will constitute much of the body. To undergo the DNA duplication that is the basis of cell duplication and hence growth, the DNA helix must unravel to be copied, "and the two new double helices grow alongside their partners," with careful matches made at every step. The copying machine must rapidly "copy the 3 billion steps in each of our cells each time the cell divides, [which] takes about 8 hours, with each of about 1000 machines [per cell] attaching about 80 new letters every second." Inevitably, mistakes are made, yet even with the array of "copying, proofreading, and repair machinery, there is on the average only about one unrepaired error in every billion to 10 billion letters copied."[43] Epigenetic patterns (marks, analogous to tattoos) are instructions about whether to activate or copy a gene; they are also reproduced during replication. Mistakes in the reproduction of epigenetic marks occur 1 in a 1,000 replications.[44] *Life's various processes are not perfect; they make mistakes!*

This points to another aspect of Life—its vulnerability. The genetic machinery makes mistakes. Its repair mechanisms are intricate almost beyond comprehension, but not perfect. Furthermore, the genes themselves are fragile and regularly damaged by radiation and chemicals. Craig

Venter's bacteria may stitch itself back together after a blast of radiation, but many other genomes cannot do so perfectly. Damages add up as we age.

In addition to DNA proofreading operations, the genome encodes proteins that can manipulate and modify the genetic material. Dawkins, giving examples of the active agency of genes, states that "the true 'purpose' of DNA is to survive, no more and no less." Snipping out DNA and splicing in of other bits of DNA are also parts of the normal stock-in-trade of the genome:

> The fact that inversions and other translocations so readily
> occur, further testifies to the casual ease with which chunks of
> DNA may be cut out of one part of the genome, and spliced
> onto another part. Replicability and "spliceability" seem to
> be among the most salient features of DNA in its natural
> environment . . . of cellular machinery.[45]

Think of this as a contingent of copy editors per cell, who, as a part of their work, liberally cut and paste. In my opinion, the presence and activities of these editors points to the self-efficacy of the organism down to the molecules, the organism able on a molecular level to delicately and very accurately groom its genome.

In the same vein, Jablonka and Lamb describe how at the molecular level, all recombination of DNA is extremely complex, with bits of DNA unwinding, breaking, and rejoining and complementary base-pairing taking place between nucleotide chains from different chromosomes. A lot of enzymes and proteins make up the cell's natural genetic engineering system. Much of this is to maintain DNA, to protect and repair it, to ensure that existing nucleotide sequences are well maintained and copied accurately.

> Cells have proteins that scavenge for and degrade molecules
> that would damage DNA; if damage does occur, there is

another set of proteins that can repair it. . . . When DNA
is replicated, there are systems that check that each nucleotide
added to the growing daughter strand is the correct
(complementary) one, and remove it if it is not. After
the new daughter strand is synthesized, it is proofread,
and if mismatched nucleotides are found, they are
corrected. . . . [Thus,] the error rate during the replication
of human DNA is about one in every ten thousand
million nucleotides. Without [these repair mechanisms],
it is estimated it would be nearer one in a hundred.[46]

If organisms didn't have these, they would not survive. With all this
in place, the authors state that it is reasonable to speculate that beneficial
mutations are not blind mistakes but have specificity. Indeed, they point
out, "directed mutation" is part of the jargon of genetics, meaning that
there are mechanisms that alter DNA in response to the signals that cells
receive from other cells or from the environment.

I see in these descriptions of cell operations a profound self-efficacy that suggests that Life takes an active, agentive role in its adaptations. Life is not solely clay that God or natural selection acts upon; rather, it is matter that contends.

PROTEINS AND RECEPTORS

DNA, copied by RNA, leads to the building of proteins via the
genetic code. The body is largely composed of and supported by
proteins. Receptors are lock-and-key devices made up of proteins.
They are integral to self-regulation and self-organization.

After the amino acids of a protein have been specified and assembled,
the protein folds, and the resulting configuration, with its peaks,
shapes, and valleys determines its function (fig.1.11).

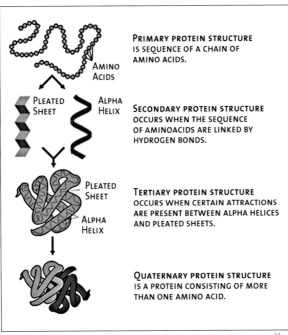

PRIMARY PROTEIN STRUCTURE IS SEQUENCE OF A CHAIN OF AMINO ACIDS.

AMINO ACIDS

PLEATED SHEET

ALPHA HELIX

SECONDARY PROTEIN STRUCTURE OCCURS WHEN THE SEQUENCE OF AMINOACIDS ARE LINKED BY HYDROGEN BONDS.

PLEATED SHEET

ALPHA HELIX

TERTIARY PROTEIN STRUCTURE OCCURS WHEN CERTAIN ATTRACTIONS ARE PRESENT BETWEEN ALPHA HELICES AND PLEATED SHEETS.

QUATERNARY PROTEIN STRUCTURE IS A PROTEIN CONSISTING OF MORE THAN ONE AMINO ACID.

FIGURE 1.11

From amino acid chain to folding to functioning protein structure.

Courtesy National Human Genome Research Institute and Wikimedia Commons[47]

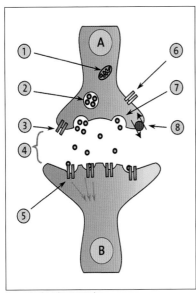

Drawn by fr:Utilisateur.Dake.
Courtesy Wikimedia Commons[48]

FIGURE 1.12

Two neurons (nervous system cells), A activating B, by neurotransmitter chemicals from A keying into the receptors (#5) of B.

1. Mitochondria (little power plants)
2. Synaptic vesicle (containers for the neurotransmitter chemicals)
3. Autoreceptor (a feedback device)
4. Synaptic cleft (space at the junction)
5. Neurotransmitter receptor (the lock the keylike neurotransmitter will fit into)
6. Calcium channel
7. Fused vesicle releasing neurotransmitter
8. Neurotransmitter reuptake pump (for recycling)

The folded protein can assume a variety of functions, such as enzymes for chemical reactions, structural proteins, and receptors. There are vast arrays of receptors on all cell surfaces; they are akin to locks whose activation or deactivation governs the actions of the cells. For example, Figure 1.12 is a schematic of the synapse (juxtaposition) of two brain cells (neurons), with neurotransmitter chemicals from A (the little circles in the synaptic cleft, or space, between the two) floating over to key into the receptors (#5) on B, thereby activating B.

HOW ORGANISMS GROW

Growth occurs as cells divide. Bacteria divide by *fission*,
and bodies of eukaryotes grow by *mitosis*. The special cell division
that results in sperm or eggs is called *meiosis*.

Let us next briefly consider how the growth of an organism, including us, takes place. All growth requires cell division and the transmission of information from the parent cell to its two offspring.[49] Genetic information resides in the chromosomes, duplicate strings of genes in turn made up of DNA. At cell division, the duplicate DNA of the parent cell is enzymatically separated and held apart. Each strand is then copied to give two new duplicate strands. This is part of a process called *mitosis*. The duplicate structure of DNA allows for its unwinding and its faithful copying of a new chain complementary to itself.[50] *Meiosis* is the process of cell division in sexual reproduction, where ovaries or testes produce cells with single strands of DNA; these cells are called *gametes*. At their union, they will form a zygote, the first cells of a newborn. *Fission* is the process by which bacteria divide. A very readable and understandable summary of the details of DNA, RNA, protein synthesis, cell division, and DNA errors can be found online at **www.talkorigins. org/faqs/molgen/**.

THE CREATION
AND FABRICATION OF FORM

During the growth of an embryo, genes switch on and off
to form tissues. It is thought that tissues are arranged in space
not by the genome, but by *fields* in which structure begets
structure. But nobody has seen a field.

It is clear that every cell has layer upon layer of profoundly intricate, faithfully reproducible, and exquisitely choreographed organized complexity. How then do these single cells knit together to create forms, the next level of order? The creation of form in the embryo is called *morphogenesis*. During the growth of an embryo, genes switch on and off to produce various cell types, but how are they to be patterned and arranged in space? Research on the ciliate *Tetrahymena thermophila* illustrates how this single-celled organism positions outer-surface organelles during growth, development, and regeneration. The evidence now is that its patterns are not dictated by the genome but spring from existing structures: Structure begets structure. Structure does so at the cellular level via *morphogenetic fields.*[51]

Tetrahymena is a pear-shaped single cell lined with lengthwise, gently spiraling rows of cilia by which it moves (fig. 1.13). It has a mouth (oral apparatus), an anus (cytoproct), and a means to eliminate fluids (contractile vacuole). Before dividing at the waist, the organism must build a new mouth at the north end of the daughter cell and a new anus and contractile vacuole at the south end of the parent cell. In addition, each ciliary row must be extended. How are these organelles constructed, and how does the cell know where to put them? Four decades of research show that preexisting cell assemblies order and arrange new cell structures, using information distinct from the genome. The mechanisms of this directed assembly fall into two classes: "local mechanisms, on the scale of molecules and large complexes, and global ones that extend over the entire

FIGURE 1.13

Tetrahymena thermophila.

cell"—the latter termed a *field*, "'a territory within which developmental decisions are subject to a common set of coordinating influences.'"[53]

Figure 1.13 illustrates the orientation of ciliary rows. In local assembly, rows spring forth first by the creation and placing of basal bodies that sprout cilia that beat in unison with others in the same row. Where these new basal bodies are built, how they migrate to the surface of the cell, and how associated structures are organized around them are all dictated by the molecular layout within the unit territory, not by any outside nuclear or cellular influence. Apparently, some aspect of surface organization, other than the cilia themselves, something more like a template, governs the layout of the entire cell outer surface.

The larger, bigger picture patterns are free of local layout mechanisms and, rather, appear to be associated with developmental fields—

that is, global positioning systems (GPS) similar to the fields found in the formation of embryos. Thus, one field lays out gradients from front to rear to position mouth and anus, while gradients around the waist lay out ciliary rows and the contractile vacuole pore. However, various methods of investigation, including electron microscopy, and biophysical and biochemical methods, have been unable to identify these fields. Such mysteries extend to innumerable other cells and multicellular organisms.[54]

Research will likely clarify the physical mechanisms underlying fields and pattern formation. But note that fields are another example of behavior patterns of living systems. Like all other patterns of behavior, whether molecular, organismic, or populational, they are highly scripted. Yet these scripts—that is, fields and embryonic development, camouflage for protection, or migration patterns—are profoundly optimized. How has all this synchronized complexity come about? The concept of adaptation holds that by some strategy of genetic variation, either by trial and error, directed change, or nonrandom processes, better and better forms survived the test of time.[55]

LIFE REGULATES ITSELF

Life, through a maze of intricate networks, is able to regulate
its physical functions. Genomic restructuring, hypermutation, and
induced local mutations are *strategies* that Life deploys.
Life is an agent in its adaptations.

Life intrinsically and intricately regulates itself to maintain its metabolic equilibrium. Cells regulate the concentrations of ions, pH, osmotic pressure, rates of metabolic reactions, and cell division, through a network of signals conveying information. These signals may be metabolic intermediates, hormones, ions, or proteins, each directed at the entire cell, membrane receptors, enzyme activation, or gene expression.

These mechanisms form extensive and intricate information networks. The what and/or when of gene activity, whether or not transcription and translation take place, is the subject of an array of regulatory devices. Prokaryotic cells, bacteria, are incredibly complex, but eukaryotic cell self-regulation is even more complicated.[56] In the vein of self-regulation, Jablonka and Lamb quote Barbara McClintock:[57]

> In the future, attention will undoubtedly be centered on the genome with greater appreciation of its significance as a highly sensitive organ of the cell that monitors genomic activities and corrects common errors, senses unusual and unexpected events, and responds to them, often by restructuring the genome.[58]

The authors state that her work suggests that when cells cannot respond to stresses effectively by turning genes on and off or by modifying existing proteins, they mobilize systems that alter their DNA. These cell behaviors to deal with stress and adversity are not random, but they also are not precisely directed. They are *strategies*. They may include increasing the global rate of mutation, as if to get lucky with a new combination. A second type is local hypermutation, a mutation in a particularly useful place, as in bacteria that mutate genes determining surface structure, to evade host immune systems; it is also not random. These contingency genes, highly mutable, can be found in snakes and snails that must constantly change poisons to capture prey. The third type of stress response system is induced local mutation.[59]

Induced local mutation occurs in response to changed conditions, occurring particularly in those genes that help the organism cope with a new environmental threat. The mutation is not random. *E. coli* in bad times shuts off genes needed for reproduction and turns on genes to make a particular amino acid when it is in short supply.[60] Microbiologist Barbara Wright, experimenting with *E. coli*, looked for mutations in a defective copy of one of these amino acid genes.[61] If this gene was to produce the needed amino acid, it needed to mutate. She looked at its rate of mutation when the amino acid was lacking and found during these stressful conditions that this specific gene underwent elevated mutation. Jablonka and Lamb explain that these elevated mutation rates depended on a shortage of the gene–activating amino acid and a cell distress signal.[62] The more mutable gene then increased the chances of finding a combination that would increase its survival rate.

Life's plasticity is illustrated in its self-regulation, mutation strategies, hypermutation, and induced local mutation. Such plasticity leads to Life's ability to adaptively respond to selective pressures. Is this plasticity ultimately a mechanical property of a mechanical system, or is it an intentional strategy of agentive Life?

Up to this point, we have characterized Life as very old, yet sharing similar cellular and molecular structures and metabolic processes. Out of these underpinnings emerge the exquisite biological organization and ultimately the diverse forms we call Life. I have intimated that Life is an agent in its adaptation to its changing circumstances.

SO WHAT IS LIFE?

Is Life the manifestation of the self-organizing and self-creating capacities of selected organic matter? And is that selected organic matter solely material, or is it suffused with God's Breath? If Life can be synthesized, will it prove the former? Science is making progress toward creating Life in the lab. If scientists can coax molecules to self-assemble to produce Life, it will suggest that even the molecules have agency, meaning that the entire universe is suffused with *Ruach*.

Science, in less than 150 years, has established an impressive array of facts that characterize Life. We now know that Life was extant 3 billion years ago. Bacteria capable of surviving extreme conditions were the first organisms, and eventually sheets of them covered the earth and provided the planet with its oxygenated atmosphere. Then, about 550 million years ago, an array of multicellular organisms suddenly appeared, followed by a second explosion of more sophisticated forms about 12 million years later. Hominids appeared 2 to 3 million years ago, with different species developing in different geographical areas at the same time and sometimes coexisting, as humans and Neanderthals did for a time. Today Life in its innumerable iterations is dazzlingly diverse.

Furthermore, all of Life uses the same molecules, lives by DNA→ RNA→protein, and shares the universal genetic code, a combination that according to Freeland and colleagues shows one in a million optimization, making it the best of all possible codes.[63] The molecular basis for Life is supported by profoundly efficient DNA repair mechanisms, the folding of a protein to produce just the right enzyme, structural components, and receptors. Life is composed of cells, prokaryote bacteria crowding every available cranny and eukaryotes capable of building complex organisms. All cells show purpose, make physics and biochemistry work for them, exist in communities, and within their communities regulate themselves. Then there is mitosis, one cell becoming two in a choreographed performance that sees our children go from 7 pounds at birth to 170 pounds when they leave for college. What is behind the formation of their unique patterns? There appear to be developmental fields that act to create organized complexity.

There are suggestions that Life is an agent in its transformations. On a small scale, bacteria appear to direct certain genes to mutate to meet changing conditions. On a large scale, myriad and widely differing organisms are able to independently create almost identical body parts and functions. What are we to make of this convergence of creativity? We can certainly conclude that Life is almost infinitely more organized and complex than we ever imagined. The Psalmist's comment that we are fearfully and wonderfully made[64] looks like a huge understatement. And for all the marvelous insights about Life that science has given us, there are vexing explanatory gaps; how does Life leap from collections of molecules to organized complexity? How can cells show purpose, community, and the ability to recruit physics? How do we explain the radical higher levels of order, and particularly the phenomenon of animated matter, that we see in living things? Is Life created whole cloth by the hand of God, Creationist style? Has God partnered with natural processes to create Life, Intelligent Design style? Or is Life the manifestation of the self-organizing and self-creating capacities of selected organic matter? *And is that selected organic matter solely material, or is it suffused with God's Breath?* I submit that this is the most fundamental question of what Life is, untestable and unanswerable, and ultimately a matter of belief, the assumption that it is only material, or the faith that it is mystical. I choose to believe the latter option. This basic assumption is the basis for many, if not all persons,' most closely held, cherished, and defended beliefs.

I shall in the following pages offer data and opinions from biology and the Scriptures to formulate the following model of Life: From all outward appearances, Life sprang forth naturalistically, from the assemblies of particular organic molecules, to produce protocells, simple beginnings. But invisibly, on a spiritual level, God has lent his breath, the *Ruach,* to these particular molecules, to complete the creation of animate Life. In doing so, he has accorded Life from its beginnings the freedom to act on its own behalf, to evolve to meet changing circumstances. Freedom entails agency. By the *Ruach,* he has made Life an agent in its development and execution. With agency, Life brings forth from its molecules consciousness, sentience, and the advancements of skills and learning on every level of being, from the molecules to their networks to the whole organism. I will show that it does this by exploiting a variety of genetic strategies, such as random variation, and/or directed genetic or epigenetic changes. It will trade or ingest DNA in another form of molecular learning. It will at times, when in danger of being overwhelmed, in jujitsu fashion recruit and absorb an invader and advance using its DNA—a process called endosymbiosis. In summary, Life owes its existence to the *Ruach,* but it is free to vary itself to meet the challenges of existence. *But a caveat! A god-of-the-gaps argument looms here.*

This model can be proved false, in that it can be called into question if science can create Life in the laboratory. And scientists the world over are racing to do just that. Go to the National Library of Medicine website at **www.ncbi.nlm.nih.gov/pubmed** and search for "the origins of life." The search brings up 1,280 papers (as of October 2010) looking at various aspects of the subject, including several papers specifically addressing the question, "What is Life?" Perusal of journal publisher SpringerLink's specialty publication *Origin of Life and Evolution of Biospheres* shows papers on such subjects as prebiotic chemistry, prebiotic amino acids, theoretical modeling, homochirality,[65] and defining Life. I focus below on the work of the team of Nobel laureate molecular biologist Jack W. Szostak and its efforts to create Life,[66] particularly as set forth in the article "The Origins of Cellular Life."[67]

The authors, drawing on an enormous amount of research worldwide, are looking for plausible pathways for the transition from complex prebiotic chemistry to simple biological assemblies able to propagate themselves and evolve. These "protocells" require two key components—a membrane to make a compartment and a lengthy molecule able to transmit functional information to progeny. Their laboratory has focused on vesicles made up of fatty-acid membranes, by which protocells could take up nutrients, grow, and divide. They have experimented with an array of genetic polymers to understand their potential for genome replication within encapsulating membranes. Their goal is to create a laboratory model of a protocell to understand possible paths for the emergence of Life on Earth. Basically, they are investigating the advanced biochemical properties of enzymes, catalysts, and the self-assembly and self-organization inherent in some carbon–based molecules. How close are they to synthesizing life? I am convinced that it lies within the realm of the possible. What will it mean if they succeed?

If scientists can, through their sophisticated manipulations of bio-chemistry, coax the molecules to create Life, I believe they will have pushed the issue of animation back from organisms to the molecules themselves. I think they will have shown that the very molecules of the Earth and the Universe have agency. This suggests to me that the *Ruach* is not confined to Earth and its living things. Rather, the *Ruach* will prove, in my opinion, to be an intrinsic property of everything that is. However, since the creation of Life in vitro is presently only a hope that scientists entertain, I am in this volume sticking with *Ruach* animating organismic Life on Earth.

Let us now examine the evidence that Life is indeed agentive.

CHAPTER TWO

LIFE IS INTELLIGENT

Single-celled foraminifera build outer protective structures from sand grains, using smaller grains to caulk the spaces left by big grains. This is intelligent behavior. Researchers observe that even the smallest cells are sentient and possess a sort of intelligence.

oraminifera (forams) are a large group of protists, amoeba–like single–celled eukaryotes. Recall a brief discussion and collage of various protists in Chapter 1. They date foraminifera back 550 million years. Forams are distinguished by netlike pseudopods (fig. 2.1), with which they construct a shell–like outer protective layer, called a *test*. They make their tests by gluing together particles from the surroundings.

FIGURE 2.1
The foraminifera *Ammonia tepida*, alive, collected from San Francisco Bay.

Courtesy Scott Fay and Wikimedia Commons[1]

FIGURE 2.2

A "tree foraminifera" from Explorers Cove, Antarctica. Image and commentary are on Sam Bowser's blog at icelabyrinth.blogspot.com.

They are very choosy in their preferences. Some select only sponge spicules; others, only quartz grains; and yet others, sand grains only of a specific size. One foraminifera selects two different sizes of sand grain, using the smaller to caulk, or fill in, the spaces around the larger ones. Researcher Sam Bowser, a cell biologist, finds this ability truly amazing.[2]

Bavarian filmmaker Werner Herzog includes Bowser's work in Antarctica in his motion picture documentary *Encounters at the End of the World*.[3] He films Bowser diving beneath the ice to collect specimens of "tree foraminifera" (fig. 2.2) and then displaying with microscopy the foram's pseudopods collecting grains and assembling their test, or tree.

Bowser point outs that the pseudopods collect and sort sand particles in a particular pattern; they choose from the rest of the environment only the grains necessary for assembling a test. In response, Herzog wonders, cautiously, if such collecting and sorting could be an early sign of intelligence. Bowser agrees that one must be cautious about coming to such a conclusion, but he notes that in the early 1900s one British scientist, Edward Heron-Allen, suggested that the work of these single-celled organisms satisfied the requirements for current definitions of intelligence.[4]

So what do we have here? First, why the cautious wonder? I suspect that the idea of intelligence in a single-celled organism would be regarded as spooky. But here is an animated being that is sentient and has computational abilities. It remembers, chooses, and exhibits intent. It is skillful. It possesses a narrow band of self-efficacy. I would call this a form of intelligence. It is a sliver of intelligence that is optimized for its specific needs. How did the creature arrive at its present optimization? Certainly, it stood the test of time; natural selection winnowed out the more poorly designed. But what was the nature of the genetic variation that specified its form? Could animation, intelligence, and genetic variation be related? Does intelligence require a brain? The foram had to have learned its craft. Here then is a case where learning did not require a brain.

In his 2007 article, "Bacteria Are Small but Not Stupid: Cognition, Natural Genetic Engineering and Socio-Bacteriology," James Shapiro asserts that bacteria possess many "cognitive, computational and evolutionary capabilities" that enable them to communicate among themselves and even to "commandeer the basic cell biology of 'higher' plants and animals to meet their own needs." He concludes that recent remarkable observations require us to "recognize that even the smallest cells are sentient beings."[5] Edward Goldsmith, in a 2000 article titled "Intelligence Is Universal in Life," notes that behaviorists assume in Neo-Darwinian fashion "that living things memorize random atoms of information . . . reinforced by success" (remember, random variation followed by natural selection); he counters that "intelligence is not an exclusive prerogative of [the] human mind. The minds of insects operate in the same way as that of [human beings]. Even a cell has a sort of intelligence."[6]

These three discussions summarize what I hope to touch on in this chapter—that there is, in my opinion, evidence that all of Life, from communities of organisms down to their molecules, possess aspects of intelligence.

INTELLIGENCE, MEMORY, AND MOLECULES

Intelligence begins with memory. All animals remember. Synaptic growth (recall the synapse discussed in Chapter 1) accompanies the acquiring of memories. Learning-related synaptic plasticity found in snails is similar to that of mammals. Molecular change follows learning.

Intelligence begins with memory and is impossible without it. Dere et al., in an article titled "The Case for Episodic Memory in Animals,"[7] write that

> behavioral evidence [shows] that various animal species
> indeed show behavioral manifestations of different features of
> episodic memory, such as . . . "metacognition," "conscious
> recollection" of past events, "temporal order memory," "mental
> time travel" and have the capacity to remember personal expe-
> riences in terms of what happened, where and when.[8]

It is common knowledge that animals remember.

Eric Kandel was rewarded the Nobel Prize in 2000 for his discoveries of molecular mechanisms underlying learning and memory. Bailey and Kandel report that "synaptic remodeling and synaptic growth accompany various forms of long-term memory."[9] Recall in Chapter 1

FIGURE 2.3

Photo by Genny Anderson. Courtesy Wikimedia Commons[10]

Aplysia californica. The creature inks when stressed.

the diagram of a synapse; this is a prime site for the plasticity of nervous systems. Kandel has long experimented with the sea slug *Aplysia* (fig. 2.3). This creature's long-term memory is associated with the growth of new synapses. Bailey and Kandel conclude that "synaptic differentiation and growth induced by learning in the mature nervous system are highly dynamic and often rapid processes that can recruit both molecules and the mechanisms"[11] that can create new synapses. An excellent interview with Eric Kandel can be accessed free online at **www.jove.com/index/ details.stp?ID=762**, "Interview with Eric R. Kandel: From Memory, Free Will, and the Problem with Freud to Fortunate Decisions." In the interview, Dr. Kandel strongly supports the existence of free will.

Getting back to *Aplysia* and memory, what does a sea slug have to do with me? It turns out that the model for learning-related synaptic plasticity proposed for *Aplysia* is similar to the models neuroscientists have developed for mammals. "This similarity suggests that the cellular mechanisms of learning and memory have been highly conserved during evolution."[12] In other words, when Life comes up with an invention that works particularly well, it retains it and uses it over and over. *Note that learning, certainly an agentive act, initiates structural changes in the nervous system.*

INTELLIGENCE AT THE LEVEL OF ORGANISMS AND COMMUNITY

A slime mold can set up a complex food transport network in hours. Honeybees gang up to smother a wasp by sealing off its breathing holes. Army ants use their bodies to level their trails. Birds can think ahead. The cuttlefish can instantly camouflage itself. Life, able to adapt to new situations, exhibits agency and self-efficacy.

The slime mold *Physarum polycephalum* is a single-celled amoeba-like creature that hooks up to its food sources by building a network of tubes connecting them. Investigators in Tokyo surrounded a single organism with fragments of oats (a slime mold delicacy) in a pattern similar to the towns and cities surrounding Tokyo. Immediately, the slime mold deployed its tubules evenly in all directions, but within hours began to refine its pattern, strengthening the tunnels between the oat flakes. Within two days, it had connected the flakes with a transport system that strongly resembled the greater Tokyo rail system, a web that took hundreds of engineers decades to design and build.[13] Figure 2.4 depicts their findings.

Astonishing accomplishments such as these are found throughout the animal kingdom. I propose that we keep in mind that it is variation, natural selection, and geologic time acting in concert with the principal actor, Life itself, that produces such stunning results.

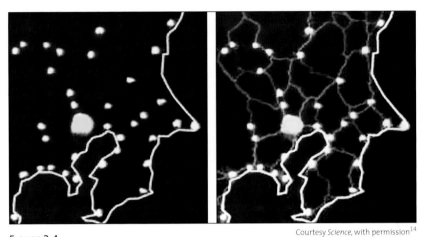

FIGURE 2.4

Courtesy *Science*, with permission[14]

Physarum polycephalum, the large dot at center, surrounded by oat flakes.
At 26 hours it has built a network similar to Tokyo's rail system.

FIGURE 2.5
Smothered to death:
Hornets asphyxiated by
honeybees.

Courtesy Elsevier, with permission[15]

Such agency is seen on a community level by honeybees of the
Cyprian strain that kill an attacking hornet by ganging up and smother-
ing it. They first surround (fig. 2.5) the abdomen of the hornet, where
its breathing holes are. Unlike most other insects, a hornet breathes by

FIGURE 2.6

Courtesy Elsevier, with permission[16]

Army ants covering holes experimentally drilled in their path. "How a Few Help All: Living Pothole Plugs Speed Prey Delivery in the Army Ant *Eciton burchellii*."

abdominal contractions. The bees press against the hornet's abdomen, blocking its ability to breathe.[17]

There is evidence that individuals within swarms can act intelligently: Army ants may use their own bodies to plug tiny potholes in rough trails (fig. 2.6). To examine how pothole filling affects the well-being of a colony, researchers inserted a variety of wood strips, drilled with holes, into the ants' principal trail. As the first ant reached a hole, it used its body to measure the fit. If the hole was small and the ant was large, it went on, leaving the hole for a smaller ant to fill. When an ant came to a hole that did fit, "It would hold a characteristic road-repair posture for as long as traffic continued to race over it. Then the ant would pop out of the hole and rush on."[18] Such acts contribute to the fitness of the colony.

Self-recognition is not a capacity in forams, but it can be seen in birds. This facet of intelligence is evidenced on the organismic level in experiments with magpies and mirrors; they check themselves out, and their reactions to their images in a mirror suggest self-recognition.[19]

Courtesy Elsevier, with permission

FIGURE 2.7

Rook raising the water level with stones, to float a worm.[20]

Courtesy Rainer Zenz and Wikimedia Commons[21]

FIGURE 2.8

Two Cuttlefish at the Georgia Aquarium. Through organs in their skin, these creatures can change colors and textures in an instant.

Rooks (fig. 2.7) think ahead and problem solve as they drop stones into a water-filled tube to raise the water level in order to float worms to within reach.[22]

Life's incredibly complex intelligence is seen on a more organismic and neuroanatomic level in the cuttlefish (fig. 2.8), which is able to camouflage itself by changing colors and patterns in waves and can furthermore mesmerize and immobilize prey with dazzling ripples of light. It is astonishing to see motion pictures of a cuttlefish moving over lighter or darker backgrounds, instantly varying its outer surface to match, or hovering over a hapless crab and arresting it with a vivid light show. The cuttlefish is able to vary its color and pattern via a network in its skin of pigmented cells connected to its eyes and brain. I don't mean to imply that this is a conscious choice on the part of the cuttlefish; rather, it is an entire network that has learned a repertoire of adaptive responses.

Common experience tells us that intelligence is all about learning to adapt to new situations. By that definition, Life—from the molecular to the whole organism, Life in all its mind-boggling diversity—is, in my opinion, profoundly intelligent.

THE INTELLIGENCE
OF SINGLE CELLS

Single cells perceive and choose. Bacteria trade DNA and can
expand their genetic capacities in minutes. This is intentional.
Cells are self-organizing, with genes spelling out parts of
the structure and system. Intelligence of the cell takes precedence
over the intelligence of the genes.

Moving from the level of the intelligence of complex organisms, we next address the intelligence of single cells. To comprehend Life at the cellular level, scientists such as Lynn Margulis, James Shapiro, and Franklin Harold have exhaustively probed bacteria and protists (single-celled organisms such as amoebas and paramecia). Margulis and Sagan's thoughts on Life derive from observations of the activity of cells.[23] They note that swimming bacteria and ciliates, when offered a variety of foods, make selections; they *choose*. *Amoeba proteus* (fig. 2.9) finds *Tetrahymena* delectable but avoids *Copromonas*. Paramecium dines on small ciliates but will settle for aeromonad and other bacteria. Forams make distinct choices of the sediments to make their shells; *Spiculosiphon* passes over many sediments to select only sponge spicules to make its

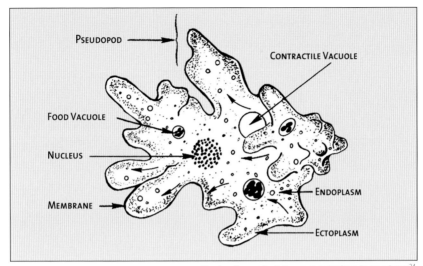

PSEUDOPOD

CONTRACTILE VACUOLE

FOOD VACUOLE

NUCLEUS

MEMBRANE

ENDOPLASM

ECTOPLASM

Courtesy Pearson Scott Foresman and Wikimedia Foundation[24]

FIGURE 2.9

Line art drawing of an amoeba.

shell. They write that without brains or hands, these determined protists choose their building materials. A chemotactic bacteria can smell a difference in chemical concentration that is a mere 1 part in 10,000 more concentrated at one end of its body than at the other. They assert that cells, alive, probably do feel. Protists reject indigestible mold spores and certain bacteria but greedily gobble up others.

"At even the most primordial level, living seems to entail sensation, choosing, mind. *Perception, choice, and sensation apply not just to human beings or animals but, if they apply at all, they apply to all life on Earth*" [Italics mine].[25] But I can imagine an objection: Where does reflex end and choice begin?

Bacteria regularly trade genetic information.[26] Having no nucleus, their DNA is loose within the cell. Unlike sexual reproduction, which vertically trades DNA, bacteria do so horizontally. They may form cell bridges through which genes are sent. Bacteria that cannot do this may transmit genes via viruses. They particularly trade information at times of drought, heat shock, when under attack by antibiotics, or to provide vitamins when they are deficient.

> DNA may separate from one dying bacterium and, either
> as pure DNA or coated with protein in a viral particle, it may
> splice into the genes of another bacterium. . . . By trading
> genes and acquiring new heritable traits, bacteria expand their
> genetic capacities—in minutes, or at most hours.[27]

I see this as a strategy, which implies intent; but how can you prove intent? This is a question that applies everywhere, in convergence, progress, and the optimization of innumerable functions and structures. Either Life is very, very lucky, or natural selection is incredibly efficient, or Life has a guardian angel, or it has a say in its fate. To argue the point further, we see purpose in bacterial function and behavior everywhere. The ability to form intent is a facet of intelligence. Again, I don't mean to imply that individual bacteria think and plan; the strategy lies in the global behavior of populations.

Franklin Harold marvels at Life as exemplified by single-celled organisms. He states,

> One senses that something is not accounted for very clearly
> in the single-minded dissection to the molecular level. . . .
>   . . . Before cells were taken apart . . . they displayed capaci-
> ties that go beyond chemistry. Homeostasis, purposeful behavior,
> reproduction, morphogenesis, and descent with modification are
> not part of the vocabulary of chemistry but point to higher levels
> of order . . . here we touch, if not the very secret of life, at least an
> essential stratum of that many-layered mystery. . . .
>   . . . How do millions, even billions, of molecules come
> to function in a collective, purposeful mode that extends over

distances orders of magnitude larger? This, in essence, is the problem of biological order.[28]

Harold's commentary suggests dissatisfaction with a materialistic, reductionistic view of life, and I take away from his statements a confirmation of Life as acting strategically and agentively over multiple layers of organization.

Harold writes that it is the cells, not the gene, that centrally organize the system. It is subtly misleading to think of cells carrying out the dictates of the genome, as if the genes were the master and cells the drones. Better to think of cells as three dimensionally self-organizing, with the genes spelling out all parts of the structure and the system. "Briefly, the genes specify [what is to be done, whereas] the cell as a whole directs Where and When . . . it is the cell that usually supplies the best answer to the question Why."[29] *I interpret this to mean that the intelligence of the cell takes precedence over the intelligence of the genes. But I shall argue in the next section that the genome has its own intelligence.*

THE GENIUS OF THE MOLECULES

An African fly can, through complex genetic rearrangements, mummify itself to survive drought. These and all genetic processes are exquisitely complex and synchronized; many have been around for 700 million years. There are also extra-genetic, or epigenetic processes, that clearly are intentional. Can we call these molecular operations intelligent? Some researchers think so. Could it be that we humans, composed of billions of such intelligent processes, have hardly scratched the surface of our own intelligence?

Can we find evidence of intelligence on a molecular and genetic level? An African fly survives severe droughts by mummifying itself in a sac (fig. 2.10), replacing its cellular water with the sugar trehalose,

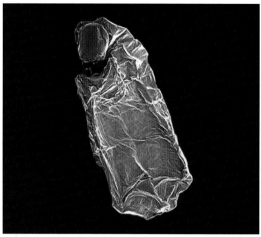

With permission from Takashi Okuda, National Institute
of Agrobiological Sciences, Tsukuba, Japan[30]

FIGURE 2.10

African fly mummifies
itself in a sac.

which turns it into a glassy state, much like melted sugar solidifies into
candy drops. The glassy sugar keeps the cellular structures from falling
apart. The fly is able to survive up to 17 years of drought, as it waits for
the next abundant rain.[31]

Trehalose is widespread in nature, being found in a variety of bacteria,
fungi, invertebrates, and plants that, like the African fly, can survive long
periods of dehydration and revive when provided with water. The sugar
also is involved in regulation of carbon metabolism and photosynthesis
and in plant–microorganism interactions. The genes involved in trehalose
biosynthesis have also been found in many organisms that do not accu-
mulate trehalose to significant levels.[32] In other words, certain organisms
switch on the expression of trehalose genes, and many others do not.

A plausible explanation might be that random variations in genes
coding for trehalose would be turned on and over time be selected for
in those organisms threatened with dehydration. In this scenario, the
organism has no agency, no say in how it is modified. Another possibility
is that a thirsty organism could switch on genes coding for trehalose and

hence mold itself for its own survival, an agentive position. A third possibility would be some combination of the two. Is there evidence for the second option? Let us look at a few of the intricacies of gene operations and ask if this is evidence for intelligence at the molecular level.

Thousands of times a second within living cells genes turn on and off, are expressed or suppressed, DNA is copied, genes are cut and pasted (spliced) or translated into RNA, proteins are synthesized, DNA is maintained or repaired, energy is transferred, and myriad other biochemical reactions occur with utter synchrony. It is as though billions and billions of orchestras were playing a dazzling composition with unimaginable elegance and precision, creating lyrics and melodies most beautiful. Within this whir of molecular activity, molecules are directed to make countless decisions a second. Gene splicing—knowing where to cut to exclude some lengths of DNA that are not desired for the synthesis of a particular protein (nontranslated regions), then the pasting together of those lengths that are to be used (translated regions)—is an example.

Jablonka and Lamb state that a gene is not simply a continuous sequence of DNA nucleotides coding for the sequence of amino acids in a protein. Rather, the DNA sequence coding for a protein is often a mosaic of translated and nontranslated regions. The translated regions, known as "exons," are interrupted by nontranslated ones, the "introns." What happens is that the whole DNA sequence is transcribed into RNA, but before this RNA arrives at the ribosomes (where the RNA will specify the sequence of amino acids to make proteins), it undergoes a process called splicing. Large protein—"spliceosomes"—excise the introns from the primary RNA transcript and join together the remaining exons. It is this processed messenger RNA (mRNA) that is translated into proteins. But there is more:

> Splicing is sometimes even more elaborate, because the exon or intron status of a sequence often is not fixed. In at least 40 percent of the RNA transcripts of human genes, different bits

can be spliced together. This means that one DNA sequence can give rise to many mRNAs and protein products. . . . The "decision" over which polypeptide will be formed depends on developmental and environmental conditions, as well as other genes in the genome. . . .

. . . How splicing is regulated—how each cell decides which segments of the primary RNA transcript are to be included in the mRNA that will be translated—is not yet understood.[33]

It obviously can't be a particular spliceosome that makes the decision; rather it has to be the complete organism, via its gene regulatory networks.

FIGURE 2.11
Nematostella vectensis, the Starlet Sea Anenome.

Courtesy Joint Genome Institute, U.S. Dept. of Energy, with permission[34]

Genetics researchers, now able to rapidly sequence the genomes of animals, are uncovering remarkable details of the genetic makeup of animals and our own species. Investigations of the starlet sea anemone *Nematostella vectensis* (fig. 2.11), a seemingly primitive animal related most closely to corals, jellyfish, and hydras, reveal it to contain 18K genes, with a gene repertoire, exon-intron structure, and large-scale gene linkage more similar to vertebrates than to flies or nematodes. The anemone genome's many segments of noncoding DNA (introns) must be delicately spliced out of genes when they are transcribed to RNA, just as we discussed in the previous paragraph. The study suggests that this advanced genetic cut-and-paste feature—one that scientists thought occurred primarily in higher animals—was present even in the ancient common ancestor of people and anemones. "Analysis of diverse pathways suggests that these gene 'inventions' along the lineage leading to animals were likely already well integrated with preexisting eukaryotic genes in the eumetazoan [a clade including all animals except sponges] progenitor."[35] These animals prove to have shared an ancestor with humans and other vertebrates 700 million years ago, yet have genetic structures and capabilities (such as splicing genes) seen in higher animals, including us. *I would only add that cutting and pasting truly were genetic inventions, and this study finds they were present very early in the history of Life. But as always there is no evidence as to how these capabilities arose; we are left to assume that they were random or that God directly created them or that agentive Life had a hand in fashioning them or perhaps some ID combination of the three. Which of these are most consistent with the evidence we do have?*

The introns in the starlet sea anemone *Nematostella vectensis* have implications for humankind's evolution. Subsequent chapters note that introns were once thought of as "junk" DNA but now are known to play a critical role in genome evolution, modulating gene expression. Intronic sequences make up a large proportion of most eukaryotic genomes. It turns out that the starlet has a large number of our introns, indicating that a large fraction of introns "present within the human genome likely originated early in evolution," in an ancestor common to us and the star-let, "at least 600 million years ago."[36] We will see in subsequent chapters how introns give evidence for the presence of natural genetic engineering, the role Life has had in creatively modifying itself.

Here is another example of molecular intelligence and intent, in Jablonka and Lamb's discussion of David Haig's idea about why some organisms have exploited genomic imprints in their extra-embryonic tissues (organisms have the capacity to "mark" or imprint chromosomes to govern their responses to cell signals).[37] Haig posits it as a conflict between father and mother on a molecular level, with both marking chromosomes or countering the other's marks. I do not mean to imply that parents consciously or deliberately mark chromosomes. This is conflict at the level of the genome.

> Each parent [marks] the transmitted chromosomes in a way
> that is for its own benefit. . . . in mammals, the X chromosome
> from the father is likely to be marked in a way that will benefit
> daughters, because the father gives his X chromosome only to
> female offspring. . . . A father will mark his chromosomes so
> that they make the offspring who receive them try to extract
> extra nutrients or care from the mother. But the mother will
> counterattack—she can mark her chromosomes in a way that
> will neutralize the marks on the paternal ones.[38]

I find this a vivid example, if indeed it is true, of intentional activity taking place on a molecular level. To me, this spells intelligence on the level of molecules. This is also an example of self-conflict—a topic to be addressed in Chapter 6—conflict I know to be true.

Jablonka and Lamb give yet another example of molecular intelligence in a discussion of "interference" RNA (RNAi) and its role in destroying abnormal RNA, which might have arisen from "invading viruses or the activities of genomic parasites [transposons]."[39] When a chromosome produces abnormal RNA, an enzyme known as Dicer recognizes the abnormal RNA and chops it into fragments. These fragments then act to further destroy more copies of the abnormal RNA, or they may deactivate the stretch of DNA that produced the original RNA. Thus, RNAi is a kind of cellular immune system. *All of this is biochemistry at work; the agency and self-efficacy lie in Life's repeated, consistent, and timely deployment of biochemistry.*

I will close this section with a statement by molecular biologist Lynn Caporale that summarizes the point I am trying to make as I talk about the genius of the molecules:

> Much as bats can see with sonar and dogs can use their exquisitely sensitive sense of smell to pick up sensations to which we humans are . . . effectively blind, the enzymes that copy, repair, and move DNA sequences live in a sense world that is different from ours. . . .
>
> . . . Since I use the word strategy in talking about genomes, I have been asked whether I am calling DNA "intelligent.". . . Is it the interaction of our brain with our environment, as we develop, that makes us become intelligent? But our genome set up the brain to experiment with the world effectively, to learn so well. . . . *If the human brain is intelligent, can we avoid considering that the human genome is intelligent in some sense, since it carries the information that in the proper context develops into a functioning human brain?* [italics mine][40]

In this chapter, we have discussed three single-celled organisms—chemotactic bacteria, forams, and slime mold—that possess astonishing computational, engineering, and construction skills. Could it be that the composite of single cells that is *Homo sapiens* has within itself similar vast capabilities. Perhaps we greatly underestimate our capacities, built as we are of billions of cells that individually can be so proficient and skillful. *Perhaps we have hardly scratched the surface of our own intelligence. This is particularly so with "mentalization," a capacity unique to humans. More on mentalization in coming chapters.*

CONVERGENCE

Convergence is the development by very dissimilar creatures of very similar solutions to a problem. Echolocation in bats and whales to navigate or find prey is an example. Convergence is organismic optimization. You see optimization everywhere, in the universe, the solar system, the physical constants, the genetic code, and in the perfection of camouflage, hunting strategies, replication strategies, eyes, limbs, immune systems, and nervous systems. It would appear that Life, using time and the resulting natural selection as a prime strategy, is the optimizer.

Another indication of the intelligence of all of Life is the phenomenon of convergence, how Life keeps coming up with similar solutions at different times and places, independently. There is a right, or optimal, answer to creatures' needs at any point in time, and Life in its innumerable iterations repeatedly and independently homes in on it. There is in convergence a goal directedness, a directionality. The Cambridge paleontologist Simon Conway Morris states, "Not only is the universe strangely fit to purpose, but so, too, . . . is life's ability to navigate to its solutions."[41] Morris' work on the Burgess shale (fig. 2.12) led to greater understanding of the Cambrian explosion, that geologic period that saw the appearance of a variety of new body plans.

Convergence is organismic optimization. You see it everywhere, in the universe, the solar system, the basic parameters, the genetic code, and in the perfection of camouflage, hunting strategies, replication strategies, eyes, limbs, immune systems, and nervous systems. What forces are doing the optimizing?

Morris states that convergence is seen in unrelated organisms: snakes, moles, burrowing frogs, and lizards became fossorial, adapted to digging beneath the earth. As in all of convergence, the evolutionary paths differed, but the endpoints were similar. It is visible in the mechanisms of balance, from insects to jellyfish to crabs to mammals. The camera eyes of vertebrates (such as humans), cephalopods (such as the octopus), and annelids (worms) bear striking similarity but evolved utterly independently of each other.

The most celebrated example is the similarity between the eyes of octopi and vertebrates, including humans, as illustrated in Figure 2.13.

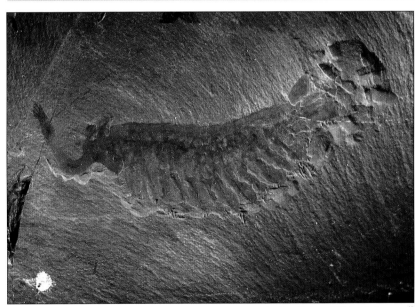

Courtesy JStuby and Wikimedia Commons[42]

FIGURE 2.12

"Fossil specimen of *Opabinia regalis* from the Burgess shale on display at the Smithsonian in Washington, DC. This appears to be the exact specimen pictured in Fig. 42 of *The Crucible of Creation: The Burgess Shale and the Rise of Animals*, by Simon Conway Morris, Oxford University Press, 1998."

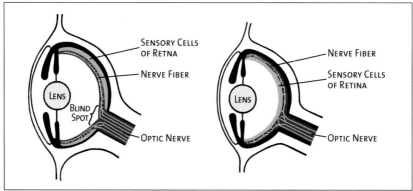

FIGURE 2.13   Courtesy Wikimedia Commons, Jerry Crimson Mann[43]

The Octopus eye and the *Homo sapiens* eye. Can you tell which is which?
The answer is in the endnote.[44]

Vertebrates and cephalopods must have diverged hundreds of million years ago. Morris notes that a camera-like eye has evolved independently at least six times. "This raises the question of how life navigates to such precise end-points, an analogy being how the Polynesians in the great Diaspora across the Pacific ever managed to find that remote speck of land that we call Easter Island."[45] But there are only so many ways an eye can work. The biggest question, then, is how, given the constraints of DNA, chemistry, and physics, these building blocks will inevitably be arranged (i.e., will arrange themselves) into the most workable, optimal patterns. Could this ordering be demonstrations of a molecular and organismic strategy?

There are myriad examples of convergence, such as echolocation, electric organs, and hearing. Mammals, birds, sharks, and insects have independently arrived at endothermy, the ability to elevate body heat above the surrounding temperature. Yet in each case these evolutionary solutions to environmental challenges are not identical; rather, optimization is unique for each species. Again, Life in its multitudinous forms constantly optimizes itself; that is, it has an uncanny propensity to zero in on the most efficient or workable adaptation possible under the constraining limits of molecular biology and physics. At the same time, freedom is allowed for a variety of blunders, blind alleys, and mistakes. Think of the Neanderthal.

MIND

Nervous system tissue is specialized for intelligence,
awareness, and learning; it has evolved from the tiniest beginnings.
There is evidence that it existed very early in Life's history.
There is an explanatory gap between mind and brain.
I argue that consciousness is the free exercise
of reason by nervous tissue lent Life by the Breath of God.

As I have argued, all living cells, down to the molecules, made animate by the breath of God, are hence imbued with awareness, skill, and intent. Such ability, intent, and awareness amount to intelligence. This intelligence is evident in whales, birds, and butterflies that migrate thousands of miles; in carrier shells that disguise themselves; and at the suborganismic level as creatures, such as Arctic and Antarctic fish that develop antifreeze proteins in their blood, interact with changing environments and ecosystems to adapt and cope with changes. Perhaps random mutations followed by natural selection hit upon antifreeze proteins; but I argue that the generation of randomness is itself a trial-and-error strategy. All of life, from molecules to organisms, is plastic. Life can learn by trial and error, but it also has other ways to be creative. Of course, over the eons, cells became specialists.

Nervous system tissue is specialized for intelligence, awareness, and learning, whereas liver cells are good at making bile, renal cells at filtration, and so on. Nervous systems have evolved from the tiniest beginnings. Denes et al. suggest that the genes patterning the nervous systems of the embryos of chordates (a phylum that includes vertebrates) and annelids (a phylum that includes worms) are surprisingly similar.[46] This extraordinary conservation[47] suggests that this patterning mechanism has been inherited largely unchanged from the bilaterian (a symmetrical creature) common ancestor and that the central nervous system is an ancient characteristic of animals. The capacities and capabilities of nervous tissue reach their peak with the elaborations inherent in the human nervous system, where awareness is raised to what we experience as self-reflective consciousness. The Breath can now fully express itself; it is sentient and able to reason. *Homo sapiens* is Life grown up.

The phenomenon of consciousness and its neural correlates are subject to interpretation. Advances in neuroscience, with its imaging of the brain during various mental and behavioral exercises, have detailed how its various activations underlie experience. Materialistic and reductionistic scientists and commentators regard consciousness and mind as no more than the firings of networks of neurons; there is no ghost in the machine. This position is termed *physicalism*. Less ideological neuroscientists, such as Christof Koch and Susan Greenfield, state,

> [We are not] attempting to explain *how* consciousness arises . . . [or] how physiological events in the brain translate into what *you* experiences consciousness.
> We are seeking a correlation—a way to show how brain phenomena and subjective experience match up, without identifying the all-important middle step of how a phenomenon causes an experience.[48]

This might be termed a pragmatic position. Others, such as philosopher and neuropsychologist Daniel Robinson, argue that mind is not reducible to its neural correlates; rather, he emphasizes the explanatory gap between brain function and humankind's rich experiences—such as making choices or the enjoyment of music or the struggle to distinguish the constructive from the destructive.[49] The elaboration of taste or ethics and morality cannot be predicted, and indeed they are qualitatively different from neural activity; the former are the processes of human experience, and the latter are processes of the brain. We might call this *nonreductive physicalism*, an agnostic position regarding the explanatory gap.

The explanatory gap between brain function and the contents of human desires, motives, and intentions parallels, and is indeed included in, the gap between the molecules and mechanisms of cell functioning and Life itself. Science is working to fill this gap and will quite possibly find a naturalistic explanation. But beyond the material characterization of Life, there remains the plausible interpretation of Life and its molecules as animated, intentional, intelligent, and agentive. In the first six chapters of this book, I am marshaling evidence for such a view, one that lends itself to the following Christian interpretation: Organisms exist by virtue of their animation by the literal or figurative Breath of God, and consciousness is an emergent epiphenomenon of agentive neural cells made intelligent by the same Breath.

Mine is not a dualist position; I also believe there is no ghost in the machine. Living things are indivisibly animatedly physical. Life is not organic molecules that are animated; rather, matter and animation compose its essential being. Think of Life as *animationmatter*. Life is a unitary whole, on loan from the Source of all Life.

SUMMARY

L ynn Margulis and Dorion Sagan summarize this chapter, "Life Is Intelligent," quite well—writing that just as Life takes in air, water, and food, so it takes in facts and experiences that may become memories. They insist that all of Life, animals, plants, and microorganisms perceive. All organisms must seek food and avoid danger.

A living being need not be conscious to perceive. . . . Most of our own daily activities—breathing, digesting, even turning a page or driving a car—are performed unconsciously . . . it is reasonable to assume that the sensitive, embodied actions of plants and bacteria are part of the same continuum of perception and action that culminates in our own most revered mental attributes. "Mind" may be the result of interacting cells. . . .

. . . Hundreds of millions of years before organic beings verbalized life, they recognized it.[50]

Later, they conclude that

the gulf between us and other organic beings is a matter of degree, not of kind. Taken together, the vast sentience comes from the piling up of little purposes, wants, and goals of uncounted trillions of autopoietic predecessors who exercised choices that influenced their evolution. If we grant our ancestors even a tiny fraction of the free will, consciousness, and culture we humans experience, the increase in complexity on Earth becomes easier to explain: life is the product not only of blind physical forces but also of selection, in the sense that organisms choose.[51]

On a personal note, the presence of sentience, purpose, free will, and intelligence support my sense that Life is transcendent. The heavens may declare the handiwork of God, and their vastness his infinity, but as I contemplate vastness and infinity, I feel lonely. However, the creatures in this chapter speak to me—the forams that build, the molds that design, the crow that thinks ahead, the cuttlefish who dazzle or disappear. I wonder at the *E. coli* that converse, compute, and trade information and the army ants that will lay down their bodies for their friends. At the heart of

Life, genomes cut and paste, and Dicers protect. All of Life converges on the optimal. I can relate to them, for I do all these things too. I also seek mastery. These are my brothers and sisters, for we share the Breath of Life. I am not alone because the Earth, and I suspect the universe, teems with God's Life.

Courtesy Wikimedia Commons[52]

FIGURE 2.14

The Cardsharps. Circa 1594 by Michelangelo Merisi da Caravaggio.
The point here is that deception, common among animals and plants, is a
form of intelligence.

CHAPTER THREE

LIFE LEARNS

All Life, down to the molecules, learns.
Adaptation is an active learning process. Many creatures have made
progress in nervous system complexity and learnability.

L iving tissue learns. We are accustomed to thinking of humans and
a few mammals as capable of learning, but the derogatory phrase
"bird brain" conveys the level of intelligence we attribute to the
nonhuman biosphere. However, biological studies are providing astonishing evidence of the learning ability of all Life, down not just to
one-celled organisms but to the very molecules that compose them and
us. I believe that learning is the key to the resilience and evolution of
organisms and their molecules. I will argue that *adaptation*, a biological term describing the ability of organisms to shift their forms to cope
with changing circumstances, though certainly subject to chance and
randomness, is by and large an active process. All organisms and their
molecular makeup are agents in their transformations. Let us look at the
evidence that suggests the uncanny ability of Life, from molecules to
cells to whole organisms, to learn.

Complex brains and advanced thinking processes have developed
from more primitive nervous systems multiple times in diverse lineages,
in such unrelated phyla as mollusks (octopuses, squid, and cuttlefish),
bony fishes, cartilaginous fishes (sharks, rays), reptiles, birds, and mammals. This convergent evolution of brains and the ability to learn includes learning by copying the behavior of others, learning to navigate
complicated mazes, making and using tools, and the use of memory to

predict the future. An octopus can learn a task by observing a fellow octopus accomplishing a maneuver in an adjacent tank. Goldfish and freshwater stingrays can quickly learn to find their way through mazes. Birds such as New Caledonian crows can manufacture and use simple tools to gain access to otherwise unobtainable foods. Florida scrub jays have been shown to recall where foods of different types were cached, what they cached, and when they did so. An African gray parrot learned to name 50 objects, could ask for objects by name, learned number labels from one to six, and even evidenced a concept of zero, or none.[1] It is not difficult to accept some degree of agency of animals. After all, most of us have viewed numerous documentaries depicting the ingenuity of nonhuman creatures. We can agree that agency and the ability to learn contribute to their survival.

ORGANISMS LEARN

Carrier shells have learned camouflage. Fruit flies learn and remember. *E. coli* can take in or give out information in the form of DNA. The green sea slug has learned photosynthesis by incorporating algae genes.
Many creatures navigate thousands of miles. Grunion have learned to use tide and sand to mate. It appears that as creatures learn, their genes follow suit and become fixed.

Carrier shells, of the genus *Xenophora*, have become expert in camouflage. These large sea snails attach shells, pebbles, or bits of coral to their shells with secretions of a cement from the foot. They move rapidly in a leaping motion, on sand or pebbly bottom, mostly in deep water.[2] Natural selection certainly favored those pioneering snails that learned to assemble this disguise (fig. 3.1). Where in this creature does the learning, and the agency involved, take place? Is there some form of consciousness

FIGURE 3.1
Xenophora pallidula.
From 80 to 100 fathoms depth off west coast of Leyte, Philippines. The elaborate structure on the top of the shell is a piece of discarded glass sponge.

Personal collection. Photo by Don Anderson

here? Is it a molecular consciousness? Are its actions genetic? If so, how did the genes get so smart? We can only say with certainty that, ultimately, it is the whole organism that learns.

The tiniest organisms learn. Jablonka and Lamb[3] state that fruit flies can learn and remember. They go on to assert that traditions can be seen in every aspect of animal life—in modes of foraging, criteria for selecting mates, ways of avoiding predators, decisions about where to live, practices of parental care, the use of communicative signs. They assert that wherever one looks, one sees them. That is, the agency of animals is everywhere. Even bacteria exhibit the ability to learn.[4] *E. coli* must contend with elaborate host immune systems, antibiotics, and changing environments. Caporale states that examining *E. coli* gives us a view of evolution that differs dramatically from the model of random letter-by-letter mutation followed by selection; bacteria are not restricted to such an unstructured approach.

Bacteria have evolved, and no doubt have acquired, mechanisms that enable them to sample and adapt information that is available in their environment and, in a two-way exchange, to share information with neighboring bacteria by sending pieces of DNA outside. DNA uptake is not an accident. Originally, perhaps, a bacterium, exploring for food, with an ancient, molecular curiosity, had taken up a dead bacteria's DNA and discovered what it could do. Modern bacteria have multiple mechanisms that they can use to acquire DNA.[5]

One of the consequences of such bacterial agency is antibiotic resistance.

Bacteria are not alone in gene transfer. The green sea slug is able to incorporate algae genes that are crucial to photosynthesis. By taking in another species' genes, animals play an active role in acquiring and

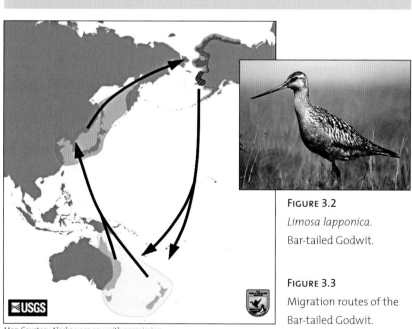

FIGURE 3.2
Limosa lapponica.
Bar-tailed Godwit.

FIGURE 3.3
Migration routes of the
Bar-tailed Godwit.

Map Courtesy Alaska.usgs.gov, with permission
Photo Courtesy Tim Bowman and Wikimedia Commons[6]

transmitting information. Animals actively participate in shaping the environment in which they live and are selected. "Niche construction" plays a significant role in social learning and the evolution of animal traditions. An example is that of black rats in a Jerusalem pine forest, how they learned to strip pinecones for their seeds and wound up living in the trees. After a number of generations, those better at living in the trees were selected. So success, as always, is selected for, but so is the intelligence of those individuals best able to figure out solutions. "Animals are therefore not just passive subjects of selection, because their own activities affect the adaptive value of their genetic and behavioral variations."[7]

As remarkable, visible, and beautiful as animal camouflage is animal migration. We marvel at how whales, seals, birds, turtles, and butterflies can annually and reliably navigate up to thousands of miles. For example, a tagged godwit (fig. 3.2) flew nonstop eight days from Alaska to New Zealand, a distance of 11,680 kilometers (fig. 3.3).[8]

In animals, this circadian behavior is an integrated system, starting with genes and leading ultimately to behavioral outputs. There has been remarkable progress identifying these circadian genes, but many remain to be discovered and identified.[9] Monarch butterflies annually undergo a spectacular fall migration, typically from east of the Rocky Mountains (fig. 3.4) to Mexico, and it may take several generations of the creatures to complete the journey. They navigate using a circadian clock located in cells in the insect's brain; the clock provides the timing to use the sun as a compass.[10] A more recent study on monarchs revealed a suite of 40 genes whose expression in the brain correlated with key migratory traits.[11] How did these living and dramatically intelligent genetic and behavioral systems come to accomplish all that they have? How to envision butterfly genes learning to migrate thousands of miles? One plausible scenario might be that proto-butterflies originated in the north during a warm period, followed the warm air south as fall approached, and returned in summers as the warm air moved north. Or perhaps they followed food sources. Genes then altered to follow suit. Recall from

Chapter 2 Kandel's studies on learning and neuroplasticity in *Aplysia*. *It appears to me that as organisms learn, genes change and the antecedent behavioral patterns become fixed.*

The questions we are raising have implications for the formations of whole life cycles. For example, California grunion spawn on sandy California beaches several times in summer, specifically for the second

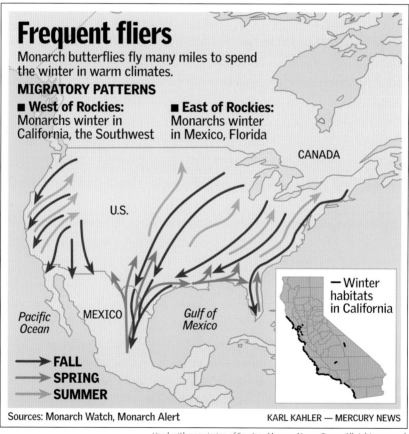

Frequent fliers

Monarch butterflies fly many miles to spend the winter in warm climates.

MIGRATORY PATTERNS

■ **West of Rockies:** Monarchs winter in California, the Southwest

■ **East of Rockies:** Monarchs winter in Mexico, Florida

CANADA

U.S.

Pacific Ocean

MEXICO

Gulf of Mexico

— Winter habitats in California

→ **FALL**
→ **SPRING**
→ **SUMMER**

Sources: Monarch Watch, Monarch Alert   KARL KAHLER — MERCURY NEWS

FIGURE 3.4

Monarch butterfly migratory routes.

to sixth nights after the full and new moon, on incoming tides. Females are swept in first, strand themselves, and drill tail first into the wet sand. There they lay about 3,000 bright orange eggs. Then males are swept in, sidle up to the half-buried females, then curve their bodies and emit milt to fertilize the eggs. The milt flows down the female's body until it reaches the eggs and fertilizes them. They then catch the next wave out, followed by the females.[12] There is a high probability that eggs and milt will make contact, certainly higher than if spawning in the ocean. So how can we explain how these creatures hit upon this novel solution to the problems, perils, and promises of mating? Indeed, how is the complex life cycle of any organism arrived at? It seems to me most probable that proto-grunion or some ancient ancestor stumbled upon this method, and the genetic rearrangements followed.

NETWORKS LEARN

Networks, particularly those made up of nervous system
(neural) cells, quickly learn. People adapt to special glasses that invert
the world. The brains of persons suffering obsessive compulsive
disorder (OCD) change as they respond to psychotherapy.
There are many more examples of neuroplasticity.

So far, we have considered whole organisms and their abilities to learn. But bacteria, butterflies, and migrating vertebrates have something in common: They exist as communities, or networks. In turn, individual organisms are complex networks or systems of organs, cells, proteins, and genes. Networks are the next level of organisms to consider. We will probe networks in their supra- and suborganismic levels in Chapter 5, "Life Is Community," but in this chapter as we plumb the ability to learn, we can ask if networks learn. Consider this example: In a series of experiments from the 1950s and shown on film,[13] experimental subjects

Courtesy aquarius3 and Wikimedia Commons[14]

FIGURE 3.5

Eric Kandel, psychiatrist and neuroscientist.

were given complex glasses to wear. The glasses blocked out all external light, and their lenses either exchanged right and left, or inverted the world. The subjects were filmed as they consistently mistook right for left, up for down, and so on. But over a period of days they adapted! After taking off the glasses, they again mistook right for left and up for down. What had changed? Visual perception, certainly. Visual systems and their networks? Or was this a shift in mind function? In a documentary I saw as a medical student, a man fitted with vision-inverting glasses reported that after a period of adaptation he perceived the world right side up. His visual networks had learned to stand on their heads! A chicken fitted with the glasses did not adapt. It would appear that the human brain is both quantitatively and qualitatively different.

Schwartz and Begley[15] give another example of such adaptation as they document human brain network changes during successful behavioral therapy with patients suffering severe Obsessive Compulsive Disorder (OCD). In these cases, functional magnetic resonance imaging (fMRI) scans demonstrated distinct improvement as they complied with and responded to Dr. Schwartz's behavioral therapy, showing again that mental and physical learning were taking place.

As noted in Chapter 2, Eric Kandel (fig. 3.5) won a Nobel Prize for studying learning and memory, first in the marine snail *Aplysia* and, later, in laboratory mice. He documented the effects of learning and conditioning on the animal's nervous systems, finding that long-term learning led to gene activation, which led in turn to new synaptic connections, which led to enduring molecular and anatomic changes in the brain. These are three examples of neural plasticity, of learning as it pertains to the nervous system. Are there instances of learning affecting other tissues? Is there evidence that the tissues of Life learn, changing as organisms learn? Indeed, is this a paradigm for how all learning and adaptation take place?

GENOMIC LEARNING

There is evidence that genomes have evolved mechanisms that create DNA mutations. A particular hotspot of genomic and molecular learning is in the area of attack and defense. For example, viruses constantly change to gain access to our cells, while our bodies just as quickly develop various forms of immunity.

Phenotypic plasticity (the capacity of Life to change its external form or behavior, its phenotype, as it adapts to environmental change) is a kind of molecular learning involving gene regulation, which involves turning on or off gene expression. But learning at the molecular level can also involve actual mutation, changes in the DNA structure of genes. Neo-Darwinism assumes that mutations are random, but Caporale states that her research leads her to conclude that mutations are not all accidental. She argues that "our genomes, and those of other life forms, have evolved mechanisms that *create* different kinds of mutations in their

DNA, and they reuse and adapt useful pieces of DNA, even to the point that there are genomic 'interchangeable parts.'" She envisions *genomes as strategically and actively generating diversity* [italics mine] and exhibiting "molecular mechanisms [that] . . . have the effect of anticipating and responding to challenges and opportunities that continue to emerge in the environment."[16]

   A hotspot of molecular learning is in the area of interactions of pathogen genomes (bacteria, viruses), the genomes of poisonous creatures (frogs, snakes, snails, scorpions, etc.), and the genomes of the objects of their attacks. Caporale discusses the toxic cone snail (fig. 3.6), which uses its venom to paralyze prey such as fish; her research shows that the snails have "evolved a *strategy* of directing genetic change to the stretch of DNA that encodes for its toxin." She adds that "other

FIGURE 3.6
Toxic Cone Shell.

Courtesy Aquarium of the Pacific, Long Beach, California

predators, too, from vipers to scorpions, seem to have special mechanisms to generate rapid variation in the very genes they need to attack their prey."[17] In like manner, the spirochaete bacterium that causes Lyme disease rapidly makes targeted changes to its outer protein coat to evade or neutralize the hosts' defenses.

Our own bodies are the objects of attack of an array of bacteria, viruses, and other microorganisms. To counter these tiny invaders' excursions, we deploy outer physical barriers (skin, mucous membranes), an innate immune system, and an adaptive immune system. All animals have an innate system, composed of macrophages (freely moving scavenger-like cells), natural killer cells (blood- or lymph-borne cells that attack viruses), and a protein that can punch holes in bacteria. Macrophages roam within a creature's tissues, extending their pseudopodia (arms) (fig. 3.7) to engulf debris or pathogens. Remarkably, the cells resemble amoebae, who get around using pseudopods, suggesting that this part of our tissues is another example of Life coming to similar solutions and designs in widely different organisms (convergent evolution). In the adaptive immune system, the DNA of the some 200 genes of blood-borne B cells (cells that make antibodies to attack the surfaces of intruders) can be cut and pasted in various combinations to produce 100 million different antibodies, to match the protein coats of every conceivable invader. That is, the genes of B cells are of a modular design that can be mixed and matched to produce incredible diversity. Molecular biologist Lauren Sompayrac[18] states that once Mother Nature gets a good idea, such as modular design, she uses it over and over.

Caporale goes on to summarize that the vertebrate immune response demonstrates how a creative genome can be structured to handle the unexpected, how it can integrate a variety of mechanisms for focused genetic change into one effective system. "Like the Lyme spirochaete, our immune system can move pieces of DNA around the genome in a targeted, strategic manner, but with even more complex choreography."[19] The genome maintains a strategic genomic infrastructure but conserves parts of antibodies used repeatedly. She states that we inherit three types of things: a large variety of potential pathogen-binding pieces, a few regions of DNA that encode the pathogen-destruction information, and creative DNA-moving mechanisms that enable us to recombine these pieces. She concludes that this enables us to create and to explore a huge variety of antibody genes very quickly, while conserving the pathogen-destroying machinery. *My thought is that such diversity through variability dramatically shows molecular intent.*

Many creatures, such as frogs and cone snails, defend against attack with their own internal toxins; for example, a Dahl's frog carries enough toxin to kill a snake. But snakes have learned to get around this defense because these frog toxins degrade in lethality over short periods of

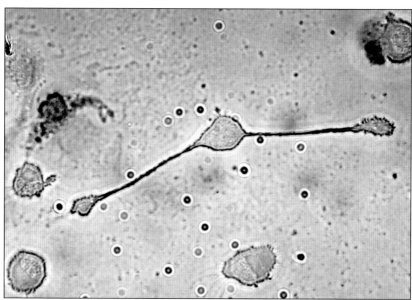

FIGURE 3.7   From magnaram, courtesy Wikimedia Commons[20]

A macrophage of a mouse forming two processes to phagocytize two smaller particles, possibly pathogens.

time.[21] The floodplain death adder has figured out the time to delay consuming various species of frog. Offered nonpoisonous rocket frogs, Adders consume them immediately, but they have learned to wait for the Dahl's frog toxin to degrade. The most likely explanation, it appears to me, is that snakes have learned to distinguish poisonous from nonpoisonous frogs based on their taste. Is the snake's decision gene based, or learned, with genetic modifications following suit? A Neo-Darwinian explanation for the frog's poison would be that over eons of time, genomes with chance mutations favoring the frog's survival would be selected. I have argued, following Colling's[22] lead, that chance mutations are a trial-and-error strategy. But could it be that the frog genome has evolved a strategy of *directing* genetic change to the stretches of DNA that encodes for effective poisons? But the snake catches on and recognizes the poisons, and its genome, in turn, adapts. Is there any evidence for these conjectures? *At any rate, I am struck by the choreography of Life, predators and prey, creature and environment, migrating creatures and the sun or earth's magnetic field, male and female. Such beautiful synchronicity is uncanny and suggests the agency of all of Life.*

Jablonka and Lamb assert that

> it is not difficult to imagine how a mutation-generating system that makes informed guesses about what will be useful would be favored by natural selection. In our judgment, the idea that there has been selection for the ability to make an educated guess is plausible, predictable, and validated by experiments; . . . "chance favors the prepared genome."[23]

Such abilities to make educated guesses (certainly a favorite method of learning) is echoed by Kirschner and Gerhart as they state that "novelty in physiology, anatomy, or behavior arises mostly by the use of conserved processes in new combinations at different times, and in different places and amounts, rather than by invention of new processes." They go on to say that "the components of living things are more like Lego blocks" and that "the regulatory components," the "RNA [and] DNA that determine the time, circumstances, and degree of activity of the processes," change. Their research shows that "evolutionary change is facilitated by simple regulatory tweaks . . . that long ago were designed so that the organism could adapt to its environment." The authors argue that "novelty usually comes about by deployment of existing cell behaviors in new combinations and to new extents, rather than in their drastic modifications or invention of completely new ones."[24] *I submit that such tinkering is clearly compatible with the idea of genomic learning.*

PSEUDOGENES

Pseudogenes are relics of genes, the result of mistakes in gene duplication at the time of cell division. Unused and discarded, they nevertheless make up a substantial proportion of our own genome. Rather than being dead, pseudogenes may form a reservoir of diverse "extra parts" that can be resurrected to help an organism adapt to its surroundings. The human genome stands out in having many processed pseudogenes. Some researchers think that the generation of processed pseudogenes has been an indispensable resource, driving dynamic evolution of mammalian genomes.

Thus far in this chapter we have moved from the undeniable learning ability of organisms to the experimental data and conjecture that suggest that suborganismic networks, such as visual networks and immunologic networks, also learn. On the gene level, there is evidence that organisms and their genomes are able to convert pseudogenes into functioning genes. Pseudogenes (fig. 3.8) are relics of genes, the result

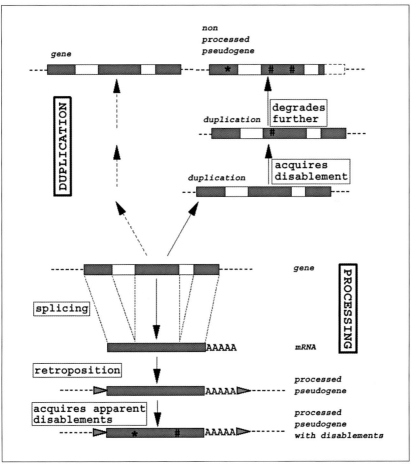

FIGURE 3.8

Mark Gerstein, with permission[25]

Pseudogene formation. From the normal gene in the middle of the diagram, normal duplication takes place (upward dotted arrow). Upward solid arrow on right shows a mutation that disables the gene. With further degradation, it becomes a classical pseudogene. Looking downward, in normal processing, introns of the gene are spliced out, and with addition of a poly (AAAAA) tail, normal messenger RNA (mRNA) is formed. But this mRNA can become retrotransposed (inserted back into the cell's DNA at a random position), creating a "processed" pseudogene. This can become further disabled.

of mistakes in gene duplication at the time of cell division. Unused and discarded, they nevertheless make up a substantial proportion of our own genome. The studies of Gerstein and Zheng have suggested that "in yeast, certain cell-surface protein pseudogenes are reactivated when the organism is challenged by a stressful new environment." They conclude that pseudogenes may be "potentially unborn genes: a resource tucked away in our genetic closet to be drawn on in changing circumstances." Discussing the reactivation of pseudogenes, they state that Nature may have "figured out a way to efficiently reuse the broken parts of genes."[26] *Parenthetically, I note the frequent allusions scientists make to "nature," "evolution," or "natural selection" as active agents in the modifications of Life. These scientists might dismiss such talk as figurative, but I think their language alludes to the deeper truth that Life in all its diverse forms has a hand in its adaptations.*

Harrison and Gerstein find that prokaryotes tend to dispense with pseudogenes, but "there appears to be less pressure to delete pseudo-genes in eukaryotes."[27] They note that "pseudogenes tend not to oc-cur in the middle of chromosome arms [but rather are often] associated with lineage-specific (as opposed to highly conserved) families that have environmental-response functions." They conclude that "rather than being dead [pseudogenes] may form a reservoir of diverse 'extra parts' that can be resurrected to help an organism adapt to its surroundings." They find that "the human genome stands out in having many processed pseudogenes,"[28] rehabilitated by reverse transcription from a messenger (mRNA) intermediate.

Sakai et al. point to the importance of pseudogenes in our own ge-nomic evolution. They note that "while gene duplications are recognized as one of the major driving forces in genome evolution, processed pseudo-genes, which are retrotransposed copies of mRNAs, have been regarded as junk or selfish DNA."[29] In their studies to detect processed pseudogenes, they extensively mapped the mRNAs to both the human and mouse genomes and then estimated the rate of the mRNA's emergence.

As a result, [their work] revealed that the rate of pseudogene emergence was about 1-2% per gene per million years, which was as high as the rate (0.9%) of gene duplication in the human genome. . . . Furthermore, 1% of the processed pseudogenes seemed to be reinvigorated by post-retrotransposition, transcription, many of them preserving the intact coding regions.

They theorize that "since the expression patterns of transcribed pseudogenes in various tissues were quite different between human and mouse, their emergence might have led to species-specific evolution." They infer from their studies that "the generation of processed pseudogenes . . . has been an indispensable resource, driving dynamic evolution of these mammalian genomes."[30]

VIRUSES

Viruses are parasites that depend on the gene operations
of healthy cells to survive and replicate. They are ingenious
in their strategies to recruit cells to reproduce them.
Though the collection of but a few molecules, they exhibit
exquisite molecular intent. However, turnabout
is fair play; sometimes, we can recruit their DNA or RNA.

Viruses have no respiration, metabolism, or ability to reproduce themselves, yet they are the most abundant life form.[31] They are cell parasites, owing their existence to hijacking the replicating ability of cells. They infect prokaryotes and eukaryotes and are thought to have originated very early in the evolution of life.[32] In Chapter 2, I mentioned genomic parasites called "transposons," segments of genes that actually jump around the genome, and Chapters 5 and 6 address them more fully. It is thought that transposons are the relics of captured and recruited

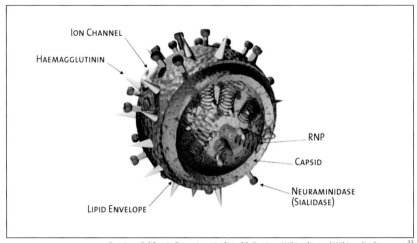

ION CHANNEL

HAEMAGGLUTININ

RNP

CAPSID

NEURAMINIDASE
(SIALIDASE)

LIPID ENVELOPE

FIGURE 3.9   Courtesy California Department of Health Services, Wikipedia, and Wikimedia Commons[33]

3D model of an influenza virus. The outer envelope is composed of lipids and two proteins, and the central core of RNA nucleoprotein (RNP). Haemagglutinin facilitates binding the virus to the cell, and neuraminidase is involved in the release of progeny from the infected cell.

viruses. To successfully reproduce, they must learn to (1) evade host defenses; (2) gain entrance to cells; (3) once inside the cell, have plans for copying the host cell's DNA and for producing the mRNA that will encode the proteins the viruses need for their operations; and (4) find a way to spread.[34] Furthermore, they need to coexist with their hosts and kill as few as possible. The fact that they are very ancient and abundant suggests they have solved these four problems very well. More than 50 different viruses can infect humans.

Viruses can spread hand to mouth, sexually, and via ticks, mosquitoes, or fleas, but by far the most popular way is by the respiratory tract. So let's zero in on the influenza A virus, a bug with which we are only too familiar. Figure 3.9 is a schematic of the virus. Figure 3.10 illustrates the steps from invasion to replication to release.

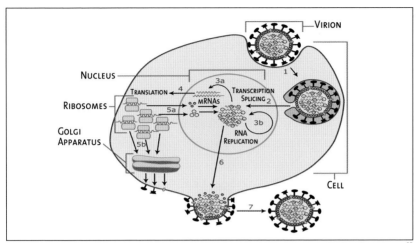

FIGURE 3.10

Courtesy User YK Times and Wikimedia Commons[35]

A diagram of influenza viral cell invasion and replication. The virus's first step (#1 on the diagram) is to bind with its haemagglutinin molecules to receptors on the cell surface and induce the cell membrane to surround it, a process called endocytosis. In the second part of step 1, the virus uses the now inverted cell membrane ion pump mechanisms to pump in hydrogen ions to acidify itself, which fuses the endosome and the viral capsid, releasing the viral genome (RNP) into the cell. In step 2, RNP uses cellular transport machinery and nuclear localization signals present on viral proteins to enter the cell nucleus. In steps 3a and 3b, the viral polymerase complexes (cells don't carry this, so the virus brings its own) transcribe and replicate viral mRNAs. Step 4 sees the newly minted mRNAs migrate to the cytoplasm where they are translated. Not shown in the diagram is something nasty that the influenza virus does. "Viral proteins actually bite off one end of cellular mRNA molecules that are present in the cell's nucleus, and use these snippets of RNA to begin synthesis of viral mRNA." Such theft "provides the virus with a ready-made cap" and focuses the cell's "protein synthesis machinery on the production of viral proteins."[36] Between steps 4 and 5a, the mRNA makes new viral coat proteins, including haemagglutinin and viral polymerase. In step 5a, these proteins reenter the nucleus, where the new viral genomes are minted and the new viruses are assembled. In step 5b, viral coat proteins are synthesized and extruded to the cell surface. In step 6, the RNA-protein complex buds from the cell surface, where a portion of now viral protein studded cell membrane is ripped off to coat the new virus. Step 7 sees the new virus on its way.[37] This entire process kills the host cell.

What of the symptoms of flu that we experience? Does this assault cause the fever, muscle aches, violent headaches, and the wiped-out feeling when we just don't want to move? Interestingly, it is our bodies' counterattacks that cause these symptoms. Fever, pain, and not wanting to move are our friends, for with high fever and immobility, our immune systems more efficiently combat infections.

So what do we have here? First, we have only scratched the surface of the intricacies and cruel elegance of this infection. We have seen here a small set of structured molecules that can, with a series of perfectly orchestrated steps, commandeer living cells for the purposes of their own reproduction. I am in awe of what basically is a house invasion where the occupants are systematically robbed, recruited to slave labor, and finally left for dead. I find this a most remarkable example of molecular intent, and I see in the serial operations of the virus a sophistication that adds up to, for want of a better word, intelligence. Finally, here is yet another example of a life cycle that is the result of specific learning on the molecular level.

Conversely, host organisms learn from viruses. Just as viruses exhibit intent, so do all organisms in their coping with, adapting to, and even ultimately benefiting from viral attacks. Several virologists, including Luis Villarreal and physician-virologist Frank Ryan, present extensive evidence that numerous life forms, after surviving viral assaults, have recruited and used viral RNA, DNA, and various viral polymerases to further their own evolution. In other words, viruses could affect the evolution of the hosts they infected.[38] Chapter 4 cites the work of James Shapiro, which suggests that transposable elements, the residual DNA of prior viral infections and once thought to be "junk" DNA, are now thought to have powerful gene regulatory functions. Chapter 5 discusses endosymbiosis, the concept that once inimical viral elements have been accommodated or recruited into the genome and now contribute to the functioning and reproductive fitness of the organism.

EPIGENETIC LEARNING

Molecular learning can take place in areas other than the genome.
It is as though Life can make and keep "how-to" notes of structural,
architectural, or gene activities and then pass these notes on
to the next generation. These notes can instruct and influence gene
behaviors and assist in adaptation to changing environments.
This is called the "epigenetic inheritance system."

Evolution is the history of Life's transformations, from its beginnings. It is clear that Life's changes are based on its propensity to generate variations of itself, followed by the naturally selective winnowing process. Neo-Darwinians insist that Life's variations are random; I have added that Life is able to use mistakes in DNA replication and/or to generate more or less effectively its own variation, making educated guesses as to what is necessary for its adaptation to changing circumstances. This learning, as well as being organismic, suborganismic, and genetic, can take place on an epigenetic level. There are several ways that organisms can transform themselves outside the genetic system. These epigenetic inheritance systems (EISs) include memories of gene activity (self-sustaining loops), the inheritance of structural and architectural memories, chromosomal memories through chromatin marking, and the silencing of genes through RNA interference (RNAi). What does all this evidence that epigenetic variations can be transmitted to the next generation mean for evolutionary theory? Because it provides an additional source of variation, evolution can occur through the epigenetic dimension of heredity. In addition, epigenetic variations are generated at a higher rate than the genetic, especially in changed environmental conditions, and several epigenetic variations may occur at the same time. Furthermore, these changes may be purposive, because changes in epigenetic marks probably occur preferentially on genes that are induced to be active by new conditions, increasing the chances that a variation will be beneficial.

This high rate of generation and a good chance of being appropriate means that adaptation through the selection of epigenetic variants may be quite rapid compared with adaptation through genetic changes.[39]

Recall the discussion in the Introduction of the five major schools of thought in the evolution controversy, as proposed by Fowler and Kuebler:[40] Creationism, Intelligent Design, Theistic Evolution, Neo-Darwinism, and Meta-Darwinism. Of these schools, only Meta-Darwinism ascribes to Life some agency in its creation and self-modification. It will prove to be the most useful in bringing about a rapprochement of evolution and Christianity. *The various phenomena explored in this chapter support, I feel, Meta-Darwinism and my thesis that Life, through its ability to learn, is an active agent in its evolution.*

MOLECULAR LEARNING IN THE EVOLUTION OF HUMANKIND

It appears that as we learn, our brains grow. The past 37,000 years has seen genes for brain growth increase dramatically in frequency. Life through its learning evolves and adapts.

This activity extends to humankind's history. Genetic evidence of the degree of our genomic evolution comes from Evans et al. who report that the gene Microcephalin, which regulates brain size, has evolved and flourished in the human evolutionary lineage. They show that "one genetic variant of Microcephalin . . . arose approximately 37,000 years ago and increased in frequency too rapidly to be compatible with neutral drift,"[41] suggesting the ongoing evolutionary plasticity of the human brain. In the same vein, the gene ASPM "is a specific regulator of brain size, and its evolution in the lineage leading to *Homo sapiens* was driven by strong positive selection" (meaning the variation was very successful). "One genetic variant of *ASPM* in humans arose [a mere]

5,800 years ago and has since swept to high frequency under strong positive selection." This implies that "the human brain is still undergoing rapid adaptive evolution."[42] These findings suggest that there is a complementary relationship between learning, gene modifications, and the growth of the brain. *I submit that all levels of Life, from the molecular to the organismic to the community, learn within themselves and from each other.* Also, think of the implications of these findings for humankind. As consumed as we and all of Life are by self-conflict, there is progress! I find this a cause for optimism.

Jablonka and Lamb write that "the current fashion among evolutionists, seen particularly in the writings of those who study human behavior, is to stress the genetic basis of behavior," that "the behavioral strategies for . . . finding a mate, or becoming socially dominant, or evading danger, or finding food, or caring for infants are to a large extent genetically determined and evolutionarily independent of each other." Such a Neo-Darwinian view holds that each strategy "has been shaped through the natural selection of genes that led to the construction of a specific behavior module in the brain." *Here is an example of the idea of Life as clay, with natural selection the shaper.* The authors, writing that all biologists would agree that learning is helpful and genetically based, raise the question "but is learning also *an agent* of evolutionary change?" [authors' italics].[43] Caporale expresses a similar view as she quotes Nobel laureate Barbara McClintock, who states that in the future, " 'attention . . . will be centered on the genome . . . sensing the unusual and unexpected events and responding to them.' "[44] *My thinking is that here is another statement supporting the idea of molecular intelligence and molecular agency acting in synchrony with and response to the environment.*

Neo-Darwinism, with its emphasis on random variation followed by natural selection to shape the species, is the dominant theory of evolution. In reviewing the work of Margulis and Sagan, Caporale, and Jablonka and Lamb, we see the emergence of dissenting views that ascribe to Life a much more active role in shaping its destiny. And dissenting views are not just a recent phenomenon. Though Darwin's views captured the allegiance of the England of his time, Samuel Butler, as noted in Chapter 4 ("Life Modifies Itself"), disagreed that Life was too inert to play a formative role in its own development. Margulis and Sagan write that Butler presented sentient life as making numberless tiny decisions— and is thus responsible in part for its own evolution. This is the plausible interpretation of the scientific data concerning Life that I take in this book.

What does this incredible ability to learn mean for humankind individually and corporately? It means that we and our race are sitting atop, within our genomes, an ancient mountain of genius, an almost unfathomable reservoir of skills dealing with every challenge imaginable. No wonder humankind is capable of creating vehicles to take us to the stars or weapons of mass destruction! So it isn't a matter of what we can do but of what we choose to do that counts.

A CLOSING NOTE
ABOUT LEARNING

As a psychiatric resident in the late '60s, I had a mentor who opened my eyes to the delights of learning by breaking through the dogmatic containers encasing my own reservoir of skills. Milton Erickson (fig. 3.11) was a profoundly gifted and disciplined psychiatrist who revolutionized the use of hypnosis for the care of people suffering chronic pain, anxiety, and a host of mental maladies. He didn't espouse a school of thought; rather, he created de novo a psychotherapy for every individual he encountered. Two of my fellow residents and I studied his prolific writings, met with him, and attended his seminars and demonstrations. In his writings, he stressed the importance of being open to learning. As a Christian, I was used to being challenged by theories that were hostile to Christianity; there was always some truth in even the most antagonistic idea. But with Erickson, I was confused because what he did seemed to bear no relationship to Christianity one way or the other. The other part of it was that his approach to therapy was extremely effective.

He was very accessible, so I decided to seek his counsel for my failing first marriage. His appearance was remarkable; suffering post–polio syndrome, he was wheelchair-bound, had the use of only his right hand, and looked close to death. After listening to my fundamentalistic assertion that the husband should be head of the wife, he told me I was rigid and launched into an hour's worth of stories about people who never changed. I felt dizzy and disoriented, and I was drawn into the emotional tone of each story. I lived the monotony of people who associated with only one kind of person, of those wedded to a party, a movement, or an ideology or who always dined out at the same restaurant. I remarked, "Yes, there is an obsessive sameness about me." At the end of the session, he looked at me hard and stated, "Take everything you know and throw it away!" I protested incredulously, "How can that be?" He grinned and replied, "The good will stick." I had the sense that I had been soundly thrashed, but I left with the exhilarating feeling that I was now free to change. The encounter began a lifetime of a passion for learning. Though I decided to stick with Jesus, I threw away the notion that with my version of Christianity I had all the answers.

FIGURE 3.11
Milton Erickson.

Courtesy Ait Salem and Wikimedia Commons[45]

LIFE
MODIFIES ITSELF

L ife has without question evolved over geologic time according to Charles Darwin's scheme of variation acted on by natural selection (NS). The source of that variation, according to contemporary Neo-Darwinists, is gene duplication followed by random mutation. Miller writes that Darwin identified NS as the efficient cause that shaped all living things, while variation, that upon which NS acts, is thought to stem from the error proneness of DNA replication (the cell proliferation that takes place within the developing embryo).[1] Colling argues that such random variation is an overarching strategy in Life's coping with changing circumstances and challenges.[2] Error plus chance leads to synchronous complexity, given enough time. This might be thought of as the safecracking model of variation; the safecracker spins out various combinations of numbers at a rapid rate until bingo, the safe opens.[3]

But there are other paths to variation: Could it be possible that intelligent genomes and organisms to some extent play a part in varying and regulating their own DNA makeup? I especially like the views of a small group of scientists, which we can term *Meta-Darwinists*, who see Life as an agent in its own intrinsic variation, transformation, and adaptation to changing environments and conditions. *But these differences of opinion actually are minor; biologists generally concur that life has a striking ability to change and even to generate change. "The design of life, ironically, includes an ability to change its own design"* [italics mine].[4]

Nikola Kojic, a biomedical engineer at MIT, asks us to imagine enlarging a spider's orb web proportionally to the size of a football field: It could stop a jumbo jet in midflight![5] In fact, orb weaver spiders spin five fibrous silks and two adhesive silks into their webs. Dragline silk, as strong as steel but far tougher, is used for the web's outer rim and spokes. In contrast, capture-spiral silk is sticky, extremely stretchy, and tough. The other five silks have mixes of these qualities. The various silks are composed of assorted amino acids strung in sequences. Silk thread contains hundreds of thousands of protein chains, each of which folds on its own and also arranges itself among other chains in the fiber. Specialized glands, one for each type of silk, secrete a thick liquid of protein and water, called spinning dope, into a storage sac. To spin, the spider moves the dope into a nozzle, from which exits the thread. Materials scientists are slowly trying to emulate these processes. Silk worms have independently evolved similar materials. Spiders have been at this for 400 million years (fig. 4.1). How on earth did these creatures develop such astonishing anatomic characteristics and the silks that materials scientists have so far been unable to copy?

I would say there are four possible ways such creatures and their products came to be: (1) trial and error through spontaneous mutation and NS, over geologic time; (2) created whole cloth by the hand of God; (3) through some ability over geologic time for organisms to intrinsically organize themselves, followed by NS; or (4) in Intelligent Design style, some combination of the three. I will take literally, for the sake of argument, biologists' consensus statements about Life's striking ability to generate its own change and design. "Natural genetic engineering," "Nature," or Life as "tinkerer" are very consistent with such a view; this chapter presents evidence for and descriptions of these means of variation. We'll weigh the contributions of epigenetics (the actions of cells that lie outside the direct purview or regulation of the genome) to variation. We'll consider further some evidence and opinions regarding nonrandom variation. Throughout this chapter, we'll look at the work

Courtesy Wikimedia Commons[6]

FIGURE 4.1

Dew drops on a spider web on a winter morning.

and opinions of James Shapiro, Lynn Caporale, Lynn Margulis, Eva Jablonka and Marion Lamb, and others whose work, I believe, suggests that Life as agent modifies itself. Let us examine first in some detail what we mean by *variation*.

VARIATION IN EVOLUTION

Organisms and cells are able to make controlled changes
to their DNA. The major source of evolutionary novelty is
gene duplication, followed by changes to the new gene.
This natural genetic engineering is done by cutting and pasting.
Two particular areas of cutting and pasting occur:
among gene elements that move about (transposons) and
in our immune system cells, which must be nimble to
respond to counterattacks. Numerous natural experiments
among hominids resulted in the human brain.

Organisms and their cells are able to make controlled changes in their DNA in numerous ways. Whole or parts of a normal chromosome can be deleted, replicated, amplified, duplicated, or rearranged.[7] Though these changes occur in somatic, not germline,[8] cells, Shapiro argues that the very existence of such cellular machinery that changes DNA in a regulated way suggests that similar processes may occur in germline cells and play a part in evolutionary change.[9] Dawkins describes "snipping out" of DNA, and "splicing in" of other bits of DNA, as parts of the normal stock-in-trade of the cellular apparatus.[10] Noting that genomes routinely invert and translocate DNA by cutting and pasting, he concludes that replicability and spliceability stand out among all the gene operations.

Single-base mutations, recombination, and deletions are sources of hereditary variation, but the major source of evolutionary novelty appears to be gene duplication, followed by progressive divergence. This would account for homology (similarities in structure, as a result of common ancestry) among proteins of widely different functions. Genomes accommodate, and often preserve, various mobile genetic elements (e.g., viruses, transposons, and plasmids).[11] Read on for the significance of such accommodations.

Jablonka and Lamb, Dawkins, and Harold, in their descriptions of kinds of DNA variability, describe some of the processes termed "natural genetic engineering." A case in point of this natural genetic engineering is exemplified by the sequencing of the chimpanzee genome and the comparison with its human counterpart, which reveals the spectrum of genetic changes accompanying human evolution. An example of this involves the human genome, where the telomere-to-telomere[12] fusion of two ancestral primate chromosomes produced human chromosome 2 (fig. 4.2). Miller has an excellent discussion of the primate gene rearrangement and splicing to produce human chromosome 2.[13]

Other changes include the human-specific pericentric inversions of chromosomes 1 and 18, as well as numerous deletions, duplications, and inversions. These examples undoubtedly represent the kinds of genetic changes underlying hominid evolution.

Ian Tattersall is curator of the American Museum of Natural History in New York City; he is responsible for its marvelous hominid exhibit. He writes basically that just as successful mammals evolved by trial and error, so did the superior intelligence of *Homo sapiens*.[14] Figure 4.3 is a schematic of hominid evolution.

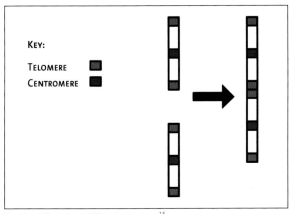

KEY:

TELOMERE

CENTROMERE

FIGURE 4.2

Diagram of ancestral fusion forming human chromosome 2.

Courtesy of Evercat and Wikimedia Commons[15]

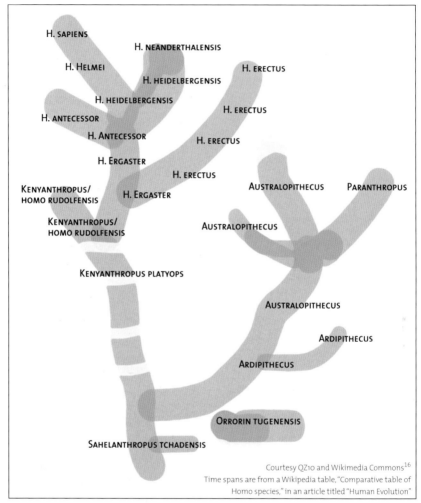

Courtesy QZ10 and Wikimedia Commons[16]
Time spans are from a Wikipedia table, "Comparative table of
Homo species," in an article titled "Human Evolution"

FIGURE 4.3

Hominid Evolution. *Sahelanthropus* spanned 7 to 6 million years ago. *Orrorin* 6
million years ago. *Ardipithecus* 5.5 to 4.4 million years ago. *Australopithecus* 4 to
1.8 million years ago. *Kenyanthropus* 3 to 2.7 million years ago. *H. ergaster* 1.9 to 1.4
million years ago. *H. erectus* 1.5 to 0.2 million years ago. *H. antecessor* 1.2 to .8 million
years ago. *H. heidelbergensis* 0.6 to 0.35 million years ago. *H. neanderthalensis* 0.35
to 0.03 million years ago. *H. sapiens* 0.2 to the present. Many of these creatures
existed at the same time, as Neanderthals and humans did.

Tattersall states that not all improvement and growth in evolution is slow and gradual; various hominids apparently developed their symbolic cognitive functions in remarkably short order, evolutionarily speaking.[17] He writes that the hominid fossil record indicates that there were from the outset several distinct hominids present at the same time, rather than there being a gradually changing linear chain. Noting the large

FIGURE 4.4

Reconstruction of a Neanderthal child, from fossil remains. Made by a research team from the Anthropological Institute, University of Zurich, using sophisticated X-ray, scanning, and modeling techniques. In spite of this remarkable likeness to a human child, Neanderthals were genetically quite distinct.

Picture by Christoph P. E. Zollikofer. Courtesy Wikimedia Commons[18]

number and diversity of known hominid species, he declares that this is evidence that humankind evolved from experiments that had given rise to multiple species, some of whom coexisted, rather than there being a linear development with fine-tuning.[19] A fine example of this is the Neanderthals, a genetically distinct group whose occurrence overlapped with humankind's (see fig. 4.4).

NATURAL GENETIC ENGINEERING

Organisms can shape and alter their genomes.
Of the human genome, 43% can transpose itself from one location to another. These transposable elements often come to function as regulators of other genes. This promotes flexibility and underlies the plasticity of living organisms.

Cells, and Life itself—as noted in the chapters on self-organization and self-regulation and as discussed in Chapter 5 ("Life Is Community")—function as carefully regulated and integrated systems; they are more or less in control of their being, unless they are overwhelmed, damaged, or dying. Within the context of such system functioning, and as an aspect of it, organisms can shape and alter their genomes. This is plasticity, and the mechanisms composing plasticity are well documented. In this section, I turn to the article by University of Chicago molecular biologist James A. Shapiro, "A 21st Century View of Evolution: Genome System Architecture, Repetitive DNA, and Natural Genetic Engineering."[20]

Shapiro points out that 43% of the DNA in the human genome can transpose itself from one location to another. Colling adds that in actuality virtually all of it can (and does) move around.[21] Our genomes are not fixed and static like the codes in your computer; rather,

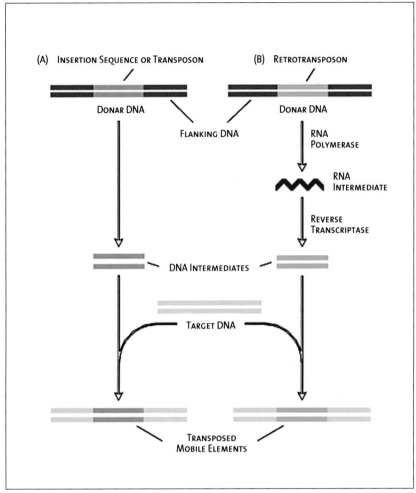

FIGURE 4.5

Two mechanisms of transposition. In transposition, the transposon gets itself
copied and then pasted into another area of the genome. In retrotransposition,
the transposon is transcribed to RNA, and via an enzyme it carries (reverse
transcriptase), gets itself transcribed back to DNA, which is then inserted into
a new stretch of DNA. In practice these movements are much more complex.
In one of the simplest uses of transposition, a transposon in a bacteria may carry
a gene that confers antibiotic resistance to a recipient bacteria.

there are DNA elements that can cut, move, and then paste themselves elsewhere, and furthermore, they can take other DNA elements with them. DNAs that can transpose themselves are termed *repetitive elements, mobile genetic elements,* or *transposons.* In addition, there are a number of types of transposons, such as DNA transposons that move at the level of DNA molecules, and retrotransposons that move by means of an RNA intermediate that can be reverse-transcribed into genomic DNA (fig. 4.5). Transposons are scattered throughout the genome and are characterized by repeating DNA sequences; hence the term *repetitive elements.* They have come to be recognized as exerting formatting and regulatory effects on the genome.

Shapiro states that molecular analysis has shown that the mechanisms of transposition likely also underlie both large- and small-scale rearrangements.

> The mechanisms underlying these rearrangements are just the kind of processes needed to explain the patterns of genome conservation and scrambling found by comparing whole genome sequences. There is abundant documentation that these mechanisms have been used in evolution.[23]

Transposons are not always rogue elements; they are usually part of tightly controlled systems that function according to cell and organism logic. Such evolutionarily significant genome elements and their effects are nonrandom.

Shapiro calls attention to the mammalian immune system as an example of the directed genetic change associated with repetitive elements. Humankind, and indeed all of Life, including bacteria, is under attack by viruses and other microorganisms. To counter such assaults, Life has developed elaborate defenses. Consider our own immune system: There are barrier defenses, the innate defense system, and the adaptive immune system. Barrier defenses include skin, saliva, acid, digestive

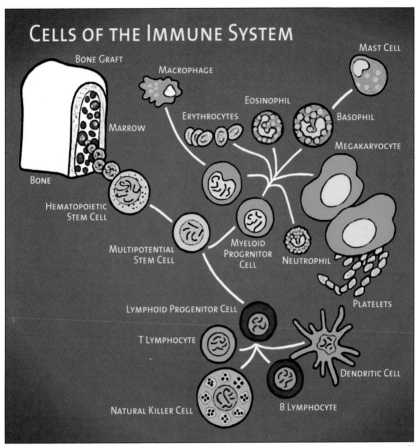

CELLS OF THE IMMUNE SYSTEM

Courtesy Jeannie Kelly and Wikimedia Commons[24]

FIGURE 4.6

Cells of the immune system emerge from the bone marrow, then differentiate into components of the innate and adaptive immune systems. Note that red blood cells and platelets also originate from the marrow. These have no immune functions.

enzymes, and mucus. The innate system includes various stationary and circulating cells (T lymphocytes, natural killer cells, dendritic cells) and proteins that can gobble up invaders or tag them for destruction (fig. 4.6). But it is the adaptive immune system that uses directed genetic change to offer the most flexible and innovative protection. B lymphocytes are the cells that undergo adaptive mutation in order to custom tailor "antibodies" (proteins that attach to viruses to facilitate their destruction) to the proteins (called "antigens") that are part of the surfaces of viruses. Here is how the natural genetic engineering takes place: The B cell reads the antigens on the viral surface and then rearranges its DNA to code for the antibodies that will destroy it. In every B cell, on the chromosomes within it that encode the antibody chains, there are multiple copies of four types of DNA modules, or gene segments, labeled V, D, J, and C. There are about 100 different V segments, 4 D segments, 6 J segments, and 10 C segments. The B cell will cut, paste, and combine these DNA segments to make the appropriate antibody. There are potentially about 10 trillion possible combinations. This B cell can then be selected and cloned, millions of times in short order, to fight off a viral attack.[25] Shapiro states that the immune system is here displaying how much control it can exert over DNA restructuring. He notes that this degree of cell control over natural genetic engineering is not an isolated case.

Shapiro concludes that transposons constitute a natural genetic engineering force that can nonrandomly carry out DNA rearrangements that are important in evolutionary change. *Cell and organismic systems regulate these repetitive elements, by which they can time and locate DNA rearrangements* [italics mine]. Shapiro closes his paper by stating that these ideas are consistent with molecular genetics but are quite different from conventional evolutionary theory; they will lead us to ask questions that could not have been imagined in the mid–20th century.

Caporale shares Shapiro's views. She notes that many find the idea of evolution difficult because of the *assumption* that random mutation accounts for changes, but she notes, "Mutations are not all accidents and . . . mutations are not always random." That each new step results in organisms getting better at finding food, fending off threats, and adapting to ongoing difficulties suggests that these changes weren't merely random.

"Over time, there emerged something that, viewing the effects now, we might call *strategies*—such as the ability to actively generate diversity . . . [making] genomes . . . more efficient at adapting and evolving." This does not set aside Darwin's theory but helps us to a greater understanding of how natural selection works:

> Our genomes and those of other life forms have evolved mechanisms that create different kinds of mutations in their DNA, and they reuse and adapt useful pieces of DNA, even to the point that there are genomic "interchangeable parts." Natural selection acts not only on fins and wings, but also on the mechanisms that change a genome. . . . "Successful" genomes—the ones that survive—are the genomes that evolve what here I will call mutation strategies.[26]

The idea that gene regulatory regions, once thought to be "junk" DNA, could be critical to shaping embryonic development has experimental support with the work of Prabhakar et al.[27] The authors focused on discovering the function of the most rapidly evolving human noncoding element yet identified, called "human-accelerated conserved noncoding sequence 1 (HACNS1)." This gene regulatory region exists pretty much unchanged in other vertebrate species, yet in humans it has accumulated 16 sequence changes in the 6 million years since the human–chimpanzee split. This is a dramatic acceleration, four times the expected value, so the authors set out to test its functional significance in human evolution. Basically, they inserted HACNS1, and analogous sequences from chimpanzees and rhesus macaques, into mouse embryos, then looked at the microscopic changes at embryonic day 11.5. The result? The human element brought about robust changes in several structures, including the anterior limb bud; the two monkey elements were much more weakly influential. Focusing on the anterior limb bud, it became clear that HACNS1 was producing a strong human-specific

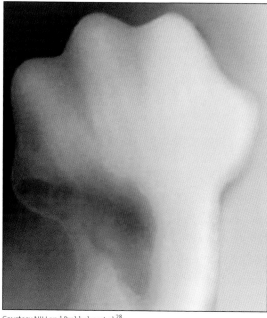

FIGURE 4.7

Human gene HCNA1, inserted into mouse embryos, activated genes in mouse thumbs and big toes. The limb bud looks human.

expression in the limb bud (fig. 4.7). The investigators concluded that the 16 sequence changes have contributed to uniquely human aspects of digit and limb patterning.

So how did these 16 sequence changes arise? And how did they arise so rapidly? "Strikingly, these human-specific substitutions are significantly clustered: 13 of 16 substitutions occur within an 81 basepair region of the 546 basepair conserved region, suggesting that this region may be particularly relevant to the human-specific function of HACNS1."[29] So what are the possibilities for the origin of these absolutely critical substitutions, changes that led to human, rather than chimp, hands? We are back to the four options: (1) a fortuitous grouping of random occurrences, (2) the hand of God, (3) an ID-style combination, or (4) some ability on the part of Life to modify itself. This leads us to Life as tinkerer.

LIFE IS A TINKERER

Organisms can put genes to work for alternative purposes.
In molecular tinkering, the modular organization of networks
of genes and proteins are like Lego blocks that can be used
to create novel structures. For example, the vertebrate jaw
came from elements that supported the gills of jawless fish.
Then organisms modified jawbones to carry vibrations,
which finally ended up as the tiny bones of our middle ear.

The analysis of DNA from a choanoflagellate, a microscopic spermlike organism (fig. 4.8) shows that it contains many of the same tools for cell-to-cell communication found in animals today. This single-celled creature branched off from the common ancestor with animals 600 million years ago. Genomes from flies, mice, and humans have considerable

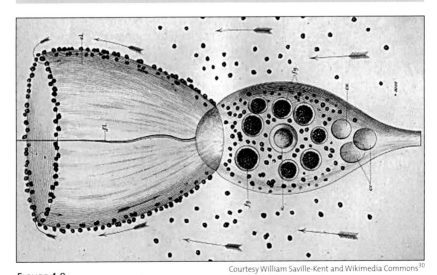

Courtesy William Saville-Kent and Wikimedia Commons[30]

FIGURE 4.8

The feeding mechanism of the related organism *Monosiga gracilis*.

similarity; now, it turns out that this creature's DNA contains as many sequences that code for proteins per gene as animals do, with many coding for proteins that are involved in vital processes in animals. Researchers say that the flagellate used genes in other roles before they were co-opted for different functions. For example, genes for proteins that help cells stick together in animals may be similar to those used by choanoflagellates to attach to the seafloor. Genes for immune systems in animals might have been used by choanoflagellate to help recognize the bacteria they eat. They even have a complete set of signaling molecules that in animals regulate communication within and between animal cells.[31]

This is an example of molecular tinkering; genes in choanoflagellate that were involved in recognizing prey, attaching to the sea floor, or signaling have been commandeered in subsequent organisms to different functions. The modular organization of networks of genes, proteins, and genomes allows a multitude of uses, much as I might use a paper clip to pick my teeth, my cell phone to tell time, or a hammer as a paperweight.[32]

Jablonka and Lamb describe tinkering as an old and well-established piece of evolutionary biology.[33] They note that new features often stem from structures that had different purposes, the vertebrate jaw deriving from the gills of jawless fish or the borrowing and modification of jaws to transmit vibrations, eventually giving mammals the tiny bones of the middle ear. Jablonka and Lamb note that even though a structure is "recruited for a new job," it often keeps its old job too. Mammalian hair, for example, most likely started as insulation before gaining roles in courtship displays, camouflage, and sensory whiskers on the snout.

Caporale likens the genome and gene families to a department store, with its sections having a variety of shoes, jackets, kitchen utensils, and so on. Life hits on useful patterns and keeps them. Through duplications and variations, genomes create gene families consisting of up to a thousand genes. Revising copies of genes or combining pieces of extant genes or resurrecting pseudogenes (discarded nonfunctional relics of genes) can lead to new proteins. Caporale writes that, for example, somewhere an ancient genome developed a protein that could cut another protein. In a sense, in addition to evolving cloth, it fashioned scissors. Saving the scissors, it could then, by gene duplication and tinkering, evolve even more sophisticated molecular scissors.

> If it could do that, it would be way ahead of a genome
> that had to rely on random mutation of random
> DNA to make more protein-cutting proteins. . . .
> Genomic knowledge can be leveraged over and over
> again . . . [to] build up a repertoire of tools and skills.[34]

Genomes use interchangeable parts, combining and tinkering with sequences of DNA, linking them in different combinations, to discover something else useful. Thus, a sequence of DNA coding for a receptor that takes cholesterol out of the blood can also be found as part of a receptor that tells cells to divide in response to a growth factor. This cutting and pasting is facilitated by the modular construction of both proteins and DNA. The modular construction of genes allows for blocks of DNA that encode protein modules to be moved about and attached to one another in different combinations. Caporale argues that this is not random, which is in addition to mutations happening randomly during the duplication of genes. In both cases, NS selects those that consistently lead to a useful new function.

I am reminded of what Craig Venter, the colorful biotechnologist and businessman who contributed greatly to the sequencing of the human genome, concluded in Chapter 1, after he described microorganisms that live in extremely strong acid or base solutions, microbes that withstand 3 million rads of radiation and after getting blown apart, stitch themselves back together, and so on: "Nature over 4 billion years of evolutionary tinkering has created a wealth of biological and metabolic templates."[35]

NATURAL EPIGENETIC ENGINEERING

The ways genes are wrapped and packaged allow them to be turned
on or off and hence influence how the organism will function in
a given circumstance. This is another source of semidirected variation
by which organisms can make educated guesses as to how
they'll meet a particular challenge of life. This again supports
the idea of Life as agent in its adaptation.

Cells are very plastic; that is, depending on environmental circumstances, they can assume different functions and morphologies,
maintaining all the while their stable DNA complement. An obvious
example is seen during embryogenesis, where cells with identical DNA
content become liver cells or blood elements or skin or neurons. Epigenesis is the means by which organisms can alter or govern which genes
are activated or inactivated to produce a desired outcome. Such gene
expression or silencing is accomplished by an array of mechanisms, most
commonly by altering the chromatin packaging of genes.

Genes and the DNA that composes them are not lying around naked
and exposed in the nuclei of cells. Rather, they are packaged to produce
a "chromatin structure." Through the modulation and modification of
chromatin, genes are activated or inactivated. Figure 4.9 illustrates chromatin structuring. In a journal article, Jablonka and Lamb argue that
chromatin modulation and subsequent gene modification allow organisms to make adjustments to environmental changes without waiting
for random genetic changes to occur.[36] Though Darwin recognized the
role of the environment in causing heritable variation, scientists at the
advent of genetics adopted the mechanism of random gene mutations independent of environment. The authors argue that this view fails to explain many evolutionary phenomena and is not consistent with emerging
data, from molecular biology to cultural studies. They note that the data
show a "genome far more responsive to the environment than previously

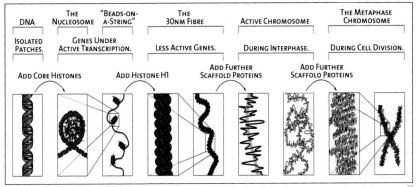

DNA	THE NUCLEOSOME	"BEADS-ON-A-STRING"	THE 30NM FIBRE	ACTIVE CHROMOSOME	THE METAPHASE CHROMOSOME
ISOLATED PATCHES.	GENES UNDER ACTIVE TRANSCRIPTION.		LESS ACTIVE GENES.	DURING INTERPHASE.	DURING CELL DIVISION.

ADD CORE HISTONES ADD HISTONE H1 ADD FURTHER SCAFFOLD PROTEINS ADD FURTHER SCAFFOLD PROTEINS

Courtesy Richard Wheeler and Wikimedia Commons[37]

FIGURE 4.9

Chromatin Structuring: How DNA is packaged. In eukaryotic cells, DNA (starting at the left of the diagram) is wrapped around histone proteins to form nucleosomes (second frame), which are in turn strung together like beads, linked by linker DNA (third frame). These nucleosome fibers are further wrapped tightly to produce less active (turned-off) genes, or loosely to produce more active (turned-on) genes. How the chromatin structure is modulated determines the accessibility of the gene and hence whether the gene is turned on or off. An array of biochemical mechanisms "marks" the DNA to modulate how the genes are wrapped. These marks are passed on to future generations.[38]

thought" and that some "variations arise in response to developmental conditions."[39]

Jablonka and Lamb wonder what the epigenetic transmission of traits to the next generation means for evolutionary theory. They note that evolution can occur because epigenesis provides an additional source of variation. They add that epigenetic variations occur more frequently, especially when the environment changes, and several may occur simultaneously.

Furthermore, they may not be blind to function, because changes in epigenetic marks probably occur preferentially on genes that are induced to be active by new conditions, [increasing] the chances that a variation will be beneficial. . . . [This] high rate of generation and a good chance of being appropriate . . . means that adaptation through the selection of epigenetic variants may be quite rapid compared with adaptation through genetic change.[40]

They go on to state their opinion that persistent, stressful, changed conditions are exactly those that may have initiated the origin of many new species. Stress awaits new arrivals to an environment for which they are not adapted, and such stress may induce epigenetic and genetic variation, a recipe for evolution. They caution that "as we see it, stress-induced variation has often been significant in adaptive evolution and speciation. . . . [but there is no evidence for this, and] *no one has good direct evidence about how new species originate*" [italics mine].[41]

Jablonka and Lamb, while acknowledging that random changes take place,[42] argue that organisms are in addition able to "bias when, where, and what kinds of variation occur."[43] Precise genomic modifications are not in an organism's interest, because environmental conditions vary. What is needed are approximate changes. They state that "many epigenetic and cultural differences are nonaccidental . . . there are many different instructive processes that lead to educated guesses. . . . evolutionary change can be very rapid, because often an induced change will occur repeatedly and in many individuals simultaneously." They call such capacity to make educated guesses "evolved plasticity"—that is, "internal (evolved) systems that generate 'intelligent guesses' in response to the conditions of life."[44]

In conclusion, I think it is plausible that, through natural epigenetic engineering methods, organisms can cope with changing environmental conditions by making educated guesses about what will be required to meet the challenges of life. This again supports the concept of Life as agent. There is, however, a downside to all this plasticity, and that is *dys*-plasticity. Epigenetic gene regulation is subject to errors and corruption, being implicated in disease processes such as cancer and in congenital disorders such as Rett syndrome,[45] schizophrenia, autism, and bipolar disorder. It appears quite likely that epigenetic mechanisms are central to drug addictions, with such drugs as cocaine co-opting transcriptional regulation, leading to chronic states of drug craving. In my practice of addiction medicine, it is painfully apparent that drugs of abuse co-opt brain function. On the bright side, epigenetics also holds promise for new and novel therapies for a variety of conditions, including those mentioned above.[46]

EYES

Eyes are an excellent example of how widely differing creatures come up with similar solutions to a problem. Molecular tinkering is seen repeatedly as organisms co-opt and redeploy basic building blocks. Genes for the control of eye development are similar in organisms as different as planaria and mammals. Molecular intent and agency are apparent in the evolution of eyes.

Life, in its 3-billion-year history, has responded to the ubiquitous light by constructing perhaps nine types of eyes, camera eyes and compound eyes the most common. From a few light sensitive proteins in bacteria to eye spots in protists to the trichromacy (color vision, coming from mixes of three primary colors) of humankind, Life has exploited and refined the physical properties of selected proteins to achieve visual perception. Morris notes that the camera eye has evolved independently numerous times, being found in vertebrates, cephalopods (squid, octopus), snails, spiders, and some jellyfish.[47] Though details of these eyes differ, it appears that varieties of living creatures repeatedly reach similar solutions to the need for vision. There are convergences as well in the molecular architecture of vision, with recruitment and modifications of the crystallins (transparent proteins used in lenses), and the opsins (proteins able to convert light into electrical signals). Morris concludes that evolutionary novelty is only skin deep, with Life constantly co-opting and redeploying basic building blocks to construct more sophisticated structures. *My argument is that Life, by virtue of having God's breath on loan, has a say in its adaptations. God is the indirect creator. It follows that Life will keep coming up with similar optimal solutions.*

The lens family of proteins, the crystallins, was co-opted from stress resistor proteins, particularly heat shock proteins, that are found even in bacteria; they have been around for billions of years. Opsins are G-protein-coupled receptors (GPCRs); they are embedded in the cell membranes of retinal cells, and they act to convert light to electrical impulses. They are combined with retinal, which comes from Vitamin A, to make up rhodopsin, found in rod photoreceptor cells; these are our night vision receptors. Other opsins make up our cone photoreceptor cells; these amino acid chains have variations that allow for the absorption of particular wavelengths of light, to enable perception of colors. Morris notes that the sites of substitution on these amino acids are extremely specific; for red-green vision, there are five sites. He points out that red-green vision and its molecular basis has evolved independently in several species; one well-known example is the convergence in red vision between a fish and mammals where two, and possible three, sites show identical substitutions.

In the same vein, Caporale discusses molecular tinkering, where DNA that codes for capturing energy from red light is copied and then modified to capture green light. She asks,

> If you wanted to build a protein that detects green light,
> where would you begin? Why start from scratch? I'd tinker
> with the DNA that encodes the red-detecting protein.
> . . . Perhaps we can get the protein to see green just by fiddling
> a little with the parts of the protein that interact with the

pigment. Before I did any tinkering, of course, I would make a copy of the red gene. . . . Over the course of evolution, genomes have, in fact, "learned" that they do not have to reinvent the wheel.[48]

Caporale goes on to point out that the ability of genomes to copy and vary genes goes way back, is universal in Life, and underlies the biosphere's tremendous diversity. "Many of the genetic concepts that are used to go from worm egg to worm are also used to go from human egg to human."[49]

What I find remarkable about this is not only the intricacy of the molecular basis of Life but also its precision. It seems to me the repeated precise modifications of opsins to achieve color vision exemplifies Life's agency, as opposed to its being solely passively subject to random mutation and natural selection.

Fernald states that though there is an incredible diversity among extant eyes, all animals share a common molecular strategy—using opsin to catch light.[50] He notes that "a family of conserved genes [meaning that Life, having invented particular genes early in its history, subsequently and through many organisms has preserved and handed down their structures] is involved in eye formation despite substantial differences in their structure and origin."[51] These particular suites of genes and their protein products have been recruited repeatedly. Especially interesting are the genes that switch on eye formation in the first place. *This preservation or conservation of particular parts of genes through eons of time again suggests molecular intent and agency.*

The Swiss scientist W. J. Gehring is known for his discovery of the homeobox, a DNA sequence found in plants, fungi, and animals (including humans) that makes proteins (called transcription factors) that switch on cascades of genes crucial in morphogenesis, the formation of embryos.[52] He and his colleagues have identified *Pax6,* a master control gene for eye development. Life, in the course of its history, has generated several very different kinds of eyes, like the camera eye, the compound eye (fig. 4.10), and the mirror eye. Because these eyes are so dissimilar, it was thought that they evolved independently, up to 40 to 60 times. But Gehring's discovery of the ubiquity of Pax6 has led him to argue for a single genesis of all eyes—indeed, their origin with single-celled photoreceptors.

Mutations influencing eye development are well known. Fruit flies have an eyeless mutation, mice have a similar mutation called small eye, and humans can suffer a hereditary syndrome called aniridia, a condition in which the eye has no iris. The genes responsible for these mutations, when cloned, turned out to be homologs—that is, members of a gene family, of a gene designated Pax6. Subsequently, he found that the mouse

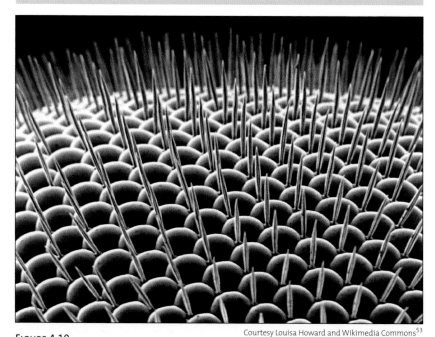

FIGURE 4.10

Courtesy Louisa Howard and Wikimedia Commons[53]

Scanning electron microscope picture of the compound eye of a fruit fly.

Pax6 gene could induce eyes on the antennae and legs of the fruit fly by triggering the fly's 2,000 other genes that were required to produce whole eyes. This and other experiments led to the conclusion that Pax6 initiates the genetic cascade to build eyes in both insects and mammals. The various Pax6 family genes found in mammals and flies do differ, but they arose from a prototypic ancestor and were modified by bits and pieces, illustrating the principle that Life is a tinkerer.

So what was this prototype eye, and how did it arise in the first place? Darwin postulated that the initial eye would be a single photo-receptor cell and a single pigment cell. The planarian *Polycelis auricularia* (fig. 4.11) has multiple eyes that exactly fit Darwin's idea, each eye having a single cell of each. Another is *Planaria torva*, whose eyes consist of

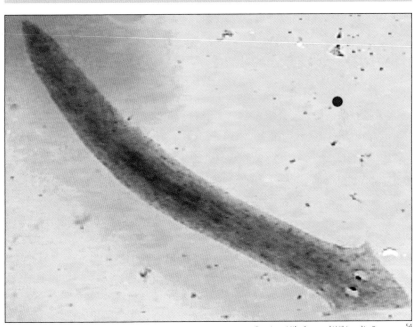

Courtesy Mike6271 and Wikimedia Commons[54]

FIGURE 4.11

Planaria.

three photoreceptor cells and a single pigment cell. These planarian eyes are likewise induced by a Pax6 gene; this conservation of Pax6 from planarians to humans suggests a single common ancestor for the bilaterian eye. Gehring therefore proposes that all bilaterian eyes go back to a Darwinian prototype, as found in planaria. So where did these single photoreceptor and pigment cells come from?

Gehring puts forward two hypotheses for the origin of photoreceptors in metazoa—that is, multicellular organisms that have differentiated cells into tissues and organs. The conventional theory is that metazoa arose from a colony of flagella-possessing cells, much like contemporary Volvox and Eudorina, where the cells initially possessed an eyespot that sent its perceptions to the flagella so that the colony could then move toward or away from the light. This eyespot would then separate into the two cell types, a photoreceptor and a pigment cell, to be melded into a primitive eye. The second hypothesis is based on observations that the eye organelle in Volvox is located in the chloroplast (chlorophyll containing organelles in algae and green plant cells). It is thought that chloroplasts were derived from free-living cyanobacteria that had been incorporated into eukaryotic cells. To prove the point, the genome of the cyanobacterium Nostoc contains a proteo-rhodopsin gene! In addition, two dinoflagellates (of which plankton and Red Tide are members), Erythropsis and Warnovia, have photoreceptor organelles as elaborate as the human eye but assembled in a single layer. These single-celled organisms are endosymbionts of some corals and sea anemones.

Based on these data, Gehring has developed his symbiont hypothesis, the "Russian Doll" model, proposing that light sensitivity first arose in cyanobacteria, which were then taken up by eukaryotic red algae as primary chloroplasts. Subsequently, dinoflagellates took up the red algae and transformed their (now ingested) chloroplasts into elaborate photoreceptor organelles. Then, because dinoflagellates closely coexist within cnidarians (jellyfish, corals, sea anemones), they may have transferred their eye genes to cnidarians—hence, the Russian Doll. I maintain that

Life, in its many iterations, actively fosters its own growth and complexity through both molecular and community networks. More about endosymbiosis is included in Chapter 5.

Life, to assemble a photoreceptor and a pigment cell into a visual organ, must have at least two classes of genes, one at the top and one at the bottom of the genetic cascade—that is, a master control gene, Pax6, and the structural gene that encodes for the pigment (rhodopsin). Gehring postulates that from this starting point, increasingly more sophisticated eye types arose by the recruiting of additional genes and then weaving them into the morphogenetic pathway. He cites evidence for two mechanisms of recruitment—that is, gene duplication and enhancer fusion—that led to the weaving of additional genes into the genetic cascade. In some cases of gene duplication, an active gene might be left behind to ensure the original function of the gene.

I am struck by the degree of precision, orchestration, utilization, and individualization inherent in the building and optimization of eyes, and how various types of eyes adapt to and use the physics of light. I think of recruitment, including gene duplications, enhancer fusions, and other mechanisms, as adding up to molecular tinkering. This appears active, purposive and intentional rather than the random and accidental changes to fundamentally passive living matter. But both forces play roles in creation—to what extent who knows? Personally, I find Life unsearchably intricate, inventive, and resourceful.

CONCLUSION

The idea that Life can modify itself is not new. It was a view articulated by Samuel Butler, a writer and contemporary of Darwin's. He is most remembered for his novels, *Erewon* and *The Way of All Flesh,* but his arguments against Darwin's theory were most articulate. Margulis and Sagan's treatment of Butler is a work of art, and the following brief summary is a most fitting conclusion to this chapter. The authors write:

For nineteenth-century Englishmen of science it was
natural and expedient to invoke Newtonian mechanics
and conceive of life as Newton's matter: blind bits predictably
responding to forces and natural laws. . . . This was [Darwin's]
new view of evolution: God . . . was Newton's God. Not an
active interloper in human affairs, it was the god of the
mathematicians, the geometer god, who made the laws and
then [in detached fashion] sat by and watched these laws
play out. To the neo-Newtonians and Darwinians, free will
[was all] but banished from the universe because the universe
was portrayed as a mechanism, and mechanisms do not
have consciousness.[55]

Darwin's natural selection, applied also to humans, made consciousness redundant. Butler, however, brought consciousness and free will
back in by claiming that Life had been shaped by how its matter engaged in life's processes, by the choices it freely made, by the habits it
developed, and by the innumerable decisions about where, how, and
with whom to live. In this way Life produced unimaginable diversity,
including us. Organisms were propagated by their power and sentience.
"This was the view that Butler attempted to resuscitate—that life itself
was godlike. There was no grand design, but millions of little purposes,
each associated with a cell or organism in its habitat."[56]

Samuel Butler thus disagreed with Darwin's mechanistic approach.
According to Margulis and Sagan, one Butlerian theme stands out:

Living matter is mnemic: it remembers and embodies
its own past. Life, according to Butler, is endowed with
consciousness, memory, direction, and goal-setting.
In Butler's view all life, not just human life, is teleological;
that is, it strives. Butler claimed that the Darwinians missed
the teleology, the goal-directedness of life acting for itself.

In throwing out the bathwater of divine purpose, Darwin discarded the baby of living purposefulness. . . . no organic being is a billiard ball, acted upon only by external forces. All are sentient, possessing the internal teleology of the autopoietic imperative. Each is capable, to varying degrees, of acting on its own. . . .

. . . [For Butler,] life is matter that chooses. Each living being . . . responds sentiently to a changing environment and tries during its life to alter itself. . . . Gradually, in tiny increments, living systems with nonnegotiable needs for food, water, and energy transform themselves in wily and persistent ways.[57]

The authors conclude their reading of Butler:

The mind and the body are not separate but part of the unified process of life. Life, sensitive from the onset, is capable of thinking. . . .

. . . We find Butler's view—which rejects any single, universal architect—appealing. Life is too shoddy a production, both physically and morally, to have been designed by a flawless Master. And yet life is more impressive and less predictable than any "thing" whose nature can be accounted for solely by "forces" acting deterministically. . . .

. . . Thought, like life, is matter and energy in flux; the body is its "other side." Thinking and being are the same thing.[58]

Most remarkably, the vision of this 19th-century Englishman is being borne out by 20th- and 21st-century science.

LIFE IS COMMUNITY

My wife and I live at a beach in Ventura County, California. Our beach is pristine, a habitat that has not yet been paved over by humankind. As I walk onto the beach, I pass a flock of gulls standing with heads pointing to the wind. They glance at me, stepping aside to let me pass, but they do not scatter. Ahead, nearer the surf, the beach teems with gulls, pelicans, plovers, sanderlings—more varieties than I can count, feasting on sand fleas, sand crabs, and anchovies.

FIGURE 5.1

California Brown Pelican about to hit the water.

Courtesy Dori and Wikimedia Commons[1]

Dolphins patrol just outside the surf, ready to chase down the barred perch, corbina, grunion, leopard sharks, and shovelnose guitarfish that feedat the surf line. We love the pelicans the most; they glide wingtip to wingtip inches above the waves or stall and spin from great heights, at the last instant folding in their wings before plunging like arrows into the water to spear unwary anchovies (fig. 5.1).

There is a bond within the families of all these creatures. In turn, the various families together form a beach community that is more than merely competitive or genetic or molecular. I love the feeling I have when in their midst, the sense that I am standing in a chaotic cathedral where a cacophony of hymns and prayers encounter no walls. Yet the genetic and molecular have their own music and create their own cathedrals—the cells, the neurons, the networks, the whole organisms that make up the communities we love and that are communities in themselves. The level of cooperation within and among them is total. These are the layers of the communities of Life that we explore in this chapter.

LIFE IS COOPERATIVE

Animals groom, talk, play, and team up. Their behaviors are more than genetic but, rather, involve learning and choice. Cooperation leads to more surviving offspring. Animals are quite able to find the right trade-offs in negotiating their needs.

My sense that Life is fundamentally cooperative finds experimental validation in the work of Joan Roughgarden, a professor of evolutionary biology at Stanford.[2] She wonders at mammals grooming each other, birds preening each other, dogs and cats enjoying our touch, birds talking, talking incessantly while they walk on the sand at the seashore. Perhaps the birds are enjoying each other's cadence, marching in tune. Think of bats hanging together, chimps hugging each other, bears that tumble about. These creatures are forming bonds, building friendships, developing a sense of collaboration, forging a team. Their physically intimate associations and sexual contact contribute to team fitness.

Roughgarden cautions against attributing such behavior to genetics, placing genes at arms' length from behavior. Is there a gene for every behavior? She states, "An animal's behavior obviously develops during its life, reflecting experience in local situations." Regarding feeding, animals are choosey. Furthermore, they interact with each other in their feeding behaviors. Does a gene exist for a bird to chase down bugs at less than one meter and ignore those farther out? No. "In fact, birds, lizards, and fish do vary their decision-making in accord with experience. . . . And their genes don't change day by day."[3] They quickly learn the best use of their time.

To what end do such intelligence, learning, choice, and bonding ultimately lead? For what purpose is there cooperation? She answers these questions by pointing out that Darwin erred by focusing on the quantity of mating rather than on the quantity of offspring successfully reared. She calls her system "social selection," where the goal is reproductive success, with cooperation leading to the most offspring raised to independence. Sex, with its random mixing of genes from both parents, is in social selection a strategy to continually balance the portfolio of genes of progeny, leading to useful genetic variations to meet changing circumstances and, hence, better survival. Sexual reproduction, with its balancing of portfolios, owes its very existence to cooperation. The parents have every conceivable incentive to work together. The failure to negotiate a working agreement leads to conflict.

So how do animals, let alone people, develop functioning working agreements? Roughgarden resorts to the bargaining game theories of Nobel Prize winner John Nash.[4] It is a matter of finding the right trade-offs between the partners, compromises where everyone's needs are reasonably met. For example, a papa and mama bird have a nest that must be guarded, fledglings that must be fed, and their own individual

needs for food, the foraging for which exposes one to danger of predation. Based on variables such as the size (and hence need for food) of each
bird, location of nest, number of fledglings, and so on, Roughgarden
uses Nash's equations to predict that papa will have to do, say, 57% of
the foraging, with mama doing 43%, to ensure the twin payoffs of individual and fledgling survival. Subsequent field observations fit the
prediction, demonstrating that these creatures are indeed capable of
negotiating their needs.

Let us further explore the idea that Life is community by looking at
molecules and some of their aspects of community.

A SOCIOLOGY OF MOLECULES

Life exists as webs of interaction; molecules themselves are arranged
in networks. Genes are not the prime movers of cells but
rather are parts of networks. Genes have meaning only within the system
as a whole. The modular nature of networks and the mobility
of transposable elements contribute to ease of rearrangement—
that is, tinkering. All this supports the idea of Life as agent.

To consider Life's molecular basis from a system and network perspective is to argue that the molecules have meaning only in the context
of their intimate interconnections. Life exists as webs of interaction, and
therefore we must consider molecules as systems and networks. For example, think of the molecular sequences in chemotaxis, where *E. coli*
senses a nutrient gradient and then swims toward it. The sequence is
between detection and the movement of its flagellae. There is a purpose-
ful chemistry of information processing within the cell. According to
Franklin Harold, "Chemotaxis is not just a matter of chemistry . . . [but]
operates within that higher level of organization, which is superposed
upon the molecular."[5] Harold goes on to point out that different bacteria

have differing molecular sequences in chemotaxis. He concludes that each organism is the unique organizer of its elements.[6]

The consensus among biologists is that biological organization is determined by the genome, that a cell's molecular makeup, its anatomy and behavior, are all established by its complement of genes. The genome then constitutes something like a recipe for producing that cell. Harold complains that stated this way, the idea that the genes determine molecular makeup and biological organization is a *Weltanschauung* (worldview) indicative of modern reductionism rather than a testable hypothesis. He is aware that genes are central in that mutations can alter an organism's features, but he points out that gene products—enzymes and structural and metabolic proteins—go on to have a life of their own. For example, knowing genes and what they encode cannot explain how a bacterium undergoes a fission that quickly produces a pair. He insists that above the biochemical dimension, there is everywhere visible a higher level of order that involves the social interactions of molecules, where direction, location, interactions, and timing generate growing cells.[7] *In other words, it is in community that molecules collectively create the exquisite organization of the cell and the whole organism.*

Jablonka and Lamb add,

> Geneticists themselves now think . . . in terms of genetic networks composed of tens or hundreds of genes and gene products, which interact with each other and together affect the development of a particular trait. . . .
>
> . . . No longer can a gene be thought of as an inherently stable, discrete stretch of DNA. . . . [Rather] a whole battery of sophisticated mechanisms is needed to maintain the structure of DNA and the fidelity of its replication. *Stability lies in the system as a whole, not in the gene. . . . The stretch of DNA that is "a gene" has meaning only with the system as a whole. . . .*
> [italics mine]

. . . If the genome is an organized system . . . the processes
that generate genetic variation may be an evolved property
of the system . . . [which] would mean that, contrary to
long-accepted majority opinion, not all genetic variation is
entirely random or blind; some of it may be regulated and
partially directed.[8]

Furthermore, these molecular networks, these linked arrays of genes
and proteins, are arranged in modules, much as your computer has moth-
erboards or hard drives that can be removed and exchanged. Wagner,
Pavlicev, and Cheverud write,

A network of interactions is called modular if it is subdivided
into relatively autonomous, internally highly connected
components. . . . Although there is an emerging agreement
that organisms have a modular organization, the main open
problem is the question of whether modules arise through
the action of natural selection or because of biased mutational
mechanism.[9]

These comments again support the idea of Life as agent.

This modular composition of living organisms sets the stage for its
transformation, to meet the changing demands and challenges of the
environment. Modules can be moved about as a unit or modified, much
as we might take apart and rearrange a Lego structure. Biologists refer
to this as tinkering.

Genes never act in isolation but only through webs of
functional connections called "genetic networks."
. . . [Such networks] include metabolic gene networks,
protein "interactomes," transcriptional networks, and the
molecularly diverse networks that underlie development.

That last category is the most complex and the one with the most direct relevance to morphological evolution. . . . Most microevolutionary "tinkering" involves changes in such genetic networks. . . . [This article] describes the ways that developmental genetic networks act as both transmitting and amplification devices for genetic change. . . . [and how] these properties [relate] to the sometimes puzzlingly rapid rates of organismal evolution.[10]

Recall that macroevolution can proceed by "Big Bangs" as well as by gradual change, as discussed in Chapter 1.

This is restated by Lieberman and Hall: "Many discoveries in evolutionary developmental biology—quite a few based on comparisons of distantly related model organisms—suggest that relatively simple transformations of developmental pathways can lead to dramatic, rapid change in phenotype." The authors go on to state that "the phenotypic effects of mutations of potentially large effect can manifest themselves rapidly, but they are more likely to emerge more incrementally over evolutionary time via transitional forms as natural selection within populations acts on their expression." They note that "future research needs to be directed at understanding how complex developmental networks, both genetic and epigenetic, structure the phenotypic effects of particular mutations within populations of organisms."[11]

Feschotte notes that "the control and coordination of eukaryotic gene expression rely on transcriptional and post-transcriptional networks." He discusses models, proposing that "genomic repeats, and in particular transposable elements, have been a rich source of material for the assembly and tinkering of eukaryotic gene regulatory systems."[12] This article fits with Shapiro's[13] work, which I referenced in Chapter 4, "Life Modifies Itself." Feschotte writes that eukaryotic genomes are rife with genomic repeats, interspersed repetitive DNA. This comes from transposable elements (TEs), which are able to replicate and move around the genome. He states that theoretical considerations and empirical studies show that TEs are best viewed as genomic parasites, which essentially owe their survival to their ability to replicate faster than the host that carries them. This conjecture, also known as the selfish DNA theory, seems sufficient to explain the maintenance of TEs over long evolutionary time as well as the wide variations in the amount, diversity and chromosomal location of TEs. . . . In spite of—and to some extent because of—this selfish and parasitic nature, the movement and accumulation of TEs have exerted a strong influence on the evolutionary trajectory of their hosts . . . [by coming to play] a major role in the evolution of eukaryotic gene regulation. . . . I explore the properties of TEs that may facilitate their recruitment as building blocks for the assembly of a diversity of systems to regulate and coordinate eukaryotic gene expression.[14]

FIGURE 5.2

Courtesy Smith609 and Wikimedia Commons[15]

A beautiful example of the "elephant skin" texture diagnostic of a microbial mat. From the w:Burgsvik beds of Gotland, Sweden.

Note the language of agency: move around, replicate faster, recruit-ment. *I also note how something that is negative, parasitic, and selfish is recruited for growth and progress.*

SINGLE-CELLED ORGANISMS
AND COMMUNITY

Bacteria formed the first communities, their microbial mats dating back 3.5 billion years. They trade genetic information through conjugation and via viruses, enabling them to flexibly adapt to stressful conditions. Bacteria communicate in a variety of ways. All of this is strategic.

Bacteria are favorites for biological study; they are individually com-plex but the simplest of living systems to evaluate. They replicate quickly. And they form communities that have specific relevance to the environmental and personal health of humankind in the here and now. Lynn Margulis has long studied and written about microbes; in a 1986 article titled "Community Living Long Before Man: Fossil and Liv-ing Microbial Mats and Early Life," she and her colleagues wrote that "microbial mats are layered communities of bacteria that form cohesive structures, some of which are preserved in sedimentary rocks as stro-matolites."[16] Recall our discussion of stromatolites in Chapter 1, "What Is Life?" These fossils go back 3.5 billion years. Their modern counter-parts are interesting, lending insights into Earth's early life. Since these communities have endured for such eons, the authors note their remark-able group persistence and speculate that they may even play roles in the larger global environment that we do not understand (fig. 5.2).

Furthermore, bacteria, in their community life, regularly trade genetic information. Margulis and Sagan write that having no nucleus, a bacte-ria's DNA is loose within the cell.[17] Unlike sexual reproduction, which vertically trades DNA, bacteria do so horizontally. They may form cell

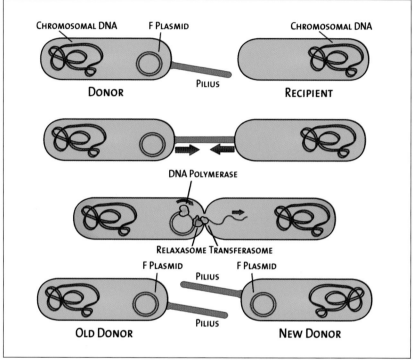

FIGURE 5.3

Courtesy Adenosine and Wikipedia Commons[18]

Schematic drawing of bacterial conjugation. "Conjugation diagram 1– Donor cell produces pilus. 2– Pilus attaches to recipient cell, brings the two cells together. 3– The mobile plasmid is nicked and a single strand of DNA is then transferred to the recipient cell. 4– Both cells recircularize their plasmids, synthesize second strands, and reproduce pili; both cells are now viable donors."

bridges through which genes are sent (fig. 5.3). This transfer of genetic material is called *conjugation,* a means of horizontal gene transfer.

Bacteria that cannot do this may transmit genes via viruses. They particularly trade information at times of drought, heat shock, when under attack by antibiotics, or to provide vitamins when they are deficient. As Margulis and Sagan point out,

DNA may separate from one dying bacterium and, either as pure DNA or coated with protein in a viral particle, it may splice into the genes of another bacterium. . . .

By trading genes and acquiring new heritable traits, bacteria expand their genetic capacities—in minutes, or at most hours.[19]

I see this as strategic, if not purposive and intentional. Regarding antibiotic resistance, one might accept that resistance is a result of gene transfer, but how can you prove intent? This is a question that applies everywhere, in convergence, progress, and the optimization of innumerable functions and structures. Either Life is very, very lucky or natural selection is incredibly efficient or Life has a guardian angel or it has a say in its fate. To argue the point further, wherever we look at bacteria, in their function or behavior, we see purpose.

It follows that bacteria communicate. Bassler and Losick describe how bacteria use a variety of means to communicate with one another and with their eukaryotic hosts:

In some cases, social interactions allow bacteria to synchronize the behavior of all of the members of the group and thereby act like multicellular organisms. By contrast, some bacterial social engagements promote individuality among members within the group and thereby foster diversity.[20]

The authors go on to describe molecular mechanisms underpinning some recently discovered bacterial communication systems. They note that bacteria can use and spread misinformation or, more dramatically, even deadly information. *I am reminded of J. A. Shapiro's comments, quoted in Chapter 2, that bacteria are small but not stupid, with sophisticated communications and sentience.*

A current hot topic in basic and biomedical research is bacteria's social congregation, called *biofilms*. Dental plaque is an example of a bacterial biofilm. Nadell et al. report on a communication mechanism that is criti-cal to the formation of biofilms.[21] The authors point out that bacteria, once thought to be fairly solitary organisms, turn out to be highly interac-tive and socially relational in complex ways. They specifically coordinate their group behavior by using a system called *quorum sensing*, with which they detect the density of other bacteria around them. This can result in biofilm formation, in which communities of cells attach to a surface and (fig. 5.4) envelope themselves in a sticky slime. Such biofilms confer resis-tance to predators, antibiotics, and host immune system attacks. They are surprisingly tenacious, as you well know as your dentist chips away your dental plaque. Bacterial biofilms also show up in medical settings and are the scourge of hospitals, medical instruments, and ICUs; they are inte-gral as well to antibiotic resistance.

Medical and basic research intensely address how to disrupt bio-films. "Despite being single-celled organisms, bacteria have social skills. Once they sense each other's presence through chemical signals,

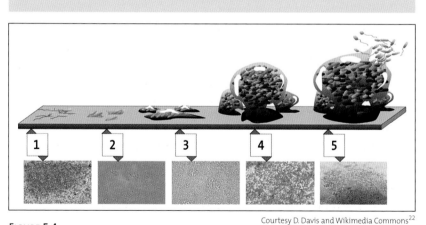

Courtesy D. Davis and Wikimedia Commons[22]

FIGURE 5.4

Five stages of biofilm development. Stage 1, initial attachment; stage 2, irreversible attachment; stage 3, maturation I; stage 4, maturation II; stage 5 dispersion, with photomicrographs of a developing *P. aeruginosa* biofilm.

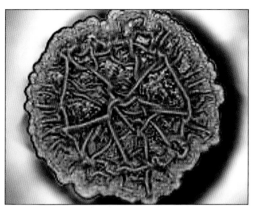

FIGURE 5.5

Colonies of *Pseudomonas aeruginosa* that make phenazines grow in Petri dishes as smooth shiny colonies. But bacteria that lack phenazines form wrinkled colonies, as shown here, probably to increase the surface area to bring more bacteria in contact with oxygen.

Science, with permission[23]

bacteria of one or more species collectively build themselves into biofilms from polymers that they excrete. . . . Up to 60 percent of bacteria live in biofilms."[24] Dental plaque, biofilms on medical devices, lining water pipes, the lungs of cystic fibrosis patients, are examples. Biofilms confer antibiotic resistance. Scientists are experimenting with a variety of methods that can break up these films.

Bacterial mats can be very thick, and biofilms inevitably bury individual bacteria. Saey describes how buried bacteria can get the oxygen they need. "Antibiotics made by *Pseudomonas aeruginosa* bacteria can serve as molecular snorkels, helping the bacteria breathe while buried in film or stuck in the middle of a colony"[25] (fig. 5.5). *Pseudomonas* is a bacterium that infects people with cystic fibrosis, leading to a sticky mucus that clogs the airways. The antibiotics, known as phenazines, are created by the bug to combat and inhibit other microorganisms. They also act as "communication signals" between organisms. It turns out that the antibiotic is an oxygen transporter; its filaments give submerged or crowded bacteria access to fresh air.

Sometimes Life is a community of one. In a South African gold mine 2.8 km below Earth's surface, scientists found a solitary organism that, isolated from sunlight, co-opts the energy of radiation from surrounding uranium in rocks to split water, which liberates oxygen, which then reacts with iron sulfide minerals to make iron sulfate, which the bacteria can eat. The water they live in is 3 to 10 million years old, is very hot at 60 degrees Celsius, and is under deep oceanlike pressure.[26] Can you imagine? An organism that lives on uranium and iron in 60-degree Celsius water, deep within the earth! This organism might be a paradigm for life on planets that have little if any atmosphere.

Social amoebae normally roam soil as single-celled organisms, consuming soil bacteria.[27] But in times of famine, they congregate to form a sluglike multicellular ball. Within this slug aggregate, specialized cells move about consuming invading bacteria and toxins, forming a kind of immune system. This behavior depends on a protein called "TirA," without which the immunity cells cannot function. It turns out this protein is related to bacteria identification proteins that are active in animals' immune systems. It is intriguing to think that the macrophages that protect us in our blood and tissues might have evolved from primitive amoebic clusters.

FIGURE 5.6

An Egyptian Plover eats leeches from the teeth of a Nile Crocodile, in a classic example of symbiosis. Illustration from *Popular Natural History* by Henry Scherren, published in 1909.

Courtesy Wikimedia Commons[28]

MERGER, SYMBIOSIS, AND ENDOSYMBIOSIS

Living forms can merge or form close alliances,
including smaller organisms living within larger ones.
Endosymbiosis is the whole-cloth incorporation and integration
of one organism by another. Discussed below is evidence that
our own brains are the result of mergers and
endosymbioses. We are mosaics.

Recall that in Chapter 1 we talked about two kinds of cells—prokaryotes and eukaryotes, the latter of which we are made. The creation of eukaryotes was a monumental evolutionary feat, and it arose through the merger, ingestions, and symbiotic alliances of prokaryotic forms. Margulis and Sagan write that symbiosis refers to intimate physical and ecological relationships, such as the African plovers that pluck and eat leeches from the open mouths of crocodiles (fig. 5.6).[29] This quid pro quo of bird and beast is an example of behavioral symbiosis. The authors note that organisms form many kinds of symbioses, but noteworthy is the exceedingly close association of smaller organisms living within larger ones. For example, humankind cannot make vitamins B and K without the bacteria in our intestines. Cows and termites cannot digest grass or wood without the bacteria in their guts.

There are innumerable other examples of life forms living symbiotically and contributing to one another's existence. Roughgarden describes how the bacteria *Rhizobia* forms nodules on the roots of pea plants.[30] *Rhizobia* takes nitrogen from the air and binds it into amino acids, which are then sent to the plant. In exchange, the plant processes atmospheric carbon dioxide into sugar, which is sent to the bacteria. The author notes that this biochemical symbiosis is highly important to the world's agricultural production, as well as to the functioning of natural ecosystems. There is an energy cost to both bacteria and plant. How the participants negotiated this partnership over evolutionary time is an interesting question. Did they co-evolve, both making changes to accommodate the other?[31]

Even more remarkable and important is the endosymbiosis that has led to the formation of the eukaryotic cell. It turns out that mitochondria (organelles that generate power for the cell in the form of chemical energy) were once free-living bacteria that were incorporated whole cloth by organisms that in turn integrated and appropriated them into the cell's function (fig. 5.7).

Not only do mitochondrial organelles look like bacteria, but their DNA differs from the DNA of the cell nucleus, appearing much more similar to the DNA of bacterial genomes.[32] These organelles appeared suddenly when digestion-resistant bacteria took up residence in larger

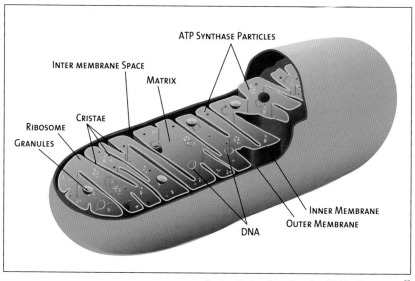

Courtesy Mariana Ruiz Villarreal and Wikimedia Commons[33]

FIGURE 5.7

This mitochondrion has a genome distinct from the cell nucleus; its DNA is very similar to that of bacteria. It produces energy for the cell and regulates the cell's metabolism. A eukaryotic cell may contain up to 2,000 mitochondria.

cells. Joan Roughgarden writes that the cooperation found here is profound, with the genes of the nucleus and mitochondria orchestrated perfectly. The author concludes that we are more than individuals; rather, we are colonies that need, for example, the bacterial flora in our mouths and guts to exist.

> We have no idea of how our ancestor cells early in life's
> history interacted with the available bacteria at the time to
> recruit them to join on a common mission. Whatever
> happened, it wasn't simply the acquisition of new genes
> through random mutation. It must have involved some
> cooperative assimilation of an entire packet of genes bundled
> up in the genome of the ancestral mitochondria.[34]

Roughgarden discusses another example of endosymbiosis, where one autonomous species of cell lives within another cell of a different species. There are corals that allow algae to enter their bodies. The trade-off is that algae cells, in exchange for the safety the coral home affords, provide photosynthetic nutrients to the coral. In addition, the coral cells can acquire genetic material from the algae (fig. 5.8). The author states,

> This is not random mutation. Instead, this process allows
> a coral cell to steer its own genetic variation in a direction
> that leads to the most breeding success. . . . a sort of directed
> mutation. This is a fundamental departure from the
> neo-Darwinian narrative of natural breeding building
> solely on randomly generated genetic variation.[35]

Margulis and Sagan suggest that another beneficial merger involved spirochaetes, known to us as the bacterial pathogen that produces syphilis and other infections.[36] Spirochaetes have prominent flagella for locomotion, and their mergers with eukaryotes could have produced the

FIGURE 5.8

Courtesy User: Haplochromis and Wikimedia Commons[37]

The hollow, cylindrical polyps of the coral *Stylophora pistillata* gather plankton with their tiny tentacles. Photosynthetic algae living within the polyps provide the coral with energy, its vibrant colors, and protection against the acidic by-products of its respiration.

cilia that propel sperm, wash our bronchial tubes, and move ova along women's fallopian tubes. The authors point out that all these cilia have a universal shaft, of 9(2) + 2 symmetry, suggesting a common origin (fig. 5.9).

Margulis argues that the earliest cells, archaebacteria such as Thermoplasma and Eubacteria such as spirochaeta, were conscious from the beginning.[38] Noting that eukaryotes have several genomes, she hypothesizes that there was a merger of the two bacteria, one ingesting, but not digesting, the other to produce a nucleated cell. These components that fused in such symbiogenesis were already conscious. The neuron (fig. 5.10) is archaebacterial in origin, with its axon deriving from the

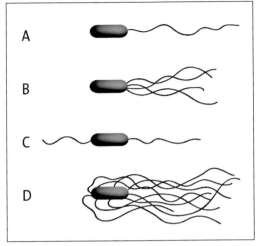

FIGURE 5.9

Bacterial flagella.

Examples of bacterial flagella arrangement schemes.

A-Monotrichous; ex. *Pseudomonas fluorsecens*

B-Lophotrichous

C-Amphitrichous

D-Peritrichous *Proteus mirabilis*

Original work created for Wikipedia, by Mike Jones. Courtesy Wikimedia Commons[39]

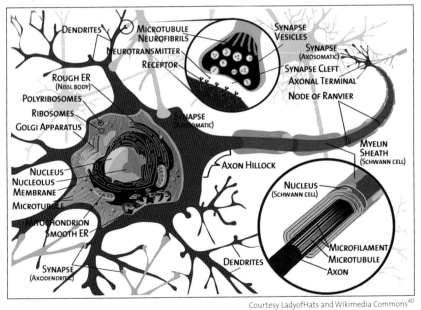

Courtesy LadyofHats and Wikimedia Commons[40]

FIGURE 5.10

Complete neuron cell diagram. Neurons are electrically excitable cells in the nervous system that process and transmit information. In vertebrate animals, neurons are the core components of the brain, spinal cord, and peripheral nerves.

undulipodium, the tail from a motile Eubacteria close to spirochaeta. The formula is Thermoplasma (archaebacteria) + spirochaeta (Eubacteria) = the first protist. From protists evolved the cells of all animals and plants. The microtubules of the component bacteria became the neurotubules of neurons. Eukaryotes have evolved by the inheritance of acquired genomes; they have gained all their new features by ingesting and not digesting whole bacterial cells with complete genomes. Our own consciousness is the extension and elaboration of the consciousness of the first living organisms. *Also, note that all learning is ingestion.*

One estimate puts the number of neurons in the human brain at 86 billion, of which 16 billion are in the cortex and 69 billion in the cerebellum.[41] So how do brain processes translate to consciousness? Koch and Greenfield admit that science "has utterly failed to satisfactorily explain how subjective experience is created." These neuroscientists note that "there is not a single problem of consciousness" (CS), but that numerous phenomena—including self-CS, the content of CS, and how brain processes relate to CS and non-CS—must be explained. They use brain scans to image "the best neuronal correlates of consciousness (NCC)— the brain activity that matches up with specific CS experience." Koch believes that "for each conscious experience, a unique set of neurons in particular brain regions fires in a specific manner." Greenfield counters that "for each conscious experience, neurons across the brain synchronize into coordinate assemblies, then disband." Koch supports his specificity by noting that just as "organisms evolve specific gadgets . . . [so] nerve cells have developed myriad shapes and functions, along with specific wiring patterns" to constitute NCC.[42]

> Qualitative, not quantitative, differences in neuronal activity give rise to consciousness. . . . A specific network of neurons is needed for a specific percept. . . . The brain works not by dint of its bulk properties but because neurons are wired up in amazingly specific and idiosyncratic patterns. . . . [reflecting]

the accumulated information an organism has learned over its lifetime, as well as that of its ancestors, whose information is represented in genes.[43]

Greenfield answers that a more plausible view of CS is that it is not generated by a qualitative distinct property of the brain but "by a quantitative increase in the holistic function of the brain."[44]

Perhaps the most remarkable of all endosymbioses is the integration of viral and organism genomes. Transposable elements (TEs), discussed above by Feschotte and in Chapter 4 by Shapiro, are thought to have originally been viruses that infected animal or plant genomes, only to become a part of the genomes, adding valuable DNA to them. British physician and virologist Frank Ryan documents, in his fascinating book on symbiosis and endosymbiosis, the molecular agency of viruses and describes how following hostile invasion, rapprochement, and assimilation, they may increase the plasticity of our genome, enhancing its potential for change at any stage.[45]

Gage, noting that TEs make up 45% of mammalian genomes, describes research showing that TEs can transpose themselves during specific moments of neuronal creation in our brains, thereby changing the genetic information of single neurons in an arbitrary fashion and allowing the brain to develop in distinctly different ways.[46] He concludes that this characteristic of variety and flexibility may contribute to the uniqueness of an individual brain. He speculates that the contributions to brain growth by ubiquitous once-viral and now-incorporated TEs add to the notion that *we humans, and all of Life, are indeed mosaics* [italics mine].

Symbiosis, merger, and endosymbiosis in general entail one body and many genomes. But in Life with all its exuberant diversity, many organisms are composed of one genome with many bodies. Roughgarden, discussing "one genome–many bodies" species, includes poplar trees, corals, tunicates, hydra, bryozoans, and sea anenomes. "In the ocean, many animals bud off duplicates of themselves that then live as colonies.

. . . The Portuguese man-of-war jellyfish is a floating colony, like a space station of animals floating through an oceanic universe"[47] (fig. 5.11).

ANTS

Ants demonstrate collective and individual intelligences.
Attine ants are dedicated farmers,
but they can be attacked by other species of ants.

It was a joy to pick our way along the forest floor at Manuel Antonio National Park in Costa Rica. The forest was drenched with rain, redolent with a hundred aromas, and filled with the calls of birds and howler monkeys. But it was the line of cutter ants, stretching for 50 yards or

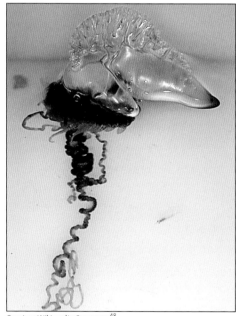

Courtesy Wikimedia Commons[48]

FIGURE 5.11
Portuguese man-of-war.

more next to our trail, each ant holding high a bright green leaf three times its size, that captivated me. What was the purpose and destination of this tiny bobbing parade (fig. 5.12)?

Leaf-cutter ants are a species of attine ants—all farmers, their crops a single species of fungus. They are transporting the leaves to nests where the leaves will be stripped and converted to mulch for the fungus farm. Various workers have specific tasks on the farm: weeding, moving the fungi for optimal temperature and humidity, applying fertilizers, protecting the crops from parasitic fungi through the use of antibiotics, and finally harvesting.

There is a collective intelligence here, a remarkable network that functions in concert like a multicellular organism; each individual seems locked into the overall function of the social system. The genius is in individual parts and the collective communications of the system. Attine

FIGURE 5.12
Leaf-cutter ants.

Photograph by Adrian Pingstone. Courtesy Wikimedia Commons[49]

ants evolved agriculture based on the cultivation of fungi 50 to 60 million years ago. Their evolutionary goals of survival and propagation are amply met; their self-organization has ensured it.

But there is experimental evidence that there are as well decision-making processes that occur on the individual level. Roces contends that in addition to the collective organization of leaf-cutting ant foraging, there are "complex individual responses that may result from the integration of local information during food collection with an assessment of colony conditions."[50] Overall, self-organization is a combination of individual and the collective.

These networks involve not just ants but the fungus as well. Indeed, there is a symbiosis here, a mutualism that has led to the evolution of nearly 50 species of attine ants and the spread of the ant-fungus cooperatives over much of the new world. But not without opposition. An unrelated species of ant, the myrmicine ant, may attack the attine nest, expel them, take over their gardens, and place their larvae next to the attine larvae, there to feed on them. The self-conflict of Life extends to ants as well as to humans.

A SUMMARY OF CHAPTERS 1 THROUGH 5, AS SEEN IN PLANT INTELLIGENCE

Plants are also intelligent beings. Plant biologist Anthony Trewavas gives striking support to the idea of Life as agent as he discusses the active (not passive) nature of plants, the role of networks in their adaptations, and the role of intelligence and learning in evolution. The section serves to review and underscore everything I have said in Chapters 1 through 5.

Central to the uncovering of the harmony between biology, evolution, and Christianity is the idea of Life as an active agent in its adaptations to its changing circumstances. In Chapters 2 through 4, and up to this point in Chapter 5, I have presented evidence that *animals are intelligent*, can learn, and are able through rearrangements in their genetic and epigenetic networks to evolutionarily modify themselves. *But animals are only half of Life's story on Earth. What of plants, the other half?* I turn to plant biologist Anthony Trewavas[51] for his interpretations of the science of plants. The following synopsis of his chapter in *The Deep Structure of Biology*[52] also serves to recap and support my arguments in Chapters 1 through 5.

PLANTS ARE INTELLIGENT

It would never occur to most of us that plants are intelligent, primarily because they don't move, as animals do. The equation of the word *vegetable* with the term *brain dead* reflects our sentiments regarding intelligence in the plant world. However, time-lapse technology and striking advances in plant physiology, signal transduction (chemotaxis in *E. coli* is analogous), molecular biology, and cell-to-cell communication tell a strikingly different story. In response to signals (light, heat, cold, wind, soil conditions, food sources, etc.), plants can change their various structures (leaves, shoots, roots, limbs, etc.) to individually optimize their foraging for resources. In addition, plants are able to predict possible upcoming changes in resources (light, water, soil qualities, seasonal changes) and then alter their form, an action called *phenotypic plasticity*. Animals respond to such changes with movement; plants, with phenotypic plasticity. "It is in foraging for food that animal intelligence becomes a premium, and it is in plant foraging that plant intelligence comes to the fore."[53] We can perceive the processing of information by animals, but the time frames are much longer for plants, as time-lapse technology makes clear. "As we acquire more knowledge about all sorts of behavioral characteristics of living organisms, not only are previous assessments of intelligence and behavior shown to be wrong, but the expanding view *enlarges our perspective of life itself*" [italics mine].[54]

Trewavas goes on to discuss the issue of intelligence, pointing out that the Latin root literally means to "choose between." He advances the idea that what we see as innate behavior of animals and plants "arose from learned, that is, intelligent, behavior in the first place, potentially by genetic assimilation."[55] (More on genetic assimilation later.) He argues that organisms exhibit foresight

> that allows [them] to come up with a behavioral solution to an environmental problem with minimal trial and error. Improved behavioral modification enables the subsequent selection of genes and gene combinations . . . that allow the strategy to develop with greater rapidity, higher probability, or lower cost. . . . Consequently, evolution becomes much faster than mechanisms that require selection of random gene combinations, just as foresight reduces the time required for successful behavior.[56]

He goes on to argue for intelligence in bacteria, protists, genomes, immune systems, swarms, and metabolic networks. He concludes that "apart from the higher animals that use the centralized activity of the brain to process information and in which classical intelligence is located, *all other biological systems possess a decentralized intelligence that is a consequence of behavior by the whole system*" [author's emphasis].[57]

PLANTS ARE ACTIVE, NOT PASSIVE
The author proposes that

> two perceptions of plant growth and behavior need to be distinguished. A common *passive* view is that plants grow according to a predetermined genetic program with rates determined merely by provided resources. . . .The *active* view of plant behavior is in complete contrast. . . . For plants facing

competition from neighbors and from other organisms in
a variable abiotic environment, intelligent adaptive behavior
is a necessity, not a luxury.[58]

He documents numerous strategies, such as exploratory speculative
growth of shoots and roots, variations of leaves to capture maximum
light, and root strategies to maximize water and minerals in highly variable soils. "Decision making about phenotypic change involves in some
way the whole plant and is, thus, decentralized."[59] Decentralization is
essential in a class of organisms constantly grazed on by animals.

PLANTS ARE NETWORKS

Plants, being both social and modular, are interactive networks
of leaves, stems, roots, flowers, and seeds. Such networks evaluate the
whole of the environment, and the whole network modifies itself to any
environmental change. As a result, there is "a very complex mixture of
communicating signals moving throughout the plant individual."[60] Signal transduction is the conveying of information about the environment
via complex biochemical networks. As a result, plants

perceive their environment in considerable detail, make
meaningful assessments of that information, and institute
adaptive phenotypic responses designed to improve
competitive ability and resource acquisition . . .
. . . Intelligence is an emergent property that results
from complex interactions between the tissues and cells
of the individual plant.[61]

PLANTS ARE AGENTIVE

Throughout the article, Trewavas discusses various agentive actions of plants. For example, plants are territorial, taking over available
space and denying it to others. But plants sense their own kind and

avoid competing with them. They in addition possess complex self-recognition systems. Plants make complex decisions on how and where to vary phenotype to garner scarce resources. Plants conduct sophisticated cost-benefit analyses in their quest for light, food, and water. Plants are capable of foresight; they can sense the future possibility that a competitor might overshadow them, and they adapt system-wide in response. "Foresight of future water availability also institutes characteristic morphological changes in anticipation and preparation. . . . programs indicate an ability to anticipate environmental change, even though it may not happen during the lifetime of the individual plant."[62] The author goes on to cite extensive evidence that plants in general learn and remember. Trewavas leaves no doubt that plants, like animals, actively contend with life's ever-changing circumstances.

PLANTS, INTELLIGENCE, AND EVOLUTION

Trewavas notes that intelligence is intrinsic to all biology, from bacteria to plants to animals. Bacteria use quorum sensing, plants use decentralized intelligence, and animals use central nervous systems. Bacteria learn by horizontal gene exchange, individual cells learn through computation, and higher animals learn by complex neural networks. "Underpinning all the forms of intelligence . . . is a network whose connection strength can be altered, enabling control of information flow and memory to be constructed."[63] Why, the author asks, is intelligence so widespread? Because it is the more intelligent who will forage the most effectively and will be naturally selected. Intelligence will beget more intelligence.

The author continues,

There are currently at least two kinds of evolutionary models relevant to this discussion. . . . The first, the neo-Darwinian view, sees overproduction, random genetic variation, and differential survival as the basis of evolution. The second . . .

places behavioral changes as the first response to environmental shifts. . . . Those that adapt most efficiently and are, thus, best able to master the current changes in the environment will experience preferential survival.[64]

Through inbreeding of the more intelligent, the new and more efficient behavior becomes genetically fixed, a process known as *genetic assimilation*. In other words, "Whatever genes the successful organism possesses go along for the ride. . . . *The very refined and complex forms of innate behavior found in reproductive rituals in animals and birds must surely originally have been learned behavior that has now been genetically assimilated* [italics mine]."[65]

The author concludes that

genetic assimilation is initiated by changes in behavior, and [in plant behavior] is expressed as phenotypic plasticity, which I have indicated is intelligent behavior. . . . *The evolution of intelligent behavior found in all forms of life, thus, becomes a central theme in the evolution of life itself* [author's emphasis].[66]

Let us go on now to investigate the idea that all of Life, down to its molecules, is in conflict.

CHAPTER SIX

LIFE IS SELF-CONFLICTUAL

"Only the dead have seen the end of war."
– Joseph B. Persico, quoting Plato[1]

Humankind is plagued by conflict. There is a murder by the fourth chapter of the Bible. Psychiatrist Karl Menninger epitomized self-conflict in his book *Man against Himself.* The animal Kingdom too is wracked by conflict. What is going on here?

n the November 30, 2007, edition of the *Los Angeles Times,* a photograph of a woman and child sitting in a glassless window and the surrounding walls riddled with bullet holes (fig. 6.1) introduced an article titled "Revenge Is Spark Behind a Somali Teen's Militancy: The

FIGURE 6.1

In Mogadishu. *LA Times,* Nov. 30, 2007.

FIGURE 6.2

Courtesy Wikimedia Commons[2]

Cain Kills Abel. Oil painting by Bartolomeo Manfredi. C. 1600.
Kunsthistorisches Museum Vienna.

Cycle of Violence Continues, with the Presence of Ethiopian Troops the Focus of a Radicalized Generation." The story was about 15-year-old Bashir Yusuf, who a year earlier dreamed of becoming a doctor, but now obsesses only on revenge and his own death. There was nothing out of the ordinary about the article; indeed, the newspapers and television newscasts regularly report innumerable incidents of war, murder, child abuse, and schism, to name a few.

The Scriptures mince no words in describing the wars within and between people. The first explicit self-conflict is recorded in Chapter 3 of the first book of the Bible, the Book of Genesis, immediately after Adam and Eve ate the forbidden fruit: "Then the eyes of both were opened, and they knew that they were naked; and they sewed fig leaves together and made loincloths for themselves."[3] By Chapter 4, there is a murder, the first internecine conflict. The event is extremely instructive, so I quote it in its entirety:

> Abel was a keeper of sheep, and Cain a tiller of the
> ground. In the course of time Cain brought to the
> Lord an offering of the fruit of the ground, and Abel
> for his part brought of the firstlings of his flock,
> their fat portions. And the Lord had regard for Abel
> and his offering, but for Cain and his offering he
> had no regard. So Cain was very angry, and his
> countenance fell. The Lord said to Cain, "Why are
> you angry, and why has your countenance fallen?
> If you do well, will you not be accepted? And if you
> do not do well, sin is lurking at the door; its desire
> is for you, but you must master it."
>
> Cain said to his brother Abel, "Let us go out to
> the field." And when they were in the field, Cain
> rose up against his brother Abel, and killed him
> [fig. 6.2]. Then the Lord said to Cain, "Where is
> your brother Abel?" He said, "I do not know; am
> I my brother's keeper?" And the Lord said, "What
> have you done? Listen; your brother's blood is crying

out to me from the ground! And now you are cursed
from the ground. . . . you will be a fugitive and a
wanderer on the earth." . . . Then Cain went away
from the presence of the Lord.[4]

Why did Cain kill Abel? What was going within him, within his mind and soul, that motivated him? What were the intents and purposes of the writer in telling this story? We'll come back to these questions in the next chapter.

Conflict is not limited to wars and fratricide. As a psychiatrist, I've made a living treating persons, couples, and families torn by divorce, dysfunction, self-hate, self-criticism, and suicide. I've worked on inpatient units with people hearing voices denouncing them as worthless, on addiction services with persons devastated by alcohol or methamphetamine, in jails with murderers or men who lust after children, and in outpatient settings with individuals wracked by trauma, depression, self-doubt, or social anxiety. Nor are these conditions uncommon; it is estimated that each of us has a one-in-three chance of suffering a diagnosable mental illness in one's lifetime. As conservative as that number is, it means that in a family of three, the odds are that one person will be afflicted. Witness the title of psychoanalyst and Christian layman Karl Menninger's best-selling book: *Man against Himself.*[5] A Catholic priest passionately exclaimed to me, "The problem with humankind isn't sin—it is neurosis!"

Men of high standing present a particularly visible form of self-conflict. Tiger Woods is one of the latest persons to jeopardize his career and family. In my private psychiatric practice, I raced against time trying to head off the self-ruin of men of prominence, working with them to curtail sexual acting out before their actions caught up with them. I wonder if men like Bill Clinton, Larry Craig, Elliott Spitzer, John Edwards, John Ensign, Mark Sanford, and numerous others ever sought counsel for their impulses.

Becoming Christian does not inoculate individuals or groups of persons from self- and internecine conflict. We regularly read of clergy who self-destruct, priests who molest children, and superiors who shield them. Such behavior occurs across denominations. I have seen congregations splinter in controversy, a priest become psychotic, and yet another sent to prison for child molesting. Verse 3 of Hymn 525 in the Episcopal Hymnal dramatizes the ubiquity of universal conflict within the Church:

> Though with a scornful wonder
>   men see her sore oppressed,
> By schisms rent asunder,
>   by heresies distressed,
> Yet saints their watch are keeping,
>   their cry goes up "how long,
> And soon the night of weeping
>   shall be the morn of song."

The situation is by no means hopeless, however; in spite of, and often because of, severe internal or interpersonal conflict, believers across the ages have sought and found harmony and healing in their faith. Furthermore, the cooperation, generosity, and self-sacrifice of church leaders and laypersons far outweigh their foibles. I have had my own issues with conflict and distress and have benefited immensely from skilled pastoral counseling and my own personal psychotherapy, and many under my care have improved or recovered likewise. The good news is that personal and interpersonal conflict is treatable.

In an editorial in the *Los Angeles Times* on April 20, 2008, writer Mark Kurlansky speculated about whether we are violent by nature or instead have to be taught to be violent, thus violating an inner "law of love."[6] He discussed nonviolence and showed how Mohandas Gandhi and Martin Luther King, Jr., made nonviolence work. He noted that biologists are of the opinion that "group conflict" has been a determining factor in the evolutionary development of numerous species, including us. In dialogue with Kurlansky, E. O. Wilson argued that aggression is hard-wired;[7] he pointed to ants. Kurlansky disagreed, noting that in the U.S. Military in WWII, at best one in four soldiers ever fired a weapon. So the military has had to train and condition soldiers to shoot automatically, in the process creating psychological problems, with veterans lamenting that they have gone against their nature. Kurlansky called on following the law of love. Wilson, a pacifist, thought we should treat violence as a normal human response, but one that has become extremely dangerous.

The violence of the animal kingdom is also distressing: Bacteria attack bacteria, viruses kill bacteria and prey on us, animals consume one another, nature shows on TV depict the bloody carnage as animals attempt to cross an African stream, Darwin's wasp lays its eggs inside a caterpillar. The wasp eggs then consume the caterpillar from the inside out, creating conflict in Darwin's mind about how a good God that created everything good could create something like this. Enslaved tiny ants may resist their captors with an army of killer nannies. Ants in the genus *Terminothorax* fall prey to do-little ants that raid the smaller species' nests and steal babies, who then do the slavemakers' housework and nurse their young. But the slave nursemaids kill a large percentage of the captors' queens and young.[8] Clark and Russell describe how bacteria kill each other, smaller bacteria infecting other larger bacteria or, much more often, bacteria killing each other by chemical warfare.[9] Some bacterial strains secrete toxic chemicals to kill off other types of bacteria that are competing to live in the same habitat. Descended as we are from the animals, we wonder who is right, E. O. Wilson or Mark Kurlansky. And what of Darwin's conflict regarding the wasp and caterpillar?

Persons persistent enough to read to this point in this book most likely read the newspapers, watch nature films, frequent the Discovery Channel and National Geographic Channel, and can agree that the world is a violent place. But the fascinating and virtually unbelievable thing is that conflict extends down to the molecules!

SELFISH GENETIC ELEMENTS

Conflict extends down to the genome. "Genes in an organism sometimes
'disagree' . . . [and] appear to have opposing effects." Some genes
are selfish, giving themselves a benefit despite being harmful to the
host organism. "The evolution of selfish genetic elements inevitably
leads to within-individual—or intragenomic—conflict.
. . . As a consequence, most organisms are not completely harmonious
wholes and the individual is, in fact, divisible."[10]

I have argued so far that creatures and indeed their genomes are intelligent and can learn. Now, Austen Burt and Robert Trivers, in their
classic text *Genes in Conflict,* marshal extensive evidence that "genes in
an organism may 'disagree' over what should happen. . . . they appear
to have opposing effects."[11] *As I read Burt and Trivers, I am immediately
struck by their language! It is the language of molecular and genetic agency;
in fact, rarely do I see authors explicitly describing genes as acting with such
intentionality. Here are the authors in their own words:*

> In animals, . . . some genes may want (or act as if they want)
> a male to produce lots of healthy sperm, but other genes in
> the same male want half the sperm to be defective. Some
> genes in a female want her to nourish all her embryos; others
> want her to abort half of them. Some genes in a fetus want it to
> grow quickly, others slowly, and yet others at an intermediate
> level. Some genes want it to become a male, others a female—
> and the reason they want it to be a female is so a quarter of
> her fertilized eggs will be defective! . . .
>
> . . . Some genes want to protect chromosomes from
> damage, while others want to break them. Some genes
> want the organism to snip out bits of DNA and insert them
> elsewhere in the genome; other genes want to stop this from

happening. Some genes want to activate a particular gene, and others want to silence it.[12]

Burt and Trivers explain that self-conflicts arise as these genes harm the organism as a whole. The benefits they give themselves negatively affect other genes in the organism. Selfish genetic elements include whole sets of chromosomes, complete genes or chromosomes, fragments of chromosomes or genes, and noncoding DNA. They disregard the host organism to increase their own numbers. This is profoundly divisive, especially as we view the molecules themselves as having agency. *"That is, the evolution of selfish genetic elements inevitably leads to within-individual— or intragenomic—conflict"* [italics mine].[13] The authors emphasize the generally remarkable cooperation within genomes, but point out that a small percentage of genes are rogues that have multiplied at the expense of the organism as a whole. In other words, Life is not of a piece, and individual organisms are in fact mosaics. *I think this is a startling example of molecular intent. It appears that the world is in conflict and therefore broken, right down to its most fundamental levels.*

DRIVE

In "drive," selfish genes are able to get into greater than 50% of a parent's offspring. There are three main strategies of drive: interfering with competing genes, overreplicating oneself, and moving toward the germline. Genes can also distort how parents relate toward competing siblings or relatives.

Normally, parental genes in sexual reproduction are dealt 50-50 to offspring. That is, any progeny will have half the father's and half the mother's genes. In "drive," selfish genes are able to get into greater than 50% of a parent's offspring. "Genes inherited in a biased manner can spread in a population without doing anything good for the organism. Indeed, they can spread even if they are harmful."[14] Such genes are said to "drive," the object being to increase their frequency in a population of organisms.

Burt and Trivers describe three main strategies of drive:

1. INTERFERENCE: Recall that in *meiosis,* or sexual cell division, gametes (sperm, egg) receive one of two homologous (similar) chromosomes. The two homologues may carry dissimilar *alleles*—that its, different genes for a trait. Drive may involve getting ahead by disrupting the transmission of the alternative allele. So a gene "might sabotage the 50% of the gametes to which it is not transmitted. . . . Or it might kill the 50% of offspring that do not carry a copy of it, thereby increasing survival of the 50% that do. . . . Note that . . . a kind of 'kinship' discrimination is being made."[15] *Notice the molecular violence—that is, sabotage or killing.*

2. OVERREPLICATION. In normal cell division, the DNA-replicating mechanisms follow Mendel's laws so that most genes are replicated exactly once per cell cycle. Transposable elements (TEs), on the other hand, are selfish genetic elements that carry their own cut-and-paste enzymes (DNA transposase), by which they can increase their copy number. These TEs are the most widespread selfish genes. Mitochondrial (the tiny power plants of cells) genes can also overreplicate themselves in selfish fashion. Yet other TEs can "cause chromosomes to break and then get themselves replicated as part of the repair process; and yet others literally jump across the DNA replication complex as the complex travels along a chromosome, and so get copied twice when normal host genes are getting copied once."[16] More about TEs below.

3. GONOTAXIS. The cell division of germline cells (meiosis) in females gives rise to one functional egg and two or three nonfunctional polar bodies. The third strategy of drive is to move genes preferentially toward the germline and away from somatic cells, when presented with the choice. By getting to the egg and staying away from the polar bodies, a gene gets transmitted to more than 50% of the gametes. "Some

CHRISTIANITY IN EVOLUTION

transposable elements are expressed in somatic cells from which they may invade nearby germline cells" and thereby get themselves multiplied. In conclusion, "A selfish gene can increase in frequency by interfering with the replication of the alternative allele, by itself replicating more often than normal, or by biased movement toward the germline."[17]

To summarize again the modes of drive, Burt and Trivers[18] note that drive is accomplished by interference with competing alleles, replicating more than once per cell cycle, and transposable elements (TE) jumping from somatic cells to the germline. That is, in general, most selfish genes spread by somehow managing to exceed their 50% allotment during sexual reproduction. In the case of transposition, TEs colonizing new locations can do so without any upper limits to the number of copies produced. In addition, there are genes involved in genomic imprinting in mammals; they can amplify their offspring by influencing how the host organism behaves toward relatives. More about this below.

ARE SELFISH ELEMENTS REALLY SELFISH?

Descriptions of varieties of drive in fruit flies, fungi, plants, and mice abundantly illustrate that Life is self-conflictual, that there is at the molecular level a most remarkable intensity of competition and violence. On the other hand, selfish elements have also sometimes "gone over to the other side." In other words, they have been co-opted to serve a useful function at the level of the individual.

Burt and Trivers answer a definite yes![19] In their textbook, they devote 10 chapters to the varieties of drive in numerous organisms, citing evidence that most (but not all) selfish genetic elements really are selfish. How can they evolve? Apparently they do so by directly benefiting themselves. But as I discussed previously, many have been recruited by the host organism to work for its benefit. In humans and other mammals, for example, TEs have come to contribute important gene regulatory functions. The recruitment or endosymbiosis of selfish genetic elements by genomes for the legitimate benefit of the organism as a whole is another twist in Life's struggles to survive and flourish. This was discussed in Chapters 4 and 5 and will be covered it again later in this chapter.

In summary, Burt and Trivers's descriptions of varieties of drive in fruit flies, fungi, plants, and mice abundantly illustrate that Life is self-conflictual, that there is at the molecular level a most remarkable intensity of competition and violence. An example of a murderous selfish element in mice is the *t* haplotype, a segment of chromosome 17; it is able to disable its brother allele, so that it, the *t* haplotype, is overrepresented in offspring. This class of autosomal killing, a molecular murder to further one's own genes, also occurs in *Drosophila* (fruit flies), fungi, and plants; in humans, gamete killers are infrequent, though several rare disorders, such as retinoblastoma and cone-rod retinal dystrophy, may occur as a result of such violence. The authors state that the *t* haplotype probably doesn't exist in humans, but "less effective killers may well exist."[20] More common in humans are transposable elements, genomic imprinting, selfish mitochondrial DNA, female drive, and selfish cell lineages. Subsequent sections will focus on genomic imprinting and transposable elements.

WITHIN-INDIVIDUAL KINSHIP CONFLICTS

Within genomes there can be conflict between genes that come from the father and those that come from the mother. Such conflict takes the form of *marks*, or genomic imprints, placed there by opposing parents, these marks then influence parental or sibling interactions.

It should be of little surprise to learn that within genomes there is conflict between genes that come from the father and those that come from the mother. Such conflict takes the form of *marks*, or genomic imprints, placed there by opposing parents, these marks then influencing parental or sibling interactions. Jablonka and Lamb discuss David Haig's[21] idea about why some organisms have exploited genomic imprints in their extra-embryonic tissues.[22] He posits it as a conflict between father and mother on a molecular level with both parents marking chromosomes or countering the other's marks.

So how will a parent mark a chromosome to benefit itself? In mammals, a father may mark an X chromosome to benefit daughters, because only they receive his X chromosome. Specifically, the father's X chromosome mark makes his daughters try to get more nurture from the mother. But the mother is not passive; she may respond by adding marks that cancel out the father's marks. *Talk about the battle of the sexes! I find this another prime example of molecular intent.* Burt and Trivers further note the evidence that in humans, imprinted genes can affect adult behavior: The mark on the father's X chromosome influences his daughters' ability and willingness to relate to her female offspring.[23] In addition, a father's mark on chromosome 2 affects handedness and may be a factor in schizophrenia.

Burt and Trivers go on to elaborate on such kinship conflicts, pointing out that warping how a progeny behaves toward relatives can be self-serving. That is, kinship (it is more likely that kin carry copies of one's own genes) leads to preferential treatment, resulting in turn with the increased likelihood of survival of one's own genes. Specifically, studies in the evolution of genomic imprinting find that the fetuses of most mammals, including us, contain around 100 genes in which alleles coming from the father and mother are expressed at different levels. Gene imprinting, the competitive marking of genes by one or another parent, offers the best evidence for transgenic kinship conflict. For example, such marks, active in a mother, may lead to her preference for progeny who received her gene over those who did not. *"An extreme version of this preference is for the father to kill the progeny without his genes so as to free up resources for those with his"* [italics mine].[24] In other words, infanticide is a vivid example of kinship conflict.

INFANTICIDE AS A FORM OF DRIVE AMONG PRIMATES

The risk of infanticide is common among primates and is not
related to conditions in the environment or the social system.
It is perpetrated by males who have not sired the mother's offspring.
It is clearly an effort to establish one's own genetic progeny
and thus is a startling example of drive.

In a 1997 paper titled "Infanticide Risk and the Evolution of Male-Female Association in Primates," Van Schaik and Kappeler note that the risk of infanticide is common among primates and is not related to conditions in the environment or the social system.[25] It is perpetrated by males who have not sired the mother's offspring. It is clearly an effort to establish one's own genetic progeny and thus is a startling example of drive. "It has been reported for numerous primate species . . . and is estimated to be responsible for 34–64% of all infant mortality in some well-studied species. . . . Primates may be more vulnerable to infanticide by strange males than most other mammals because primate infants develop slowly,"[26] leaving large periods of vulnerability to infanticidal males. Also, infants of primates can be found easily, because they stay close to their mothers.

The authors write that "most primate females are permanently accompanied by at least one male. . . . this association serves to reduce the risk of infanticide by strange males."[27] The authors found that "male infanticide is almost invariably associated with the disappearance or disabling of protective males, because of take-overs by outsiders or dominance upheavals inside groups, and can be provoked reliably by experimentally removing the dominant adult male."[28] This is one more example of the drive to perpetuate one's own genes involving murder. It is interesting that infanticide, except among the severely mentally disturbed, has become very uncommon in *Homo sapiens*, an example of what Francis Collins describes as the development and internalization of the moral law.[29] Also, note that permanent accompaniment of males and females to protect their young evolves into love and marriage in our species.

Female chimpanzees can likewise kill infants; for an interesting article on female infanticide among primates, go to **http://primatology. net/2007/05/14/female-led-infanticide-among-sonso-chimpanzees/**. Shown there is a photo of Passion and Pm, a mother–daughter Chimp duo who cooperated in the killing and cannibalization of at least two infant offspring of other females. The researchers note that chimp behavior can be as inscrutable as human behavior.

TRANSPOSABLE GENE ELEMENTS

Transposons are genes that literally move around the genome in cut-and-paste fashion. Transposable elements do not always act to the benefit of the genome and its organism; rather, they drive. They can exert profound effects on their hosts, causing "a bewildering array of chromosomal rearrangements." On the other hand, they may be beneficial and thus be important sources of mutation in that they can be domesticated by the host. *The unity of the organism is an approximation, undermined by these continuously emerging selfish elements with their alternative, narrowly self-benefiting means for boosting transmission to the next generation.*

Barbara McClintock was a plant geneticist who in 1983 won a Nobel Prize for her work with the genetics of maize. For many years, she wrote about the phenomenon of genes that acted autonomously by literally moving about in the genome, particularly in the times that the organism was stressed. These genes were called "jumping genes," or transposons; they can cut and paste themselves into different areas of the genome. Jablonka and Lamb write that McClintock's work suggested that the first strategy for cells under stress is to turn genes on or off or modify existing proteins.[30] If this strategy fails, the next strategy is to mutate by mobilizing systems that produce genetic variation. This is a semidirected response to severe environmental pressures. "No longer can we think about mutation solely in terms of random failures in DNA maintenance and repair."[31] But it is now recognized that transposable elements do not always act to the benefit of the genome and its organism; rather, they drive.

Transposable elements (TEs), according to Burt and Trivers, are the most widespread selfish element, accumulating by copying themselves to new locations in the genome.[32] A single organism may have up to hundreds of active copies of a single TE scattered across its genome. TEs can also jump into other, separate species and as a result have colonized all eukaryotic species, including our own. They furthermore have evolved numerous subtypes with differing strategies of drive. They can exert profound effects on their hosts, causing "a bewildering array of chromosomal rearrangements."[33] On the other hand, they may be beneficial and thus be important sources of mutation, in that they can be domesticated by the host. "Just such an event was critical to the evolution of the vertebrate immune system." These benefits notwithstanding, "they are still best considered as parasites."[34]

About half of humankind's genome is derived from TEs. There are three classes of TEs—DNA transposons, LINES and SINES, and LTR retroelements. The first is a cut-and-paste affair, as shown in Figure 6.3 below.

LINES and SINES (long or short interspersed nuclear elements, or retroposons) reverse the transcription process to copy themselves and, like a fax machine, send the copies to a new location. LTR retroelements are even more complicated, but the general idea is the same. An image and an excellent commentary can be found at **www.thenakedscientists.com/ htML/articles/article/jamilcolumn1.htm/**.

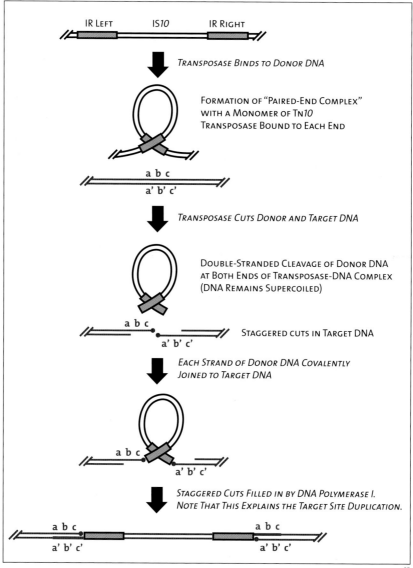

FIGURE 6.3

Figure by Stanley Maloy, San Diego State University College of Sciences, with permission[35]

Transposase, or molecular scissors, cuts away the transposon DNA, moves freely to attach to target DNA, severs it, and then inserts the transposon in the new DNA stretch.

So what are the consequences of TEs? As previously noted, they can harm the host, reduce fitness, and cause disease. They put a burden on the physiology of the host cell. They can cause mutations that lead to genetic diseases, but they can also cause mutations that benefit the host. TEs "can cause duplications, deletions, and rearrangements of host genetic material in a bewildering number of ways, most harmful to the host, but some . . . beneficial.[36] Last, the host cell might incorporate and use a TE's mechanisms. It may produce insertions that increase genome size. The authors wonder if selfish genes drove salamanders stupid. "It has been argued that large genome size in salamanders has set sharp constraints on their mental evolution. . . . Salamanders and lungfishes have the largest genomes of any animals, and they have the simplest nervous systems of any vertebrate."[37] Burt and Trivers write,

Perhaps nothing has impressed us more than the steady discovery of a vast, hidden world of selfish genetic elements inhabiting every species studied. From an evolutionary perspective, these elements are to a degree their own independent life forms, sometimes even with their own distinct evolutionary histories, always with genetic interests that diverge from those of the rest of the organism. They are often the simplest of life forms—one or a handful of genes and perhaps some noncoding repeats (if even that). . . . In our own species these effects include fundamental aspects of the genetic system itself—its size, organization, and degree of recombination—intense internal conflict over early development, and later internal conflict over juvenile and adult behavior. *The unity of the organism is an approximation, undermined by these continuously emerging selfish elements with their alternative, narrowly self-benefiting means for boosting transmission to the next generation. The result: a parallel universe of (often intense) sociogenetic interactions within the individual organism—*

*a world that evolves according to its own rules, as modulated by the
sexual and social lives of the hosts and the Mendelian system that
acts in part to suppress them*[38] [Italics mine].

TRANSPOSABLE ELEMENTS
AND HUMAN DISEASE

Twenty-five human genetic diseases are attributable to TE-mediated
rearrangements. A particular type of transposable element called "human
endogenous retrovirus" (HERV) has attracted considerable medical
research. HERVs are the result of retroviruses that over millions of years
have invaded human and primate genomes and are now passed down the
generations according to Mendelian laws. Primate and human genomes
are littered with these elements; it is estimated that they make up about
8% of our genomes. Some of them transcribe proteins that have been
implicated in cancers and multiple sclerosis, but to date, their
significance is controversial.

Although the harmful effects of TEs inserting themselves have been
extensively documented, it is likely that in their resulting genomic
instability they pose the greatest hazard to their host genomes. Though
they periodically generate important evolutionary innovations, genomic
alterations involving TE sequences are far more often damaging or of
no consequence. Twenty-five human genetic diseases are attributable to
TE-mediated rearrangements. Some of these rearrangements, such as
those involving the MLL locus in leukemia and the LDL receptor in
familial hypercholesterolemia, represent recurrent mutations that have
independently arisen multiple times in human populations.[39]

A particular type of transposable element called "human endogenous
retrovirus" (HERV) has attracted considerable medical research. HERVs
are the result of retroviruses that over millions of years have invaded

human and primate genomes and are now passed down the generations according to Mendelian laws. Primate and human genomes are littered with these elements; it is estimated that they make up about 8% of our genomes. Some of them transcribe proteins that have been implicated in cancers and multiple sclerosis, but to date, their significance is controversial.[40] Evidence from animal models clearly points to HERV's involvement in causing cancer, but evidence for a role in human cancers is likewise tenuous.[41] "The transcriptional activation of human ERVs (HERVs) in the brains of patients with some neurologic diseases suggests that ERVs may participate in certain disease processes in the central nervous system."[42] Experiments with mice suggest that HERVs express themselves in the brain and may contribute to pathologic events through proteins they produce.[43] Research in these areas is therefore complex but promising.

COPING WITH ROGUE ELEMENTS
BY SILENCING THEM

Eukaryotes constantly struggle against TEs by deploying small molecules of RNA that destroy the intruding TEs. This amounts to a kind of cellular immune system against rogue elements.

In the constant struggle of eukaryotes against TEs, organisms have basically employed "RNA interference (RNAi)," the deployment of small RNAs in their defense. Although details of defense vary, all organisms deploy a three-step approach. First, transposon detection gives rise to the production of small RNAs. Second, the number of small RNAs that target active transposons is increased through "slicer" molecules. Third, the growing number of small RNAs is incorporated into complexes that either silence transposon transcription or act epigenetically to repress transposons through chromatin modification or DNA methylation.[44]

Scientists came upon RNAi quite by accident in the late 1990s. The new science of genetic engineering allowed researchers the ability to manipulate genomes of plants and animals by injecting them with foreign genes. But such experimental tricks were constantly meeting with frustration; the organisms were somehow silencing the new genes. For example, petunias with new genes to make them a deeper purple instead

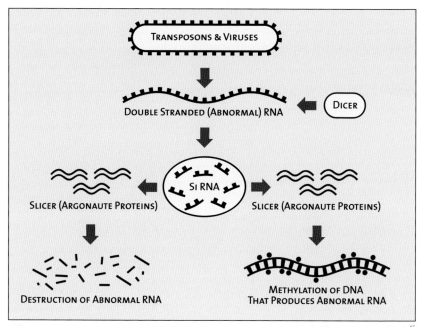

Adapted from Jablonka and Lamb[45]

FIGURE 6.4

Rogue elements such as transposons and viruses produce a double-stranded RNA, which is detected by the enzyme Dicer. Dicer chops up the abnormal RNA into 24 to 30 nucleotide RNAs (small interfering RNAs, or siRNAs), which will be turned against the rogue elements. SiRNAs combine with Argonaute proteins, a family of proteins with a crucial role in silencing mechanisms, to carry out methylation and destruction of rogue DNA. Slicer is the endonucleolytic (destructive to nuclei) activity of some Argonaute proteins.

turned out white or variegated (interspersed purple and white). Something was interfering with the experimental gene. This phenomenon turned up in numerous instances and organisms, and the mechanism is now recognized to be a kind of genomic and cellular immune system against rogue elements through the use of small RNAs.[46] Figure 6.4 summarizes the mechanism.

LIFE AND JIUJITSU:
USING ADVERSARIES FOR GROWTH

Because TEs deploy an array of proteins that can bind, copy, break, join, or degrade nucleic acids—in essence, processes that might be of interest to host cells—it is not surprising that Life has figured out that mobile DNA can serve as a dynamic reservoir for new cellular functions. One intriguing suggestion is that a massive movement of transposable elements following stress-induced epigenetic changes was responsible for the rapid emergence of many evolutionary novelties.

Because TEs deploy an array of proteins that can bind, copy, break, join, or degrade nucleic acids—in essence, processes that might be of interest to host cells—it is not surprising that Life has figured out that mobile DNA can serve as a dynamic reservoir for new cellular functions. Vollf writes:

> [TE] genes encoding transposase, integrase, reverse transcriptase as well as structural and envelope proteins *have been repeatedly recruited by their host during evolution in most eukaryotic lineages* [italics mine]. Such domesticated sequences protect us against infections, are necessary for our reproduction, allow the replication of our chromosomes and control cell proliferation and death. . . . Many new candidates for domesticated sequences

have been revealed by sequencing projects. Their functional analysis will uncover new aspects of evolutionary alchemy, the turning of junk into gold within genomes.[47]

Muotri et al., calling some transposon families "the necessary junk," point out their impact not only in germ cells but also in stem cells and somatic cells:

Transposable elements have been shaping the genome throughout evolution, contributing to the creation of new genes and sophisticated regulatory network systems. Today, most of genomes . . . allow the expression and accommodate transposition of a few transposon families. The potential genetic impact of this small fraction of mobile elements should not be underestimated. Although new insertions that happen in germ cells are likely to be passed to the next generation, mobilization in pluripotent embryonic stem cells or in somatic cells may contribute to the differences observed in genetic makeup and epigenetic gene regulation during development at the cellular level. *The fact that these elements are still active, generating innovative ways to alter gene expression and genomic structure, suggests that the cellular genome is not static or deterministic but rather dynamic* [italics mine].[48]

Continuing these thoughts, Jablonka and Lamb suggest that TEs moving en masse during stressful periods accompanied by widespread epigenetic changes led to rapid self-modifications among organisms. Since 45% of the human genome is composed of TEs, it is likely that they were instrumental in our own rapid evolution. Expanding on the role of TEs in evolution, the authors write that TEs' mobilization in bad times produce potentially useful genetic variation by moving in or out of a gene's regulatory regions. In so doing, they likely produce significant mutations, "because they cause changes that affect whether, when, and where the gene responds to the signals that turn it on and off."[49]

IMPLICATIONS OF
LIFE AS SELF-CONFLICTUAL

Life is cursed in that it must struggle and conflict with others to make a living. For much of Life, making a living is often at the expense of others. Paul laments the futility, bondage, and pain the creation experiences as it groans for release. Although Life has responded to adversity by coping, growing, and evolving, conflict disrupts the community of Life, upon which all Life depends.

In all the preceding chapters, we have developed a view of Life that includes marvelous ingenuity, intelligence, agency, and exquisite co-operation. Much of Life involves beauty and bonds of affection, but Life also continuously struggles to adapt to and survive changing environments. Furthermore, the biblical curse in Genesis 3:17-19 appears to apply to all of Life, down to the molecules:

> And to the man he said, "Because you have listened to the
> voice of your wife, and have eaten of the tree about which
> I commanded you, 'You shall not eat of it,' cursed is the
> ground because of you; in toil you shall eat of it all the days of
> your life; thorns and thistles it shall bring forth for you; and
> you shall eat the plants of the field. By the sweat of your face
> you shall eat bread until you return to the ground, for out of it
> you were taken; you are dust, and to dust you shall return."

This passage vividly dramatizes the struggle to survive. Later, Scriptural passages will attest that survival is often at the expense of others.

And that is what this chapter is about—that survival, even down to the molecules, of any one element of Life may at times mean the devouring of another element of Life. Life is not a zero-sum game by any means, for Life on balance is a glorious affair. But there is abundant conflict, suffering, and misery as all the players struggle to make a living, inevitably at another element of Life's expense.

Out of this struggle to make a living and to eke out an existence, Life has over the eons flourished and grown, culminating in Life grown up, *Homo sapiens*. It clearly is *that which is*, but is it what God intended from the beginning? *This chapter is, of course, a discussion on a biological level of what is known in Christianity as "sin." Yet this study casts sin in a much different light. It emphasizes the self- and internecine conflictual basis of sin.* It doesn't say *why* Life is self-conflictual. That is left to Christianity to answer.

The study makes crystal clear that all Life, not just humankind, is tearing itself apart. St. Paul was aware of this when he wrote the following:

> For the creation was subjected to futility, not of its own will
> but by the will of the one who subjected it, in hope that the
> creation itself will be set free from its bondage to decay and
> will obtain the freedom of the glory of the children of God.
> We know that the whole creation has been groaning in labor
> pains until now; and not only the creation, but we ourselves,
> who have the first fruits of the Spirit, groan inwardly while
> we wait for adoption, the redemption of our bodies.[50]

It stands to reason that God did not intend that the creation should turn out this way. God saw that everything he made was good (integrated, self-cohesive, inherently constructive).[51] Rodin's *The Prodigal Son* (fig. 6.5) expresses for the whole creation the longing for recovery and release.

Yet ironically, Life has *used* adversity and self-conflict to evolve, cope, and grow. Precisely *because of* self- and internecine conflict has it

FIGURE 6.5

The Prodigal Son, by Auguste Rodin, at Victoria and Albert Museum.

honed its intelligence and its substrates, culminating in the big brain of *Homo sapiens. It is paradoxical that God has seen to it that conflict has become the means of developing friends with whom he can relate.* The curse in Genesis "By the sweat of your face shall you eat bread"[53] has led to a creation capable of knowing and loving him.

The bottom line: Certainly, Life has had to struggle to survive, and selfishness stands out, but the end product of Sin (with a capital S) is self- and internecine conflict. *And the end product of self- and internecine conflict is the disruption of community. In its essence, self-conflict is the antithesis of community.* The disruption of community impedes and hampers Life. Life *is* community. Life does not exist for long without community. Community is integral to Life's functioning. Humankind may be Life grown up, but it remains inextricably in community with *all* creation.

THE SEVEN DEADLY SINS

The Church has focused on moral transgressions,
as exemplified by the Seven Deadly Sins, when in fact
the more fundamental problems are the wars
within and between us.

The church since early in its history has focused on seven particular vices as being most representative of sin.[54] *Pride, gluttony, lust, anger, envy, sloth,* and *greed* are diagnostic categories with which we can all identify. I can certainly locate one or more of these within myself at one time or another. The Seven Deadly Sins are thus a litmus test for the state of our morality. There is, however, a kind of institutional quality about them, and there is a danger that they could be dismissed as ritual or, conversely, that they could become an obsessive preoccupation, a focus on externals, the pride of keeping all the rules, or the denouncing of oneself for failure to do so. Manning cautions against the pitfalls of spiritual perfectionism, moralism, legalism, and unhealthy guilt, pointing out that these are prescriptions for more, not less, self-hate.[55]

I have found within myself, and I find it in my patients, that the Seven Deadly Sins are more like fever, chills, body aches, and cough, certainly problems in themselves, but symptomatic of a deeper and more fundamental disease process. In other words, I try to look beneath them to the underlying self-conflict that generates them. Consider studying the seven words italicized above to see what the underlying self-conflict might be, what self-conflict they might share in common.

SELF-CONFLICT IN HUMANKIND

The root of war is shame; the consequences of self-hate are ubiquitous. Humankind tends to paper over self-conflict with false pride or the idealization of others, and pays the price of loss of the ability to mentalize, which leads to more war.

Shame is at the root of all human self-conflict. Recall that shame was the first expression of self-conflict by Adam and Eve after they ate the forbidden fruit. Thus, shame is a more primary hurt, an injury that must be accepted and handled with care for healing to take place. It was shame that underlay humankind's first recorded internecine act, Cain's attack on Abel. Adam and Eve's act of covering their nakedness is in reality an expression of self-hate. These are strong words, but with them we begin to recognize the universality of low self-esteem, and we get a glimpse of what was behind the ferocity of Cain's attack on Abel.

The consequences of self-hate are enormous and ubiquitous. The fallout includes all the self-defeating behaviors we can imagine— depressions, anxieties, and a panoply of self-destructive actions. But even more frequently, humankind covers over shame and self-hate with a reactive narcissism that includes both a personal inflation of self-esteem and a tendency to idealize select others. Hubris, the first, can conceal our sense of inferiority, but putting up a false self directly interferes with our relationships with God and others. With the second, the ideal-ization of others, we abandon our critical faculties to religions, political parties, movements, or charismatic persons so that we can feel a sense of belonging and importance. Christians in particular can get caught up in morality, appearances, and piety and develop a self-righteous or guilty persona or focus on and follow magnetic leaders. But the price we pay is drastic; through hubris and/or idealization, our capacity to *mentalize*[56] is neutralized. I will address the critical human capacity of mentalization in subsequent chapters.

It will be toward the solution to self- and internecine conflict and the restoration of Life as Community that God will act, as we shall see in the following chapters.

Courtesy Yair Hakli and Wikimedia Commons[57]

FIGURE 6.6

Peaceable Kingdom, by Edward Hicks. Oil on canvas, circa 1834.
The National Gallery of Art, Washington D.C.

PART TWO

EVOLVING

CHRISTIANITY

AND THE

REDEMPTION

OF LIFE

IN CONFLICT

CHAPTER SEVEN

CHRISTIANITY AND A PLAUSIBLE GENESIS
THE OLD TESTAMENT

Life is agentive but conflicted. The Breath of God animates Life
and underlies its capacity for intelligence and choice.
There is one reality: Life, using chronos time and digital language,
occupies Reality's south pole, Earth. Heaven, where the Godhead reigns,
is the north pole; its time is kairos time, and its language, metaphoric
and allegorical. Adam and Eve are denizens of Heaven; their
disregard for God and the resulting self-conflict are inherited by Life.
The boundaries between Heaven and Earth are fuzzy, permeable,
and in places thin. God's glory fills all Reality. He will take the initiative
in restoring Life's relation to him, for Life's ultimate safety.

I t is time to explicate the harmony intrinsic to Christianity and evolutionary and biological science. I have in the chapters up to now presented an interpretation of the biological data. My vision is that Life is animated, intelligent, and capable of learning and modifying itself; that is, it is agentive. Life exists only in community, but its inner and collective harmony is threatened by conflict. Christianity can inform what we know about Life, and a deeper understanding of Life can enlarge our appreciation for how God creates, cares for, and loves all Life.

Life's animation—its agency, its intelligence, its creativity, its capacity for self-regulation and self-modification—sharply distinguishes it from the nonliving. Furthermore, nonliving objects don't form relationships or war within or between themselves. The explanatory gap between animated agentive Life and the nonliving is profound. Science has dissected *E. coli* down to almost every conceivable component part, but we can only say that it moves, not what moves it. Judeo-Christianity, though, tells us what animates us: the Breath of Life. *A caveat, however:* With that statement we have just moved from science to religion! But that is what we've set out to do. The idea of the Breath fills the explanatory gap between matter and its animation with a religious understanding. Breath is the first point of rapprochement. *But a second caveat:* This is a god-of-the-gaps model. Recall at the end of Chapter 1 the discussion of this model's vulnerability: If science can create Life in vitro, it casts doubt on the model. But if the molecules can be coaxed into Life, it would appear that the *Ruach* (i.e., Breath of God) fills the molecules of the universe and not just Life.

By virtue of the Breath, Life is intelligent and agentive. Through its agency, Life *chooses.* God has granted Life, within limits, a measure of choice. With choice comes the freedom to rebel, which leads to self-conflict. Life in this respect mirrors the heavenly ancestors, Adam and Eve. The remarkable parallels between the ancient progenitors and Life constitute the second point of meeting of Judeo-Christianity and evolutionary biology. So far, so good. But a glaring discrepancy exists between the first 11 chapters of the Book of Genesis and the scientific worldview of our day. If 40% of Christians don't believe in evolution, it is likely that they are rejecting a 4.5 billion-year-old earth as well as evolution itself. What follows is a cosmology faithful to the Scriptures and the biological and evolutionary sciences.

Suppose we consider that there is an ultimate single Reality, but one characterized by two dissimilar domains. Imagine a single Reality with two poles, Heaven and Earth. Heaven the spiritual pole, the Godhead preeminent; its time is kairos[1] time, and its language, metaphorical, allegorical, and analogical. Its denizens are Adam and Eve, Cain and Abel, and Noah, as well as the angels and the devil and his retinue. Adam and Eve are free; they have palpable boundaries that distinguish them from their Creator. They have choice. In this domain, Adam and Eve heed the bad advice of the serpent and move against God, which instantly separates them from him and immediately precipitates shame—the prototype of all self-conflict. In the timelessness of kairos time, the creation, Adam and Eve, and their act of disregard—and its consequences—become "that which is."[2]

Life in all its iterations inhabits Earth, the south pole of Reality. Its time is chronos[3] time, and its language is digital. God is intimately involved with Life, animating it with his Breath and incessantly providing it with information by his Word. God has lent his Breath to all living, and like its counterparts Adam and Eve, Life is free to develop itself, but on Earth and within the constraints of biochemistry and physics. Sadly, however, Life, like the heavenly ancestors, is contaminated by self-conflict. In a sense, Life is the Earthly embodiment of Adam and Eve.

The Godhead's Breath is lent to Life, resulting in Life's agency and laying the groundwork for self-modification and evolution. The distance between agentive Life and God is not geographical but, rather, a function of the degree of our spiritual blindness and deafness. God, in fact closer than our own breath, constantly instructs and converses with all of Life, whose agency culminates in humankind. A fuzzy boundary separates Heaven and Earth, allowing glimpses of Heaven.

We humans tend to be blind to the subtle mystical aspect of Earthly reality and, more so, to the purely mystical reality of Heaven. Yet at times we do perceive, and some among us have reported seeing a ladder going up to Heaven, a burning bush, a flaming chariot, Jesus transfigured, the four Horsemen, or the Heavenly Jerusalem. And there are windows to the mystical that at times open up to ordinary persons. Think of the "thin places" of the Celtic tradition, experiences that seem to allow passage between heaven and earth. Recently, while attending a Eucharist at St. Paul's Episcopal Cathedral in San Diego, it seemed to me that the high vaulted ceiling reached to and encompassed Heaven, time became kairos time, and the entire experience spanned heaven and earth, both poles of a single reality. In addition, dreams and trances have afforded many people a glimpse or two. These foretastes are powerful anchors to the truths we have learned. Think of "stove pipes" bridging the two domains; by them we can transcend ordinary waking and experience something of the Divine.

The two domains, Heaven and Earth, separated by a veil, can be likened to the floor plan of Eastern Orthodox churches. The nave and narthex, open to the congregation and the outside, represent Earth, while the sanctuary (altar area) represents Heaven. The veil between them, which I call the fuzzy boundary, is represented by the iconostasis, a beautifully ornate wall (fig. 7.1) with doors. The church building is also thought of as Noah's Ark.

Author fi:Käyttäjä:Pertsaboy. Courtesy Wikimedia Commons[4]

FIGURE 7.1

The iconostasis of Uspenski Orthodox Cathedral, Finland, as seen from the nave. The cross-adorned door at center is the Royal Door, through which only the priest and acolytes enter.

So what follows is the theological interpretation of Life as agent, as put forth in the first six chapters of this book. My starting assumption, and it is the core assumption of Judeo-Christianity, is that Life is animatedly physical—a position, if you will, that we can call *animated physicalism*. Life's animating principle is the Breath of God; Life is "animationmatter." This religious model corresponds to external evidence (which is science), is internally coherent, and is of practical use— and for the Christian is consistent with revealed truth. *Again, as stated earlier, a word of caution. This is a god-of-the-gaps model. If science indeed succeeds in coaxing molecules to Life, I would say that it is not just Life but the molecules themselves that are suffused with the Ruach. But until that happens, I'll stick with the Breath and Life.*

Central to the model is the Fall. At the moment of their realization of their separateness and freedom from God, Adam and Eve listen to and follow very bad advice, choose to act against God, and instantly become subject to self-conflict, resulting in chaos, evil, and spiritual death. Earth and its inhabitant, Life, are Adam and Eve's heirs and inherit the choice to act against God, with its resulting self- and internecine conflict. In this chapter, and indeed in the remainder of the book, we will see how God takes the initiative to resolve the conflicts within and between individuals, by calling us to himself and restoring Life as Community. We start with the Old Testament and the Breath of Life.

THE BREATH OF LIFE

The phrase "breath of life" occurs frequently in the Scriptures; it tells us that the Breath, on loan from God, gives Life. The Breath is the source of intelligence and creativity. Death is the withdrawal of the Breath.

In my biblical concordance there are 76 references to the "breath of life" and "breath of God."[5] Let us look at a few of these references:

"Then the Lord God formed man from the dust of the ground, and breathed into his nostrils the breath of life; and the man became a living being." (Genesis 2:7)

"For my part, I am going to bring a flood of waters on the earth, to destroy from under heaven all flesh in which is the breath of life." (Genesis 6:17)

"In his hand is the life of every living thing and the breath of every human being." (Job 12:10)

"As long as my breath is in me and the spirit of God is in my nostrils." (Job 27:3)

"But truly it is the spirit in a mortal, the breath of the Almighty, that makes for understanding." (Job 32:8)

"If he should take back his spirit to himself, and gather to himself his breath, all flesh would perish together, and all mortals return to dust." (Job 34:14–15)

"By the word of the Lord the heavens were made, and all their host by the breath of his mouth." (Psalm 33:6)

"When you hide your face, they are dismayed; when you take away their breath, they die and return to their dust."(Psalm 104:29)

"Therefore the Creator of the world, who shaped the beginning of humankind and devised the origin of all things, will in his mercy give life and breath back to you again, since you now forget yourselves for the sake of his laws." (2 Maccabees 7:23)

Courtesy NASA, ESA, and the Hubble Heritage Team (STScII/AURA)[6]

FIGURE 7.2

"By the word of the Lord the heavens were made, and all their host by the breath of his mouth" (Psalm 33:6). Image is of galactic dust at the center of a star-forming region 9,500 light years away, in the direction of the constellation Cassiopeia. This dust has the potential to form stars.

"Nor is he served by human hands, as though he needed anything, since he himself gives to all mortals life and breath and all things." (Acts 17:25)

So what do we have here? It is the Breath that gives Life, animating the dust. It is on loan to all of Life, including humankind. Death is the withdrawal of the Breath, and without it, all Life returns to dust. Life is ultimately completely dependent on God to sustain it with his Breath. I particularly like the quote from Job that it is the Breath that makes for understanding. If Life, as I have argued, is intelligent and creative, it is the Breath that provides that sentience, intelligence, and creativity. But notice, the Breath, having been lent to Life, is now separate and distinct from God, making Life itself separate and distinct from God. In the Genesis account of Adam and Eve (beginning at Gen. 2:7), the two ancestors clearly have their own boundaries, agency, and free will. Last, I find it astounding to realize that I have been lent and have within me such a reservoir of genius, a Breath that I share with all creatures going back billions of years.

THE WORD OF THE LORD

The Word templates Life's forms. The Word itself has agency and becomes manifest in Jesus. God incessantly dialogues with Life, which responds with its best educated guesses.

If it is the Breath that animates the dust, it is the Word that templates its form. *Word* appears 722 times in the Scriptures, according to my pocket Bible concordance. As the Scriptures use it, the Word itself has agency, having distinct communicative qualities, at times instructing or commanding or creating. In modern parlance, God's Word conveys information, and Life runs on information. In the first creation account in Genesis, God's Word first *calls light out from the formless void covering the face of the deep,*[7] then the various structures of the universe, then the earth, then the animals. Notice that God didn't create something out of nothing; it is as if there exist vast potentials, which God unleashes, as in "Let there be light!" So it is with Life: "By the Word of the Lord the heavens were made, and all their host by the breath of his mouth."[8] The Word of the Lord is a distinct dynamic entity, and ultimately that dynamic entity is identified in the person of Jesus: "In the beginning was the Word, and the Word was with God, and the Word was God. . . . All things came into being through him, and without him not one thing came into being."[9]

So just how does this dynamic entity, the Word of God, call out from Life's vast potentials its evolution, its adaptations, its innumerable structures, to enable the creation of its endless forms most beautiful?

An aspect of God's relationship with people can serve as a paradigm: God is constantly talking to people, if they have the ears to hear. "Now the Lord said to Abram, 'Go from your country and your kindred and your father's house to the land that I will show you. I will make of you a great nation.'"[10] The Scriptures are replete with the Word of the Lord coming to people, culminating in humankind's encounter with the Word face to face. And it is not a monologue, but a dialogue, which I will discuss further in Chapter 9 on prayer. Extrapolating from how God dialogues with us to Life and its unfolding, I suggest that the Lord is constantly dialoging with every level of Life, even with its molecules, guiding, instructing, providing it with templates, inspiring its morphogenesis, with Life at all its levels responding with its educated guesses, just as we pray and then take our best shots in our everyday lives.

ADAM AND EVE, CAIN AND ABEL, AND NOAH

Adam and Eve and Life are parallel. As the ancestors are free,
so is Life, itself free to be selfish, suffer, and murder.
Life's alienation from God initiates a vicious cycle of exile and self-conflict.
The Noah story is an allegory, derived from the Gilgamesh epic,
that wonders if starting over could solve the problem.

The biblical vision of Adam and Eve and the concept of Life described in this book are parallel in numerous ways, starting with their endowment with the Breath. Adam and Eve are God's ultimate creation, certainly intelligent, and furthermore hungry to increase their reach, if succumbing to the temptation to eat from the tree of the knowledge of good and evil is any indication[11] (fig. 7.3).

Life, too, reaches an apogee of intelligence with *Homo sapiens,* with our big brains and self-reflective consciousness; Life's intelligence,

FIGURE 7.3

Courtesy Wikimedia Commons[12]

The Fall of Man. Oil on Canvas, Jacob Jordeans. Museum of Fine Arts, Budapest.
Image from Web Gallery of Art.

creativity, sense of community, and struggle for existence all find their
logical extreme in humankind. And Adam and Eve, as is Life, are
self-conflicted almost from the beginning; the biblical writers lay self-
conflict's etiology with the ancestors' very first exercise of free will,
which results in alienation from God.[13] And the first manifestation of
self-conflict occurs immediately; they realize they are naked and are
ashamed! *Ultimately, it is as if Life is Adam and Eve, or vice versa.*

Life, too, is wracked with self-conflict, as we have seen in Chapter 6. And as Adam and Eve are free, so is Life altogether free, within the constraints of biochemistry and physics, to spread into innumerable life forms, but also free to be selfish. Life's freedom must of necessity extend to the freedom to suffer, to be vulnerable to the vagaries of errors, chance, and misfortune. How could Life be considered free if it, and we, were not allowed to suffer?

And free to murder. God prefers Abel's sacrifice of the firstborn of his flocks to Cain's offering;[14] God sees Cain's anger, and warns him that "sin is lurking at the door." He seems a narcissistic sort of fellow, and his narcissism leads to a lack of empathy with God. He rises up against Abel and kills him. But what is his rage? I think his rage is *toward God* but is displaced onto Abel. *Another move against God.* And why is his rage so powerful, so murderous? *Shame, or self-hate, is at the heart of this internecine conflict!* Cain's fear is that God's displeasure with his sacrifice is a rejection but, furthermore, a condemnation, a pronouncement that he is unlovable. I find all the time that troubled people at heart fear they are unlovable. Such a core belief leads to a reactive narcissism and the kind of acting out discussed in Chapter 6, the foibles of men of high estate. The Old Testament and Jesus repeatedly challenge our reactive narcissism, for it hides the wounds that most need healing.[15] Paradoxically, it will take the ultimate move against God, the crucifixion of God himself, to begin to put a dent in such beliefs.

Note that we are only four chapters into the Bible and we have profound self- and interpersonal conflict, with alienation from God (Cain ends up a fugitive wanderer). A vicious circle of exile and self-conflict ensues. I have tried to demonstrate that Life in its entirety suffers the same problem. But the biblical writers first ask "Well, *what if* God wiped all Life from the earth and just started over, would Life, and particularly humankind, be any different?" Enter the vision of Noah and the Flood.

First I want to establish the allegorical quality of the Noah story. Though as such it conveys truth, the story is derived from a myth of antiquity. In their book *The Bible and the Ancient Near East,* Jewish scholars Cyrus Gordon and Gary Rendsburg describe the various creation and flood myths extant in the ancient Near East, and particularly the greatest literary accomplishment of Mesopotamia, the Gilgamesh Epic.[16]

In the story, as taken from tablets such as that shown in Figure 7.4, Gilgamesh is a tyrant, part man and part god, who fears death and longs to live forever. In his quest for everlasting life, he seeks out the only

FIGURE 7.4
Deluge Tablet
(Babylonian,
Gilgamesh).

Courtesy Wikimedia Commons[17]

man who had ever become immortal. Here are the words of Gordon and Rendsburg: "That was the Babylonian 'Noah,' named Utnapish-tim, who with his wife had become immortal after the Flood."[18] When Gilgamesh finds Utnapishtim, he is surprised, for he appears mortal like himself; he implores him to reveal the secret of his immortality. Per-suaded, Utnapishtim decides to tell him the whole story, which includes the flood of Babylonia. "While the Hebrew and Babylonian creation accounts are radically different, their flood epics are quite similar and come from a common source."[19]

Utnapishtim tells Gilgamesh that he lived before the Flood in the city of Shuruppak. The gods had decided to destroy mankind with a flood. However, one god, Ea, liked Utnapishtim and set out to tell him how he could save himself from the Flood. He was told to abandon his possessions and to build an ark according to exact specifications. He was to take aboard his wife, the seeds of living things, plenty of supplies, and a crew.

> The Babylonian account is more detailed and realistic than the biblical version because the Mesopotamians were more advanced than the Hebrews in material civilization in general and specifically in the arts of naval construction and operation. . . .
> The rains came and, as in the biblical narrative, the ark landed on a mountain from which Utnapishtim sends out first a dove, then a swallow, and finally a raven before he determines, much like Noah, that the earth was dry.[20]

After the flood, the god Ea makes Utnapishtim and his wife immor-tal. Unfortunately, this will never apply to Gilgamesh, who now must face death and its attendant fears.

It is therefore plausible (Gordon and Rendsburg offer five additional reasons for thinking it so) that the Hebrew writers adapted the flood sequence of the Gilgamesh Epic to their purposes. But if so, to what

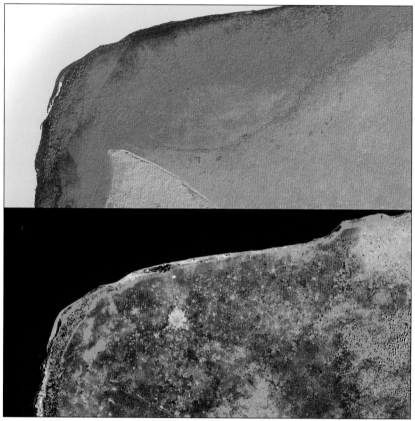

Courtesy Wikimedia Commons[21]

FIGURE 7.5

The top picture is a shaded relief image of the northwest corner of Mexico's Yucatan Peninsula generated from Shuttle Radar Topography Mission (SRTM) data, and shows a subtle, but unmistakable, indication of the Chicxulub impact crater. Most scientists now agree that this impact was the cause of the Cretaceous Tertiary Extinction, the event 65 million years ago that marked the sudden extinction of the dinosaurs as well as the majority of life on Earth. The pattern of the crater's rim is marked by a trough, the darker semicircular line near the center of the picture. . . . The bottom picture is the same area viewed by the Landsat satellite. The circular white area near the center of the image is Merida, a city of about 720,000 population. Notice that in the SRTM image, which shows only topography, the city is not visible, while in the Landsat image, which does not show elevations, the trough is not visible.

end? Recall that the Hebrews saw self-conflict and its subsequent moral failing as humankind's fatal flaw and the ultimate obstacle to union with God; it must be remedied for a reconciliation to take place. The story of Noah and the flood is thus a "what if?" story. What if God took a "righteous" man such as Noah and his wife, wiped out the remainder of humankind, and started over? Would the effort work? No, God concludes, "I will never again curse the ground because of humankind, for the inclination of the human heart is evil [prone to being self- or other destructive] from youth."[22] In other words, the Hebrew writers understood that self-conflict was endemic and discarded the quick fix of simply starting over.[23]

It is noteworthy that there have in fact been several mass extinctions during geologic time, the most spectacular being the extinction of the dinosaurs due to a giant asteroid's impact on Mexico's Yucatan Peninsula about 65 million years ago. The Chicxulub impact crater is still visible (fig. 7.5).

The presence of several mass extinctions in geologic time gives pause for a sobering thought: Humankind is as vulnerable as any species to extinction from a catastrophic cosmic or geologic event.

The first 11 chapters of Genesis relate a series of allegories, including two creation stories, stories of Adam and Eve and their offspring, mythical gods who impregnate the daughters of men, Noah and the Flood, and finally in Chapter 11, the story of the Tower of Babel. I have suggested above that the stories represent the mystical aspect of a single reality. The first chapter introduces something of the nature of God, that there is one God who creates the universe and all of life and who delights in his creation, calling all that he made very good.[24] Furthermore, he relates specifically to individuals; we see him interact intimately with Adam and Eve, Cain, and Noah (who listens to God and carries out the appropriate action of building the ark). The next 10 chapters of Genesis focus on the derelictions of humankind and God's subsequent distress. For example, Genesis 6:5-6 says,

The Lord saw that the wickedness of humankind was
great in the earth, and that every inclination of the thoughts
of their hearts was only evil continually. And the Lord
was sorry that he had made humankind on the earth,
and it grieved him to his heart.

These stories and their punch lines are the Scriptures' initial efforts
to *mentalize*—that is, to describe and name key thoughts, feeling states,
intents, and actions of God and humankind, the two principle players
in the drama of Life.

MENTALIZING

The process of mentalizing can enhance one's comprehension of the
Scriptures. We all mentalize as we attempt to "make meaning"
of the minds of persons we encounter. Grasping the intent of another
involves using focus, imagination, empathy, context, and prayer.
The process can be productively used to discern meaning in Bible
passages; we can even know to some extent the mind of God.

The Scriptures, consisting of about 1,600 pages of often contradictory essays spanning thousands of years, describe how God, loving
his creation and humankind but faced with Life's self-conflict and brokenness, sets out to redeem it and us. Given that the Bible is replete
with allegories, parables, visions, dreams, and trance experiences that
strain my ability to understand and with miracles that often stretch my
credulity, how can I hope to fathom and make sense of it at all, let alone
in this very brief discussion? I therefore introduce my method, derived
from a process in psychiatry and psychotherapy called "mentalizing,"
an idea originally formulated by U.K. psychiatrist Anthony Bateman
and U.K. psychologist Peter Fonagy.[25] In my psychiatric practice, I am

continually challenged to make sense of, to grasp and understand, the minds and mental states of suffering people, and I have found that mentalizing enables me to "make meaning" of their dilemmas and persons. Parenthetically, one of the great rewards of my work is to see people blossom as they realize they have been heard, understood, and accepted. I find that the process of mentalizing likewise assists me in putting together a credible, pragmatic, and satisfying interpretation of the Scriptures. We all attempt to mentalize all the time, and certainly pastors try to mentalize, as in writing their Sunday sermons they plumb biblical characters and the contexts of their actions.

Mentalizing is something everyone tries every day, albeit often inaccurately. Indeed, we are constantly trying to make meaning of the people and events around us. In mentalizing with a patient, I focus on and try to determine, appreciate, and understand the *mental state* of another, with an eye to eventually comprehending that person's *intent*. I use my imagination to put myself in that person's place, and my feelings to try to empathize, to gain an awareness of the feelings surrounding his or her mental state. I use my intellect to ask myself what the context is of the person's mental state. I have learned to pray, little arrow prayers—"What's going on here?"—and I listen for the answers with my "third ear." Finally, I am dialoging with that person, and the dialogue is a progression, and the enlightenment mutual. I do the same with the Scriptures. With this approach, whether or not a miracle actually happened or whether or not there was actually a Flood or whether or not there was an actual, literal Adam and Eve is not important, for what I am looking for is the motivation, the intent, the character of a biblical figure or event, or the intent of the writer, so that I can better understand my own being and even the mind of God. Yes, we can grow in our knowledge of the mind of God. In fact, it should be a primary goal in our relationship with the Almighty. Jesus said, "And this is eternal life, that they may know you, the only true God, and Jesus Christ whom you have sent."[26]

THE PATRIARCHS,
AND MOSES AND THE EXODUS

God, to repair our relationship with him, made his first move by focusing
on a particular people, the Hebrews. Abraham heard him, listened,
and responded, becoming the Patriarch for three present-day religions.
Moses followed suit. The Ten Commandments try to limit conflict with
others and within ourselves, as God calls us to "come up higher."

Humankind, arising from the animals, took Life's genius and
internalized it as superior intelligence and self-reflective consciousness, but also took Life's inherent self- and internecine conflict and
externalized it as sophisticated violence against the self and others. God,
knowing our intrinsic ineradicable violence and desiring to effect a
reconciliation with us, made his first move by singling out a particular
people, the ancient Hebrews, and calling them. Or perhaps God has
always been making overtures to humankind, and one man, Abraham,
a real historical person, actually heard him and implemented what he
heard.[27] *The utterly remarkable thing about this is that God speaks to us also,
and we have the capacity to hear him!* The capacity to hear God and the
exercise of that capacity effects reconciliation with him. Everything
God subsequently does is to try to get us to hear him and ultimately to
know him and act accordingly. It seems entirely plausible to me that the
creation stories of Native Americans are Old Testaments, their perceptions of what they have heard from the Almighty.

Abraham went on to become the Patriarch for three present-day
religions—Christianity, Islam, and Judaism—his offspring throughout
the Old Testament struggling to discern his voice and will, sometimes
succeeding, often failing, all the while being buffeted and challenged by
the vagaries of life. Such is the experience of one particular Old Testament figure, Moses, for he is the pivotal hero in Hebrew history, both
for his role in the Exodus and for the giving of the Law; the Exodus and

the Law reveal aspects of God's saving action.[28] In the Exodus, God, through Moses, guided the Israelites to freedom from slavery in Egypt. This dramatic event is celebrated by Jews to this day, and it illustrates for all humankind for all time that God can act, for those who call on him, to liberate us from the multitude of bondages to which we may fall prey. During the Exodus, God revealed himself on Mt. Sinai in the burning bush, telling first Moses (fig. 7.6) and hence the world that he

FIGURE 7.6

Moses mosaic,
Cathedral Basilica
of St. Louis,
St. Louis, MO.

Picture courtesy TheWB and Wikimedia Commons[29]

cares for each of us personally. He gave us the Law, particularly the Ten Commandments, giving humankind guidelines for living in community, both with God and each other.

As such, the Law was God's initial effort to enable us to put aside selfishness and conflict with others and within ourselves, and the Law continues to this day to call us to "come up higher." Most of all, the Law attempts to enable us to form and maintain *community*. Unfortunately, though the Law and laws in general constrain our selfish elements, rules are not very effective in penetrating to the depths of our being; in fact, many of us find rules irritating. Eventually, God implemented his ultimate plan, to send his only son, for relationships, not rules, attract us.

However, I do not mean to disparage the teaching of the Ten Commandments and rules in general. What we teach to and model for adults and especially our children is profoundly important. In my practice as a psychiatrist, I may work with people, particularly young persons, on their propensity to lie, steal, retaliate, or gossip. Perhaps 80% of the people I see were physically or sexually abused or neglected as children. Such abuse has a variety of fallouts, but one stands out: There was no one present to teach them not to steal or lie or try to get even, let alone revere God, love neighbors, or honor parents. For example, one young woman I recently worked with, a victim of profound neglect, described repeated acts of verbal cruelty toward others. As she became aware of the pattern, she complained that the behavior was compulsive, and she felt helpless to stop it. I told her, "My sense is that meanness is something we learn or maybe haven't yet unlearned. In nature, there is a lot of cruelty, but it is unthinking cruelty. As humans developed big brains and self-reflective consciousness, we attained the ability to choose. And learning to choose harmlessness, compassion, forgiving others, and asking for forgiveness lead to a fuller life. Your parents were too much into their own stuff to help you do all that. So you are starting to work on it now. It is never too late."

THE TRAINING OF THE INNER PERSON

In Israel's spiritual journey, the struggles of the inner person,
the remorse, shame, guilt, fear, and the problem of suffering became
the motive for crying out to God. In stories of David, warrior and
king, the poetry of Ecclesiasticus, and the struggles of Job,
the Hebrews progressed in their relationship to God.

The first 17 books of the Old Testament concern the efforts of Israel to consolidate itself as a community belonging and dedicated to God. Conflict was the only constant as Israel battled its enemies, and its kings vied for power, all in the context of its people wavering in their commitment and devotion to God. Violence was everywhere, wars and murder commonplace (fig. 7.7). There were great warriors, such as Joshua,

FIGURE 7.7
David and Goliath,
oil on canvas, by Caravaggio.
Prado, Madrid.

Courtesy Wikimedia Commons[30]

powerful spiritual leaders such as Samuel, and gifted holy men such as Elijah and Elisha, who out of their devotion to God inspired the people. The greatest hero of all, however, was King David, though he too was flawed, prone to vanity and attracted to beautiful women, especially to Bathsheba, wife of Uriah the Hittite, whom he had murdered. Here there was a shift to the inner man, as David confessed his sin. David went on to author many of the Psalms, those marvelous heartfelt poetic prayers expressing praise, worship, supplication, and contrition to God.

Psalm 51 is a Psalm of David, when the prophet Nathan confronted him after he had gone in to Bathsheba:

> Have mercy on me, O God, according to your
>   steadfast love;
> According to your abundant mercy blot out my
>   transgressions.
> Wash me thoroughly from my iniquity,
>   and cleanse me from my sin.
> For I know my transgressions, and my sin is ever before me.
> Against you, you alone, have I sinned,
>   and done what is evil in your sight,
> So that you are justified in your sentence
>   and blameless when you pass judgment.
> Indeed, I was born guilty, a sinner when
>   my mother conceived me. . . .
> Create in me a clean heart, O God,
>   and put a new and right spirit within me.
> Do not cast me away from your presence,
>   and do not take your holy spirit from me.
> Restore to me the joy of your salvation,
>   and sustain in me a willing spirit. . . .
> The sacrifice acceptable to God is a broken spirit;
>   a broken and contrite heart, O God, you will not despise.

This Psalm models the fundamental brokenness due to self-conflict and its admission, confession, contrition, openness, love for God, and dependence on him for restoration. Note that being guilty from conception has nothing to do with sex; rather, the phrase expresses what I have tried to get across in this book, that we and all of Life are intrinsically flawed. Also note that the Psalmist is in the action stage of readiness for change.[31]

The training of the inner person progressed with the Wisdom literature, in books such as Proverbs, Ecclesiastes, and the Song of Solomon and in the Apocryphal books, such as Ecclesiasticus. I particularly like Ecclesiasticus 41:1-7, which addresses our elemental fear of death.

> O death, how bitter is the thought of you
> to the one at peace among possessions,
> who has nothing to worry about and is prosperous
>   in everything,
> and is still vigorous enough to enjoy food.
> O death, how welcome is your sentence
> to one who is needy and failing in strength,
> worn down by age and anxious about everything,
> to one who is contrary, and lost all patience!
> Do not fear death's decree for you;
> remember those who went before you and those
>   who will come after.
> This is the Lord's decree for all flesh;
> why then should you reject the will of the Most High?

One of my favorites is the Book of Job, an outrageous book full of extremes that deals with the problem of suffering with a most subtle sense of humor. Job was a responsible and ethical man of great wealth, but he lost it all through a series of setbacks and misfortunes (fig. 7.8). His friends see this as God's punishment; after all, God rewards righteousness and punishes sin, doesn't he? Job insists he has done nothing to deserve this and eventually hurls a challenge to God to tell him face-to-face what he has done wrong. God obliges with this elegant poem:

> Then the Lord answered Job out of the whirlwind:
> "Who is this that darkens counsel by words without
>   knowledge?
> Gird up your loins like a man, I will question you,
>   and you shall declare to me.

FIGURE 7.8
Hiob
by Gerhard Marcks,
St. Klara Kirche,
Nurnberg.

Photo by Andreas Praefcke. Courtesy Wikimedia Commons[32]

Where were you when I laid the foundation of the earth?
    Tell me, if you have understanding.
Who determined its measurements—surely you know!
    Or who stretched the line upon it?
On what were its bases sunk, or who laid its cornerstone
When the morning stars sang together
And all the heavenly beings shouted for joy?[33]

The poem goes on for several pages, and Job never gets an answer to why he has suffered, but the inexplicable joy of seeing God face-to-face is enough for him, and he revives. Subsequently, Job's fortunes are restored. The story is a marvelous dramatization of the seeming contradiction of a good, omnipotent, and beneficent God allowing people he supposedly loves to suffer pain and loss, or the conundrum of why bad things happen to good people. We'll return to this question in Chapter 10, "God on Trial."

THE PROPHETS

After the glorious reigns of David and Solomon, threatened conquest by neighbors gave rise to intense self-examination. Invasions and conflicts within engulfed Israel. They longed for a messiah to lead them to safety.

After the glorious reign of David and his son Solomon, internal and then international conflict again reared their ugly heads. First the kingdom splintered into two, and then the Assyrians invaded. Babylonian king Nebuchadnezzar overran the country, destroyed the Temple, and sent the Hebrews into captivity. During these profoundly stressful times, prophets proclaimed, or purported to proclaim, the Word of the Lord. They were not soothsayers, but they could see the threats bearing down on the nation, and they linked these threats to the nation's

FIGURE 7.9

Courtesy Doré's English Bible & Wikimedia Commons[34]

The Glory of God, circa 1883 by Julious Schnorr Carolsfeld. The vision of prophet Ezekiel (Ezekiel 1:4-28).

apostasy and straying from God's ways. There are several whose writings made it into the canon of the church, and their literature predicted subjugation by overwhelmingly powerful and inimical neighbors. Hosea used his personal suffering as a metaphor; his wife was repeatedly unfaithful, and he likened Israel to her and even gave names to his three children that symbolized the nation's unfaithfulness.[35] Joel predicted the incipient judgment of God against Judah and projected a coming "Day of the Lord." Amos noted the vast disparity between rich and poor.

Micah accurately predicted the Babylonian invasion. Habakkuk predicted the invasion of Judah by the Chaldeans, and in his book he arraigns God, asking a variation on the theme of theodicy. Why are the strong allowed to burden the weak? The mystic visionary Ezekiel strengthened the Babylonian exiles with his vision of the most High (fig. 7.9) and the reanimation of the nation (fig. 7.10).

Yet each prophet uniquely saw God as ultimately intervening for the people. Isaiah 42 and the chapters thereafter have a number of poetic messianic allusions. I particularly like Isaiah 50:4-6:

> The Lord God has given me the tongue of a teacher,
> that I may know how to sustain the weary with a word.
> Morning by morning he wakens—wakens my ear to listen
> as those who are taught.
> The Lord God has opened my ear, and I was not rebellious,
> I did not turn backward.
> I gave my back to those who struck me, and my cheeks to
> those who pulled out the beard;
> I did not hide my face from insult and spitting.

Though this clearly prefigures the character of Jesus and alludes to his passion, I can aspire to these qualities for myself.

Joel likewise points to change that is coming, as he writes first of the devastation left by invading armies, but then the coming "Day of the Lord," in Joel 2:28-29:

> Then afterward I will pour out my spirit on all flesh;
> your sons and your daughters shall prophesy,
> your old men shall dream dreams, and your young men
> shall see visions.
> Even on the male and female slaves, in those days,
> I will pour out my spirit.

Courtesy Bilder-Bibel, Leipzig & Wikimedia Commons[36]

FIGURE 7.10

Ezekiel's Vision of the
Valley of Dry Bones
(Ezekiel 37:1-14)
1866 by Gustave Doré.

God's intervention in history with Jesus and the sending of new Breath to Life is foretold in these passages. Notice that all of Life, not just humankind, will receive God's spirit. And the events will initiate the beginning of the end to all of Life's self-conflict, as is foretold in Micah 4:2-3; this will come about as individuals and societies open themselves to direction:

"Come, let us go up to the mountain of the Lord,
    to the house of the God of Jacob;
that he may teach us his ways and that we may
    walk in his paths."

For out of Zion shall go forth instruction,
    and the word of the Lord from Jerusalem.
He shall judge between many peoples, and shall arbitrate
    between strong nations far away;
they shall beat their swords into plowshares,
    and their spears into pruning hooks;
nation shall not lift up sword against nation,
    neither shall they learn war any more.

Even this very brief—indeed, miniscule—sample of the Old Testament affirms that God's breath, lent to life, animates it; the Breath is intelligent. The Word instructs and dialogues with Life, which like Adam and Eve, is free. But Life is broken, and its brokenness, combined with alienation from God, is a vicious circle. God takes the initiative to set things right, creating a focus by choosing the Jews. He establishes a dialogue with Abraham and enables Moses to lead the Jews out of slavery, giving them the Law, a first step in training them to put aside self- and interpersonal conflict. The passages chosen for this little synopsis show David confessing his transgression, Ecclesiasticus consoling us regarding death, the suffering of Job offset by the presence of God, Isaiah rejoicing in the gift of a tongue for teaching, and Joel predicting that God will ultimately pour out his spirit on all flesh. Through these and numerous other steps, God was not only present with his people but was laying the groundwork for the visit of his Son, Jesus, the next step in Life's redemption.

CHAPTER EIGHT

THE
NEW TESTAMENT

Whether we are fallen angels or emerging beasts, God is calling
us to come up higher, to transcend self-interest, put aside our fears,
and love all the creation and one another, to realize fully Life as
God intended it to be. But in the Old Testament, God could take us only so
far, for survival struggles and conflicts are written into Life's and
our genes. Life needed a new Adam. Enter God's son, Jesus.

L
ife, able to modify itself by the Breath and Word of God, has in
geologic history branched out in all directions to produce innumerable elegant, or not so elegant, forms to adapt to changing
environmental conditions. Preeminent among Life's achievements has
been the maximization of its intelligences through various tinkerings of
ever more complex nervous systems, culminating in the last seconds of
geologic time in the big brain of *Homo sapiens*. At the same time, Life
has contended within itself with selfish rogue elements in its genomes
that would corrupt it, and outside itself with intense competition for
limited resources and the extremes of predation from particles as small as
viruses to the inevitable presence of creatures higher up on the food
chain. Substantial amounts—no, most—of Life's ingenuities and resources
have been involved in frenetic arms races, a fact that humankind is only
too familiar with. We seem to express the best and worst of evolution,
capable of unimaginable acts of love, compassion, intelligence, creativity, and cooperation on the one hand and equally capable on the other of
holocausts, nuclear annihilation, and unbounded greed, as in the latest
financial meltdown.

FIGURE 8.1

The Savior of the World.
El Greco (Domenikos
Theotokopoulos).
1600 CE. National Gallery
of Scotland.

Courtesy Wikimedia Commons[1]

Self-conflict is the label I have given for Life's propensity to consume itself; in a way, such consumption is perfectly understandable. After all, everybody has to make a living, and the struggle to survive has wrought ever more elegant life forms. We have questioned if such is the way God intended it; the Scriptures say it is not. It is fair to say that it is *that which is,* certainly implying that God accepts the situation and is working within it. But to say that the survival of the fittest can become excessive is an understatement. After all, humankind's problematic behaviors— our rage, our fears, our greed, hunger, lust, and pride—are only elabora- tions and extensions of the Darwinian struggle to get ahead. However things became as they are, whether we are fallen angels or emerging beasts, God is calling us to come up higher, to transcend self-interest, put aside our fears, and love all the creation and one another, to realize fully

Life as God intended it to be. "I have come that they may have Life, and have it abundantly," Jesus said.[2]

We have seen how God has taken the initiative in setting things right, first by his focus on the 12 tribes of Israel, just as later Jesus would begin his ministry with 12 disciples. The Jews, the patriarchs, Moses and the Law, and the prophets could take themselves and humankind only so far, for survival struggles and conflicts are written into Life's and our genes. In other words, humankind needed a *new* Adam, and God has provided him in the person of his son Jesus. And just who is this man Jesus? More likely than not, you have heard about him all your life; let us look at him carefully. I hope that my perspective will be illuminating.

JESUS AND THE GOSPELS

The New Testament differs from the Old Testament like day and night. A major difference is the energy field of the Holy Spirit. Using mentalization skills, we focus on Mark's Gospel and immediately see that something happened to the people therein.

The transition from the Old to the New Testament is as abrupt as the breaking of dawn after a long and very dark night, a precipitous shift from persons struggling to articulate dim visions to one who is utterly qualitatively different. The difference is the *energy field;* Jesus (fig. 8.1) embodies energy, and all the New Testament crackles with it. It is at first hard to see or hear, within the flat words on a page or in words uttered or chanted on a Sunday morning, the 9 million volts that surround this man, not some flashy external display, but an inner transformative energy. We tend to gloss over words such as *power or Holy Spirit,* or if we hear of events such as Jesus' healing a leper or feeding 5,000 people or walking on water, we instantly dismiss them as not credible. But if

FIGURE 8.2

Statue of St. Mark, by Nicolo' di
Piero Lamberti, 1393–1437. Museo
dell 'Opera del Duomo, Florence.

Courtesy Jastrow and Wikimedia Commons[3]

I apply my mentalization skills to the writer of any New Testament
book, as I try to get inside his or her head, and most important, as I
try to grasp the writer's *intent,* I begin to see that the writers are trying
to clothe with words the core phenomenon of an energy field that is
barely imaginable, much less believable. With the image of energy field
in mind, the reactions of the crowds, the apostles, the eye-witnesses,
become understandable; words such as *astonished* or *astounded* abound,
and as you read on and hear about the subsequent actions of people, you
realize that at the most basic level *something utterly revolutionary happened
to them.* The label the Scriptures give to this energy field is "Holy Spirit," but I fear that such a label has been so routinized by 2,000 years of

theologizing that the essential quality of 9 million volts of transformative electric energy has been obscured or even lost.

At the beginnings of Christianity, virtually everything written about Jesus came from his followers; it was through the lenses of faith and belief that writers wrote for and to their communities of believers, the church. According to Luke Timothy Johnson, Paul's letters, written around 50 to 68 CE, are the earliest documents about Jesus and the then nascent Christianity; the Gospels (Greek for "good news") came later.[4] He writes that the majority of scholars hypothesize that Mark's Gospel was the first of the Gospels, with Matthew and Luke using his Gospel independently as a written source. Mark's Gospel, with even a brief examination, can give us a feel for how all the Gospel authors both related Jesus to the Old Testament writings that preceded him and described the unique dynamism that he projected (fig. 8.2). We can accomplish this by examining Mark's first chapter, a brief description of the middle sections of the text, and a synopsis of his narrative of Jesus' crucifixion and resurrection. I suggest, if you are not familiar with Mark's Gospel, that you read it before proceeding.

THE GOSPEL ACCORDING TO MARK

Mark dramatizes his good news of the life, death, and resurrection of Jesus, much as a modern motion picture abruptly changes scenes. We read of electric energy, lightening fast actions, devout prayer, the healing of bodies, and ultimately, the forgiveness of our opposition to God and the healing of its main consequence, self-conflict. Jesus opposes legalism, resulting in his crucifixion. In his mightiest act, God raises Jesus from the dead.

The Gospel starts with a description of John the Baptist, who is proclaiming a baptism of repentance for the forgiveness of sins; that is, we are told at the outset that this "Good News" pertains to the solution

FIGURE 8.3

Christ in the Wilderness.
By Tracey Clarke, with permission.
The image captures a man
hunkering down under the conflict of
whether to use his power for his own
aggrandizement or to put his ego
aside in his service to God.[5]

to the dilemma of self-conflict. John then predicts the coming of a much more powerful baptizer, who will baptize with the Holy Spirit: That is, the nuclear energy of Jesus will remedy our moving against God—our resistance, our opposition—and the resulting self-conflict. John then baptizes Jesus, and as he comes up out of the water, Jesus sees "the heavens torn apart and the Spirit descending on him like a dove": The energy is cataclysmic, but harmless, not destructive. A voice comes from heaven, "You are my Son . . . and the Spirit immediately drives Jesus out into the wilderness." Things are happening with lightning rapidity. In the wilderness he is tempted (fig. 8.3) by Satan. He is fasting and praying and confronts the temptation to misuse his energy as power to rule and dominate. Finished with the wilderness, Jesus calls several fishermen to follow him, to become fishers for people; the nascent community will be the means of dealing with humankind's—and indeed all of Life's—conflict with God and self. Note that in the first 16 lines of Mark's Gospel, the word *immediately* is used three times; there is no delay, and no intervening medium or agent. This dramatizes the energy. Next, he enters a synagogue and teaches, and "they were astounded at his teaching." He has come to instruct us, because learning is another solution to our conflicts, and the people are electrified by his *words,* which are, after all, the words of the Lord. Next, he encounters a man possessed, and he calls out the unclean spirits. He has the power to call out not only our potentials but also our terrifying self-conflicts, another solution to our Sin. After several healings and a nights' sleep, he gets up in the dark to pray.

Prayer is the source of his energy. A leper asks for healing, and Jesus, moved with pity, commands the uncleanness to come out; the leprosy immediately leaves him, showing another characteristic of Jesus—his compassion. The chapter closes with a comment that crowds now seek him. This chapter is like a modern movie, one scene abruptly changing to the next, showing over telling, all contributing to the 9-million volt effect.

The second chapter moves to the heart of Jesus' coming, to free Life from the bondage of our conflict with God and ourselves; it is the Good News in miniature, save for his final act to destroy death (spiritual death) by his death and resurrection. The chapter begins with a paralytic brought to him, to whom he says, "Son, your sins are forgiven." In other words, "I adopt you, sins and all, and your oppositional self-conflict is no longer an obstacle to the Father's and my communion." Some legal scholars are sitting by, and they pick up on this: "This is blasphemy. Who can forgive sins but God alone?" To punctuate the point that he indeed has this power, he heals the man, to everybody's total amazement. He then calls on a tax collector (an overt sinner, whose visible contradiction is to be a Jew and serve the Romans at the same time) to follow him and ends up dining with a group of such sinners. This causes more scandal among the legal scholars, to which he replies, "I have come to call not the righteous but sinners." There is ultimate truth in this passage, for he indeed comes to free us from self-conflict, but the irony is that there are in fact no righteous people in existence, for we are all tainted by self-conflict. *The real danger in life is not self-conflict, but its*

Courtesy Wikimedia Commons[6]

FIGURE 8.4
St. John and Jesus at
the Last Supper.
Valentin deBoulogne,
circa 1625.

denial, for when we deny our brokenness, we put ourselves outside God's reach.
This butting of heads with legalism will ultimately lead to Jesus' death,
which he knows is imminent.

These themes are repeated frequently in the body of the Gospel.
Jesus teaches, performs a number of miracles, forgives sins, is repeatedly compassionate, and foreseeing that his stands against legalism are
going to get him killed, prepares his disciples for his death. The accounts of his miracles can be a stumbling block to 21st-century rational
minds. Again, I try to *mentalize,* to understand Jesus' intent in these
passages, insisting that it is Jesus' mind-set that is critical for me, not
whether or not a given incident is a literal fact. Attitudes such as his utter

dependence on God, prayerfulness, compassion, forgiveness, great humility, resoluteness, strong boundaries, iron courage, and an unconditional acceptance and passionate love for people, warts and all, shine forth. There is no trace of violence in him. Let us now fast-forward to his crucifixion.

All four Gospels have roughly similar accounts of Jesus' crucifixion, and in all, the vignettes of Jesus' words and actions inexorably progress toward this penultimate event, where humankind will once again move against God. It is the one incident in Jesus' life that is mentioned in other than Christian chronicles, confirming it as a historical event. Mark's Passion account (the name given to the whole train of events) spans Chapters 14 and 15, with Chapter 16 describing the resurrection. Readers not familiar with the events surrounding his death and resurrection should read these chapters now. Chapter 14 gives an account of Judas' intent to betray Jesus, the Last Supper (fig. 8.4), Jesus' agonizing

Photo by the Rev. Michael Bell, with permission

FIGURE 8.5

"Father, if you are willing, remove this cup from me; yet, not my will but yours be done."[7] Garden of Gethsemane, Basilica of the Agony, Jerusalem.

Courtesy Wikimedia Commons[8]

FIGURE 8.6

The Crucifixion. Giovanni Battista Tiepolo. Oil on canvas. St. Louis Art Museum,
St. Louis, Missouri.

prayer in the Garden of Gethsemane (fig. 8.5), and Judas' return with an
armed crowd; he betrays Jesus with a kiss, and Jesus is taken before the
high priest, interrogated, and condemned.

At Jesus' trial, Peter denies him three times. Next, in Chapter 15, he
appears before the Roman Procurator, Pilate, who gives in to the shouts
of the crowd to crucify him, and he is led off and crucified, along with
two thieves (fig. 8.6). Everyone has turned against him. Once nailed to
the cross, he makes in Luke's Gospel a statement that accepts Life as it is,

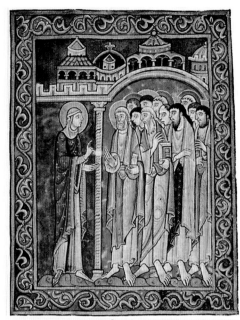

FIGURE 8.7

Mary Magdalene announcing the resurrection to the apostles. St. Albans' Psalter, St. Godehard's Church, Hildesheim, Germany. Unknown artist, circa 1120 A.D.

sins and all: "Father, forgive them; for they do not know what they are doing."[10] Darkness comes over the land at noon; a centurion facing him is moved to exclaim, "Truly this man was God's Son!"[11] The irony here is that in Mark's Gospel this centurion and the demons are the only ones who recognize Jesus' divinity. Several women, including Mary Magdalene and Jesus' mother, watch from a distance. He breathes his last and is taken down from the cross and entombed.

Mark's account of the resurrection in Chapter 16 is quite brief. The three faithful women who witnessed Jesus' death went to his tomb on the third day, after the sun had risen, to anoint him, but they found the stone at the entrance rolled away. They entered the tomb and saw a young man, sitting to the right. After reassuring them, he told them that Jesus had been raised; they were to go and tell the others (fig. 8.7). Soon, Jesus appeared to Mary Magdalene, then to others, and finally to the 11 disciples. The other three Gospels have more detailed accounts. According to McKenzie, the earliest literary witness of the New Testament is 1 Corinthians 15:3–8.[12] There Paul describes Jesus' appearances to Peter, then the 12,[13] then to more than 500 at one time, "most of whom are still alive, though some have died,"[14] then James, and finally to Paul. It is tempting to argue that resurrection is the convincing demonstration of Jesus' claim to divinity, but McKenzie writes that in the New Testament "the resurrection is not an argument for faith, *but rather is that which faith first apprehends* [italics mine], the risen and glorified Jesus." He concludes,

> The resurrection is the climactic achievement in the
> saving deeds of God. To recognize the event as a fact is
> nothing: to accept it as a saving deed is to believe in it
> and to receive the salvation which is achieved by it.
> . . . it is faith in the resurrection, not observation of the
> fact, which is blessed by Jesus.[15]

IMMEDIATE EFFECTS OF THE RESURRECTION: ACTS OF THE APOSTLES

The energy field, the Holy Spirit, becomes identified with
the Breath of Jesus. The Holy Spirit is poured out on the disciples,
who then pour out with the good news that God is with us.

The accounts of people recorded in the Acts of the Apostles, the first book to follow up on Jesus' resurrection, document an utterly different mind-set from Old Testament persons and, for that matter, different from the mental patterns of Jesus' disciples. Reading Acts for the first time is a bit offensive: People spoke out seemingly recklessly and confronted the authorities dangerously, even to the point of death, and there was even a scene resembling intoxication or mass hysteria. But the greatest skeptic or cynic, if he or she really paused to mentalize, would have to agree that *something happened* to these people; something radically changed them. A diagnosis of insanity wouldn't fit, for insane people withdraw, become less accessible, and are more often vindictive or combative; these people loved each other and readily forgave the hostility of others. What happened was that the energy field surrounding Jesus was poured out on his followers and, indeed, on all flesh! As I mentioned above, the code word for the energy field is the Holy Spirit. And the energy field, or the Holy Spirit, is Jesus' *breath*! My text is John 20:22-23 (Jesus is speaking to his Apostles): "When he had said this, he breathed on them and said, 'Receive the Holy Spirit. If you forgive the sins of any, they are forgiven; if you retain the sins of any, they are retained.'" Jesus' breath was united in these men with the Breath of Life, relieving Life of the fixity of distrust and self-conflict and enabling them to pass along the favor!

PAUL'S LETTER TO THE ROMANS

Paul, a persecutor of Christians, is blinded by a vision of Jesus. His Letter to the Romans is an all-time masterpiece. In it, he shows that we are brought to wholeness by Jesus' faith in God. But has Jesus' sacrifice really made a difference? I can see the benefits in my own life, but what of the totality of Life? The answer lies in evolution! We have seen in this book that the evolutionary changes producing our species took many millions of years. It took time to get us to this place, and it will take time for the implementation of God's plan to make us safe and sound.

Paul comes to occupy center stage in the Acts of the Apostles, being first mentioned as present at the stoning of Stephen.[16] Paul, at this time known as Saul, was a persecutor of the early Christians, but on the road to Damascus, he had a dramatic conversion experience, a vision in

FIGURE 8.8

The Conversion of St. Paul. Nicolas-Bernard Lepicie, 1767.

which Jesus appeared and inquired as to why Paul was persecuting him (fig. 8.8). Paul then became Jesus' most ardent missionary, much of the remaining book chronicling his travels, teaching, and preaching. Paul's

FIGURE 8.9

Saint Paul. El Greco
(Domenikos
Theotokopoulos),
circa 1605. Sarasota,
The John and Mable
Ringling Museum of Art.
Author Taty 2007.

Courtesy Wikimedia Commons[18]

letter to the Romans, according to Luke Timothy Johnson is univer-
sally regarded at Paul's masterpiece.[19] In it, he vividly and emphatically
outlines humankind's and indeed all of Life's problem as self-conflict
devolving from hostility toward God, with its reversal set in motion by
Jesus' faith, as he lived out his life, death, and resurrection. I suggest the
reader peruse *The Message,*[20] a modern translation of the Bible, to get the
best feel for the work, all the while keeping in mind that Romans was
written 2,000 years ago in the style of ancient Greek rhetoric, a method
of argumentation in which Paul poses rhetorical questions, apostrophes,[21]
abrupt responses, and dialectical arguments (fig. 8.9).

In Chapter 1, Paul, before interpreting the meaning of Jesus to humankind and to Life, describes humanity as failing (though they should

know better) to honor God and thank him, leading to a number of consequences, including loss of sound judgment, confusion, sexual acting out, and a host of character failings. The "wrath" of God here is the inevitable suffering consequential to such behaviors, not God's lashing out and inflicting pain. Paul is not moralizing but, rather, is trying to contrast the human condition against God's transcendent deity and his "giving them up" (he uses the term three times) to their behaviors—that is, allowing things to run their course.

Well, I think to myself, I'm not like that litany in Chapter 1; I don't have dishonorable passions, at least not very many, nor am I full of envy, murder, deceit, and the like. But not so fast, Paul says in Chapter 2, lest I believe I am not one of them, think again. Pious religion is a thin cover for self-conflict, and adherence to the law doesn't get to the heart of self-conflict, which he summarizes succinctly in Chapter 7. Circumcision, an outward religious observance, is external and physical, while real circumcision is a matter of the heart, spiritual and not literal. In Romans 3:9 he writes, "All men, both Jews and Greeks, are under the power of sin." Note that Paul here personifies sin as an oppressive force, and he is trying to tell us that we are powerless in its grip. I think of Step 1 in Alcoholics Anonymous: "We admitted we were powerless over alcohol—that our lives had become unmanageable."[22] Though we may escape or avoid overt maladies such as alcoholism, we still suffer at the molecular level from self-conflict and, if we will admit it, from our own special behaviors that stem from it.

But God has no intentions of abandoning Life to the consequences of its actions. Even patience and forbearance, though present, are not the last word, for by themselves they would add up to God's capitulation to Life's self-conflict. Romans 3:21-24 indicates God's intervention in sending us Jesus.[23] Verse 22 can be read as "Christ's faith" or, alternatively, "faith in Christ." Johnson states that it is Christ's faith that restores Life, which, with human consciousness at the forefront, is incapable of initiating and sustaining a right relationship with God, at least at the outset.[24]

Similarly, when as a medical student beset with emotional problems, I received pastoral counseling from an Episcopal priest, the Rev. S. Dunham Wilson, who told me he would hold the faith, hope, and prayers for me at a time when I was incapable. I had the experience of being restored,[25] and with a newfound faith in Christ I have been able in my subsequent work as a psychiatrist and addictionist to pass soundness on to others. We need to embrace weakness and powerlessness, in the sense of being dependent on the Good Father, a posture that Life, with its ingrained self-reliance, views with suspicion and has difficulty accepting.

To reinforce his idea that *Jesus' faith,* even unto death, initiates our own restoration,[26] Paul turns to Abraham, a type of Christ, and shows that it is through his faith that many are saved—that is, brought to safety and soundness. At this point in the readings, I have an objection. OK, I follow the logic of Jesus' atoning death on the cross and his faith that overcomes our self-conflict, but in practice, I see the world, people, indeed all of Life still ravaged with self-conflict. Where is the effect? I can see the benefit in my own life, but what of the totality of Life? I think the answer lies in evolution. We have seen in this book that the evolutionary changes producing our species took many millions of years. It took time to get us to this place, and it will take time for the implementation of God's plan to make us safe and sound. The first step in this evolution was Abraham's believing God, trusting that he would make good on his promises. The next great step in evolution is Jesus and him crucified and raised from the dead. He was and is Life,[27] *and by accepting his death, he took on Life's cursedness (under the power of self-conflict), as it is written,* "For anyone hung on a tree is under God's curse."[28] Thus, I am optimistic about Life's long-term prognosis.

In Chapter 5, Paul talks of being put right with God through Jesus' faith, with resulting peace and the ability to endure suffering. He marvels that Jesus would die for us and how that act proves God's love for us. He repeatedly uses the word *reconciliation,* enabling the first two paragraphs to graphically tell us that God and Jesus are *with* us. He then sharpens the sense of immediacy of Jesus' presence in us by likening Jesus to a new Adam. The former Adam, whom I have likened to Life, is weak, self-conflicted, embattled, alienated, and alone, while the new Adam, Jesus, provides a *grace* best thought of as the energy field that generously bolsters and strengthens us with the presence and goodwill of God.

I had an experience that has led me to believe that the new Adam is literally present within us. I approached the Episcopal Priest Fr. Wilson, mentioned above, with a specific complaint. I was a womanizer, and though I was aware that my impulses contradicted my wish to authentically love others, I couldn't stop. Early in my counseling I had a dream, one so vividly real that it was indistinguishable from waking. In the dream I was talking with a Roman Catholic priest (remarkable in itself, for my mother had tried to imbue me with her rabid anti-Catholicism), who told me that Jesus had the answers to my acting out.

At first blush, a Catholic priest is a convenient symbol of the ability to live without sex, but this was no ordinary figure. He remains one of the most remarkable persons I have ever encountered; he glowed with an inner radiance, an energy field bar none. He had crooked front teeth, and later in the dream I saw him smoking a cigarette. Well, it so happened that I had crooked front teeth, and at the time smoked, so he was possibly part of me, but I could go no farther. I now believe, and the belief has an emotional resonance, that he was my new Adam, not perfect by any means, present by the grace of Jesus, and waiting to be called out. And in time I got my healing.

Paul, in Romans 6, asks us to exercise, to our best ability, our will to stop sinning; he doesn't review the list of various ways of acting out from Chapter 1, but that presumably is what he is referring to. But then in Chapter 7 he reminds us of the ineluctability of self-conflict, proceeding to paint in painful personal tones the *absolute most graphic and direct description and definition of self-conflict* found anywhere in the Scriptures. I quote Romans 7:14-25 from the NRSV:

For we know that the law is spiritual; but I am of the flesh, sold into slavery under sin. I do not understand my own actions. For I do not do what I want, but I do the very thing I hate. Now if I do what I do not want, I agree that the law is good. But in fact it is no longer I that do it, but sin that dwells within me. For I know that nothing good dwells within me, that is, in my flesh. I can will what is right, but I cannot do it. For I do not do the good I want, but the evil I do not want is what I do. Now if I do what I do not want, it is no longer I that do it, but sin that dwells within me. So I find it to be a law that when I want to do what is good, evil lies close at hand. For I delight in the law of God in my inmost self, but I see in my members another law at war with the law of my mind, making me captive to the law of sin that dwells in my members. Wretched man that I am! Who will rescue me from this body of death? Thanks be to God through Jesus Christ our Lord!

Immediately thereafter, in Chapter 8, Paul expands on the above last sentence:

For the law of the Spirit of life in Christ Jesus has set you free from the law of sin and of death. For God has done what the law, weakened by the flesh, could not do: by sending his own Son in the likeness of sinful flesh, and to deal with sin, he condemned sin in the flesh. . . . To set the mind on the flesh is death, but to set the mind on the Spirit is life and peace. . . . if Christ is in you, though the body is dead because of sin, the Spirit is life.[29]

And not only us humans, but the whole creation as well, is suffering from the curse of self-conflict, but Paul is hopeful:

I consider that the sufferings of this present time are not worth comparing with the glory about to be revealed to us. For the creation waits with eager longing for the revealing of the children of God; for the creation was subjected to futility, not of its own will but by the will of the one who subjected it, in hope that the creation itself will be set free from its bondage to decay and will obtain the freedom of the glory of the children of God. We know that the whole creation has been groaning

FIGURE 8.10
St. Paul writing. From an early 9th-century manuscript version of St. Paul's letters, written in the Monastery of St. Gallen. The picture is believed to be one of the earliest depictions of Saint Paul in European art.

Courtesy Wikimedia Commons[30]

in labor pains until now; and not only the creation, but we ourselves, who have the first fruits of the Spirit, groan inwardly while we wait for adoption, the redemption of our bodies. For in hope we were saved. Now hope that is seen is not hope. For who hopes for what is seen. But if we hope for what we do not see, we wait for it with patience.[31]

There are eight more chapters to Romans, some of them devoted to Paul's concern for his fellow Jews and many filled with advice for living the good life and the building of communities where people love one another, both of which are after all antidotes to self-conflict. All in all, it is an exuberant, passionate, generous, and elegant book, and without doubt Paul's masterpiece.

A PSYCHIATRIST'S LOOK AT ROMANS

Self-conflict is an inherent part of Life.
From my work as a psychiatrist, and as one who has his
own self-conflicts, I have a variety of thoughts that
I believe can add light to Paul's writings.

It is no accident that as I read various works on evolution and the biological sciences, and even before I learned about genes that conflict, I picked up on self-conflict as an inherent part of Life. I have, of course, encountered it in myself, but it has been my bread and butter for more than 40 years, where, in my work, I have been privileged to be invited to peer within the deepest recesses of suffering peoples' hearts and minds. Consequently, as I study the Letter to the Romans, I have a variety of thoughts that I think add light to Paul's writings (fig. 8.10).

My basic premise is this: Despite their selfish genes and genetic quirks and errors, people are consistently trying to make the best choices for their lives, an exception being those people with antisocial personality disorder, and even that grouping is by no means homogeneous.[32] Normal infants are hard-wired for attachment, and this gives rise to one of the two basic drives of the self—the drive for communion, the other the drive for individuation—to realize and become the unique person God intended one to be.[33] When these twin drives are frustrated through childhood abuse, neglect, overprotectiveness, or traumas or by genetic maladies such as schizophrenia, autism, bipolar disorder, attention-deficit disorder, and a host of biological or physical conditions, then false selves can be put up, masks, if you will, resulting in a variety of acting-out behaviors, the symptoms of which can look a lot like the litany of ills Paul lists in Romans 1:26-31. In other words, Paul's litany may not be the result of inborn self-conflict but, rather, the outcome of childhood abuse, neglect, and/or trauma. That is not to excuse them, for we all are ultimately responsible for playing the hand dealt to us, whether it is a history of childhood cruelty or a genetic flaw. Paul's letter tells us how to play the hand.

Paul's list of character flaws in Romans 1:29-31 is very reminiscent of narcissistic personality disorder. These persons have false selves consisting of grandiosity, pride, and the devaluing of others. They are very brittle people, have enormous pain inside, and protect themselves and maintain their egg-shell self-esteem with the actions described in Romans 1:29. Inevitably, they have been subject to childhood abuse, usually physical, but often as children they were dismissed, their presence devalued; these actions are guaranteed to distort personalities. Persons exhibiting the character traits that Paul details deserve our compassion, not judgment, and I am sure Paul did not mean it as judgment but, rather, as a generic discussion indicative of a separation from God that applies to all of us. Victims of childhood abuse, neglect, or trauma are prone to feeling even more alienated by virtue of their experience, but on the other hand they may be crying out to God. That said, they can also be very difficult people.

A desire for revenge is implicit in much of Romans 1:28-32, and its antidote is forgiveness, the exercise of which is central to Jesus' teaching and example. In my work in addiction medicine, I find histories of physical and sexual child abuse and neglect to be very common in drug and/or alcohol users. Almost invariably, sufferers of addiction with such traumatic histories are deeply resentful and bent on getting even, their revenge taking the form of self-destruction. Often, their substance use is a way of telling significant others or the world, or even God, to go to hell. This impulse is often deeply buried and quite subtle, and it can be very salutary to have it empathically brought to light. People quickly come to see that revenge is only hurting themselves, and they are often quite open to the option of forgiveness; however, for severely traumatized people, this can take a lot of time.

Romans 1:26-28 is often used as evidence for God's abhorrence of homosexuality, which is a source of controversy in Christianity at this time. I shared this abhorrence as a young man, particularly after having been approached on three occasions by men. As a psychiatrist, however, I saw a substantial number of gay men for various other complaints, chiefly depression, panic attacks, and agoraphobia, and I came to see that they were conscientious persons living their lives as constructively as possible. My own judgmental attitudes toward them remained, though I kept my opinions private and did my job. About that time I chanced to read *The City of Joy*, by Dominique Lapierre.[34] The story is of a Polish Catholic priest who ministers in the City of Joy, a Calcutta slum. The priest had a completely different attitude than I did; he cared for and indiscriminately liked, loved, and enjoyed being with an array of homosexuals, cross-dressers, transsexuals, prostitutes, and beggars. Reading the book was for me an affective experience, and I yearned to be able to love with such abandon.

As my work progressed, I was particularly privileged to work in depth with three gay men. Two of them were troubled by promiscuity, sexual addictions that were rooted in the distorting effects of childhood abuse, and in our work together, they attained sexual continence, though their sexual attraction toward men remained. The third man I saw for an anxiety disorder, and as I got to know him I found him to be a most generous, self-sacrificing, and compassionate person. He was not promiscuous, but was committed to a long-term relationship in which he was very happy. These three men were all Christians, deeply committed to God and their churches; the only thing different about them was that they were gay since their earliest recall.

What can we say about the root causes of homosexuality? Pillard and Bailey, in a review of behavioral genetics research on sexual orientation, found that family, twin, and adoptee studies indicate that homosexuality runs in families, with the hypothesis that genes account for at least half of the variance in sexual orientation.[35] Kendler et al. found familial resemblance for sexual orientation, greater in monozygotic twins than in dizygotic twins, though family environment was also possibly a factor.[36] Rahman found inconclusive the evidence that sexual orientation in humans may be laid down in neural circuitry during early fetal development or that prenatal sex hormones could influence future sexual orientation.[37] In summary, biological and genetic studies show that homosexuality can run in families, but the smoking gun of causality has not been found.

Joan Roughgarden, a professor of biology at Stanford, notes the diversity of gender expressions, reproductive rituals, sexual practices, and family constellations of animals.[38] In a given species, there can be aggressive or alpha males, overtly feminine males, masculine females, and feminine females. In many species, males guard the eggs. Male seahorses carry the eggs in their mouths. Same-sex sexuality among animals is commonplace. For example, especially well-studied male bottlenose dolphins engage in homosexual activity, a male placing his erect penis in another's male genital slit, nasal aperture, or anus. They may form lifelong pair bonds and together forage and look out for danger. With the death of a partner, the widower searches for a new companion, usually failing unless he finds another widower. Homosexual male-male and female-female pairings are well documented in lizards, birds, and fish, as well as mammals. This study of Life tells us that variations in gender expression and sexual orientation are part of *that which is.*

It thus appears that human homosexuality, rather than representing underlying pathology, is a variant found throughout nature. Like their heterosexual counterparts, homosexual men and women can act out promiscuously, such acting out indicative of severe self-conflict. Paul, in Romans 1:24–32, is singling out lusts of every kind, not homosexuality, as symptomatic of separation from God. Motivated individuals in our time, sensing the self-harm devolving from promiscuity, can, with competent psychotherapy, enjoy sexual continence. Changing sexual orientation is another matter. At this time, I can find no convincing experimental evidence that psychotherapies or counseling meant to change sexual orientation has any lasting effects. Though there are self-reports in the popular press and case reports in the psychiatric literature of persons making changes, credible scientific studies in this area have yet to be carried out.

My studies on evolution and my clinical psychiatric practice have persuaded me that biological structures, as well as behavioral patterns, are malleable. However, when it comes to sexual orientation, it appears to me that there is a spectrum, ranging from those men and women homosexually oriented from a very early age and hard wired to others more confused than hardwired and, if self-motivated, possibly capable of change. *My concern for Christianity at present is that some church denominations have made homosexuality an ideological issue and in the process have lost emotional contact, empathy, and compassion for a whole segment of humankind. In other words, they have sacrificed their ability to mentalize (more on this crucial capacity in upcoming chapters).* I deplore judgmentalism and coercion toward homosexual people, and I favor a theology of inclusion regarding them and, for that matter, all people.

A SEGUE TO PRAYER

I name three ways to
experience the presence of Jesus and God.
There are many others.

In the context of arguing that Life is mystical, I have presented synopses of the Old and New Testaments that dramatize how God reveres Life and sets out to restore its integrity and bring it back to him. The spare and sparse words of the Scriptures can move us deeply when we plumb and contemplate them, yet feelings fade with time, and they easily become words on a page. Furthermore, as I said above, we tend toward blindness to the heavenly aspects of reality.

It follows that sustaining an affective sense that Jesus is God is difficult. I have a friend named Jack Smith. I could write to you all about Jack Smith, but until you met him, touched him, and heard his laugh, he would only be words on a page. I strongly identify with the man in Mark 9:24 who runs up to Jesus and says, "I believe; help my unbelief." The experience of others must come from the outside. Such experiences are available; our brains have receptors to hear the inaudible and see the invisible. But we must put ourselves in the paths of experience. If I want to get run over by a truck, I must drag myself from my upstairs apartment to the street.

Here are three ways to experience Jesus and the presence of God. Recall that all Life is community. One needs a good church or a 12-step program, but be advised that some churches can be mausoleums. Look for meetings or congregations that are skilled in and practice mentalization. In addition, there should be certain urgency; I prefer the spirituality one would find on an aircraft carrier in a combat zone. Second, the Scriptures, studied and mentalized by a group, are a blessing. I meet weekly with a group of men, where over breakfast we pore over and mentalize the readings for the week. The third and chief means of keeping in touch with the Godhead is prayer, which we turn to in the next chapter.

Image copyright of Marco Burali, Tiziano Capecchi, Marco Mancini
(Osservatorio MTM), with permission[39]

FIGURE 8.11

"Praise him, sun and moon:
Praise him, all you shining stars!
Praise him, you highest heavens,
and you waters above the heavens!"
(Psalm 148: 3-4).

The Magnificent Horsehead Nebula is some 1500 light-years distant, embedded in the vast Orion complex. It is five light-years "tall."

CHAPTER NINE

PRAYER

Does prayer work? It certainly has for me.
Through prayer I have found purpose, direction, insight,
and the sense that I am not alone.

So far in this book I have presented data to show that Life is very old, starting with single-celled organisms, the tree of Life springing from them, all of us cut from the same cloth. Life, endowed with intelligence and the ability to learn, can creatively modify itself but is tragically self-conflicted. I suggested that this concept of Life, combined with the Breath and Word of God, makes for a plausible genesis. The Scriptures show how God has set out to redeem Life from its resistance to him and its self- and internecine conflict by calling out its constructive capacities, thereby carrying it to safety and soundness (salvation). In the last seconds of geologic time, he has sent his son Jesus to become the next Adam, whose faith Life can seize upon to realize its potential as sons and daughters of the Most High. In terms of philosophical tests for truth, the construct put forth in this book corresponds with the findings of science and the witness of Scripture and is internally consistent, but is it pragmatic? Does it work? Are people's prayers answered? Can we hear the voice of God as Abraham and Samuel did? Is God really on our side, or is he poised to punish us when we sin? Can God really heal our conflicts?

I was raised in the Episcopal Church; attendance was mandatory, and I recall as a teen kneeling during services and thinking to myself that this was a lot of nonsense. When I left for college, I was free, and I

FIGURE 9.1   Courtesy Antandrus and Wikimedia Commons[1]

Cuyama Valley, about 90 miles north of Santa Barbara, California, in the springtime.
The Sierra Madre Mountains are in the distance.

gave God no more thought. After a stint in the Navy, I took a position-
in-training in my chosen field, petroleum engineering, to pursue my
vague but grandiose plan to make a million dollars. Instead, I wound up
in the Cuyama Valley (fig. 9.1), in a little remote oil field town, sharing
a house with some other guys, feeling very lost. One day, while working
in the pump shop, I was given a pump to assemble. The supervisor was
watching, and when I had finished, he snatched the pump from me,

disassembled it, and showed me that I had put one of the valves in upside down. My emotional reaction was telling: *I didn't care.* Petroleum engineering is a perfectly good field, but it was proving not to be my niche. Furthermore, I had no idea of what else to do with my life; I was stuck. There weren't any open doors anywhere.

My sense of immobilization went on for months. I drank a six-pack a night, but the parties of college and Navy days had emptied out, replaced by a deadness I now identify as joylessness. I listened over and over again to my record player, the Kingston trio singing "It takes a worried man, to sing a worried song; I'm worried now, but I won't be worried long." But I had a script tucked away in the back of my mind: If all else fails, I can turn to God. Later in life, I told a Christian friend about my script, but he scoffed at my foxhole faith. I replied, "Well, it beats the script a lot of my patients have—if all else fails, I can always kill myself."

So one evening, in the living room by myself, I prayed, no words particularly, more the glance of an injured man in an ER, looking at the doctor who holds his life in his hands. What I got back changed my life forever—a Presence, a warmth, an energy, and perhaps most of all, a sense of love, that I was not alone. Ever since, I have accessed that Presence in my prayers, much as I might search about with my hands in a pitch-black room, locating him, sketching out his face with my fingertips. And as I make contact, I get my breath, inhaling, feeling a little step, an added depth to my inspiration, telling me I am home. I began praying regularly and started reading whatever I could get my hands on.

In my training program I was assigned to work on a drilling rig (fig. 9.2). One day the driller, as he reeled up the elevators, told me to grab a wire line that was hanging from it. I did, and the steel rope came down on me, coiling around me, knocking my hard hat into the cellar, and striking hard my right forearm. The tool pusher came over and checked me out, asking me if I'd like to see a doctor. I was taken to a physician, his office gleaming bright and smelling like rubbing alcohol. As he examined me, I asked him about becoming a doctor—was it a possibility?

FIGURE 9.2
A drilling rig.
Photograph by
Brudersohn.

Courtesy Wikimedia Commons[2]

He looked me up and down, a roughneck, shirt and jeans smattered with drilling mud and oil, and replied, "No, you aren't smart enough."

I continued to pray, and I was no longer worried. I eventually quit that job, and moved to San Francisco, to join a bunch of college friends living there on Castro Street (fig. 9.3). I found work, but the job proved even worse. By this time, I knew that I would have to go back to school.

FIGURE 9.3
Castro Street,
San Francisco.

Courtesy Steve Parker and Wikimedia Commons[3]

In the office where I was working, I met an engineer who was going nights to law school at the University of San Francisco (USF), and he invited me to attend a class with him. In the class I fell asleep.

I recalled my friend Tim in college, who believed in action: He would say, "Do something, even if it is wrong," so I decided to enroll in the adult extension night classes at USF. I chose a class, and stood in line to register. In front of me was a guy to whom I poured out my dilemma; he grinned and said, "Oh yeah, I can identify with where you are at. I work for Greyhound Bus Company, but I don't fit there, so I've started classes at USF to be a dentist." At that instant a lightbulb lit up my head, and I said, "I'll start classes to become a physician." In the ensuing days, I wondered if this was just another unrealistic scheme I was thinking up, but door after door flung itself open, and in another two years, I began studying at the UCLA School of Medicine. As I prepared for medical school, I relied on prayer, so much so that it was the foundation of my life.

Even though I was confident of my new path, I became inexplicably beset with anxiety. On a sunny Saturday morning atop a hill in San Francisco, I poured out to a girlfriend my vague feelings and confused thoughts; I had no idea what was bothering me. She listened sympathetically but could offer me no insight. I had an impulse to go to a downtown bookstore; books had worked for me before. At the store, on a lower shelf to my right, I seized a title, paid for it, and walked out. *Prayer Can Change Your Life,* by William R. Parker and Elaine St. Johns.[4] I rushed home and opened it; I recall that it suggested I look at myself and add up my characteristics. I listed them: a penchant for airplanes, women, and drink; a swagger; a petroleum engineer. The revelation plunged into my mind: I was trying to prove myself a man! So why the anxiety? My present job didn't fit my caricature of what a man was. My anxiety fell away. The first of many insights and healings.

Prayer, a consistent dialogue with the Most High, works. As this dialogue has progressively freed, guided, inspired, comforted, corrected, and healed me, so it has myriad others, past and present. The substance and effects of this dialogue are mostly subtle and indirect yet at other times more visible, but always present in prayer is the energy field. Jesus said, "If you then, who are evil [distrustful of God and self-conflicted and therefore chaotic and unpredictable], know how to give good gifts to your children, how much more will the heavenly Father give the Holy

Spirit to those who ask him!"⁵ To the question of whether we can hear the voice of God as Abraham and Samuel did, the answer is, as I hope to show below, a definite yes. But first, I'd like to consider an attitude that I find indispensable when praying: *that which is*.

THAT WHICH IS

"That which is" is a mind-set that focuses on the present.
Prayer works better with a present focus.
A serene acceptance of unavoidable circumstances is a result.

Everyone is familiar with the idea that only the present exists; the past is gone, except to inform us about what was, and the future is only a potential. Yet we spend a lot of time obsessing about "if only" and "what if," which includes worrying about misfortune and, ultimately, death. God's beautiful poem to Job at first seems to dodge Job's complaints that things should not be as they are.⁶ Rather, the poem has the net effect of bringing Job sharply into the present, which is more than satisfactory for Job and all that he needs. Likewise, the passage on death in Ecclesiasticus 41:1-7, quoted in Chapter 7, said to me, "Death is what is, and it's OK." Finally, if you look closely at the Gospels, you find that Jesus is firmly rooted in the present; his every act is in the here and now, of course, but virtually every statement he makes is voiced in the present tense. He explicitly supports the present when he says, "So do not worry about tomorrow, for tomorrow will bring worries of its own. Today's trouble is enough for today."⁷

I had a simple experience with prayer that illustrates the point. One morning, when I was a younger man, I awoke and simply could not get out of bed. Lying there fixed to the mattress, I prayed, "Lord, get me out of bed." It wasn't a command but, rather, an entreaty. The effect was dramatic: It felt like my body weight doubled, and I sank deeper into the

FIGURE 9.4

Courtesy Emmanuel Brunner and Wikimedia Commons[8]

The Grotto of Massabielle at Lourdes.

bed! I thought to myself, "Wow, that didn't work!" After a few seconds reflection, I prayed, "Lord, I don't want to get out of bed!" I instantly felt like a feather, and I jumped out of bed. The former statement expressed what I thought *should be,* but the latter was a confession of *what is.* Perhaps much of the power of confession lies in the acknowledgment of that which is.

Here is another prayer that has worked for me. There have been times when I simply do not have the strength to continue on. So I've prayed, "God give me strength." It doesn't work; I get an image of a room covered with broken glass, and I'm praying for the strength to crawl over it. No good. So I have changed the prayer: "Lord, I'm feeling really flat. Give me enthusiasm, give me interest!" With enthusiasm and interest I fly over the field of broken glass. In this case, enthusiasm and interest are intrinsic to the energy field, and he is only too glad to share it. And he has never failed to answer that prayer.

I often need help discerning what is. I was working one day at a mental health clinic in a poverty area. As an unkempt 400-pound schizophrenic woman walked into my office, I went into an instantaneous depression, like being in an elevator that suddenly drops 10 floors. Amazed, I prayed, "Lord, what is going on here?" The thought flashed into my mind, "You think you have to fix her; all you need to do is renew her prescriptions!" Perhaps enlightenment is having a realistic sense of what is. Or enlightenment may pertain to properly dealing with that which is. Some years ago my wife and I relocated to Ventura County from Los Angeles County. As I drove into the new area, I prayed, "Lord, help me meet some people I can love." Instantly, a thought plunged into my consciousness: "Learn to love the people you meet!" Notice that these two examples have to do with intuition. We'll consider below how prayer, God's voice, and intuition connect.

This acquiescence to what is was brought home to me by a psychiatrist who was a quadriplegic, confined to a motorized wheelchair that he operated with the movement of a finger and thumb on his right hand. Before the accident that paralyzed him, he had been a fine athlete. He said, and I don't know if the quote originated with him, "The more I struggle against what is, the more things stay the same; when I accept the present, change becomes possible." The story is similar to a documentary I watched on PBS: the experience of a man who in his 30s suffered a stroke that left his left side paralyzed. The documentary was of his sixth trip to Lourdes (fig. 9.4), describing all the pathos, drama, and pageantry at this center of Catholic Christian healing. After the man had been lowered into the healing waters and had emerged and a little time had passed, the commentator asked him (and I couldn't tell if the commentator was being sarcastic or sympathetic), "Well, did you get your healing?" The man replied quietly, reverently, firmly, his left side still immobile: "Yes, I got my healing!"

Nowhere is the struggle with *that which is* more apparent than the battle people have with alcohol and/or drug dependence. Alcoholics Anonymous (AA) has adopted the prayer of Reinhold Niebuhr, which is worth memorizing and repeating often by all of us. This version is one I found on a wall at Mt. Calvary retreat house in Santa Barbara, California:[9]

> God give us serenity to accept what cannot be changed,
> Courage to change what can be changed
> And wisdom to distinguish the one from the other;
> Living one day at a time, enjoying one moment at a time,
>   as the pathway to peace,
> Taking, as God does, the world as it is, not as I would have it,
> Trusting that God will make all things right
> If I surrender to the divine will.

So far, we have looked at *that which is* from the standpoint of suffering, but there are other aspects as well. Over against *that which is* are future- and past-oriented attitudes such as *what should be, what if,* and *if only.* Whole segments of religious people fear going to hell: "What if I go to hell?" leads to anxiety and great preoccupation with the way things *should* be. As you can well imagine, these attitudes are components of self-conflict.

Ultimately, *that which is,* is positive; when we focus on gratitude in prayer, we will find Life as it is on balance much more positive than negative, particularly when we look on it through the eyes of faith. For example, I was greatly bolstered, as I researched the science of evolution, to realize that each of us has within the incredible genius of our genomes, with their astonishing molecular creativity honed over billions of years.

MEDITATION

Meditative states provide the inner states within
which effective prayer can take place.
Such states follow quiet focus on breathing
and the acceptance of inevitable intrusive thoughts.

Several Psalms suggest that we can access the presence of God: "I waited patiently for the Lord; he inclined to me and heard my cry."[10] "As a deer longs for flowing streams, so my soul longs for you, O God."[11] "Give ear to my prayer, O God; do not hide yourself from my supplication."[12] "For God alone my soul waits in silence; from him comes my salvation."[13] As the quotes intimate, patience and silence are key. Meditative practice leads to the inner space in which one can move closer to the Most High.

To meditate, I like to sit upright, in a comfortable position, though I can also meditate lying prone or supine in bed. A quiet place free of distractions is important. As I start the meditation, I immediately encounter a racing mind; I go with it, allow it to race, listening to it. "I'm in a hurry; I want to get on with my writing." This is Adam, my Adam, working, working, so I pray, "Lord Jesus, my new Adam, pull me into this meditation, so that I can take time, as you did, to seek out the Father." Next, I am aware of tension in my neck, so I focus on my breathing—in, out, in, out. The tension lessens, but now my daily to-do list starts coming. Adam again. He says "The sprinklers for the yard aren't coming on; I need to adjust them." A dozen other "to-do" thoughts come to mind; I acknowledge them and promise to remember to take care of them later. As I calm down, ideas for this paragraph I am writing come to mind. These are inspirations; I have pencil and paper handy, and by writing them down, they get discharged from my mind to the paper. More focus on breathing—in and out. Quieter. Again I pray, maybe out loud, "Lord, you are the center of all things, and I am at the periphery; pull me into you, that I may experience you." More quieting of the mind. I pray:

O God of Peace, you have taught me
that in returning and rest I shall be saved,
In quietness and confidence shall be my strength,
Lift me, I pray,
by the might of your Holy Spirit,
To your presence, where I may be still,
And know that you are God.

Now I focus on returning, resting, quiet, confidence, until at last I am really into this meditation, and finally God is here, present. He has been here all along; I just finally found him. I inhale and get the extra step of breath, that little extra bit of inspiration. I do nothing now but wait in silence, as the psalm says, and like the deer at the flowing stream, I am home.

At this point in the meditation, there occurs a payoff. I start to have insights, sudden flashes of ideas or solutions to things of concern to me. For example, recently I attended a gathering where everybody seemed very accomplished, leaving me stuck with the frustrating sense that I was a wannabe somebody (my Adam again). In a meditation soon after, I found the means to reorient myself outward, realizing that real success consists of being a blessing to others. I then prayed for others, resolving for the day to listen for the needs of others, readying myself to take action to meet those needs. I finish with the "Our Father." Now I can go outside and fix the sprinklers, then get to the keyboard to write.

There are thousands of books on prayer, meditation, and mystical theology. I wore out two copies of William Johnston's *Mystical Theology*; the book is a compilation of Eastern and Western mystical prayer practices and is an excellent source for meditative practice.[14] Another source is Buddhist Jack Kornfield's *A Path with Heart: A Guide through the Perils* and *Promises of Spiritual Life*.[15] Meditation is at the heart of Buddhist spiritual practice; these gentle people meditate effectively, and we can learn a great deal from them. The book contains very practical advice for handling the numerous intrusive thoughts that emerge as one attempts to quiet the mind. Particularly helpful is the gentle acceptance of and patient listening to each intrusion, giving each thought credence, inviting each thought to go along for the ride. I have found that such intrusions are largely the worries, concerns, fears, and wishes of my Adam and Eve, as they clamor to be heard and struggle to survive. Banishing them from the garden of meditation does not work, for they are us, and we don't rise above them so much as we carry them along to the heights and depths God calls us to.

PRAYING WITHOUT CEASING

Praying without ceasing is the on-the-spot
dialogue with the Most High.
It is a highly productive and gratifying form of prayer.

When I was a second-year medical student, I was blessed with the wise counsel of my first mentor, the Rev. S. Dunham Wilson, an Episcopal priest. One morning I went to his house; he greeted me at the door, invited me in, and said, "Me and Jesus are working on my hi-fi." I thought it was a curious statement, but later I realized it was my first introduction to the possibility of carrying on a running dialogue with the Most High. I went on to hone the skill of mentally shooting little arrow prayers to God during tense therapy sessions with my patients, then listening with my third ear to the intuitive thoughts that plunged into my awareness. I was on the faculty at St. John's (Roman Catholic) Seminary, Camarillo, California, where in courses on pastoral counseling, I taught seminarians the skill; I dubbed it "Praying without ceasing."

There is a chapter on "praying without ceasing" in my book, *Christianity and Change*.[16]

The Scriptures cite numerous instances where Abraham,[17] Jacob,[18] Moses,[19] Samuel,[20] David,[21] Solomon,[22] and many others heard the voice of God. We may find it a little difficult to believe such phenomena occur outside the pages of holy writ, but I take the above instances to mean that humankind really can hear the advice of the Almighty. Furthermore, I believe God is constantly talking to everyone; let those with the ears to hear, hear! Specifically, in a tense situation, pray from within your mind, then be alert for and pay attention to intuitions as they pop up. I learned a lot from German psychoanalyst Theodore Reik in his book *Listening with the Third Ear*.[23] Dr. Reik had an uncanny ability to listen, suspend judgment, and pay attention to fleeting impressions or details caught out of the corner of his eye. Is intuition God's voice? Maybe not all the time, but if you are praying, that is where you look. It takes practice and experimentation, however. For example, as I was first trying this out, I was playing golf, and drove a ball into the rough. As I looked for the ball, I prayed, and the thought "Look to the right" popped into my mind. I later found the ball to the left. I interpret this to mean that this form of prayer is meant for mind-to-mind situations. God simply will not tell me which stock to buy or which horse to bet on.

I am most attuned to prayer during counseling and therapy sessions with patients. People, when they seek out a psychiatrist, are inevitably at an impasse within themselves; they are stuck. As they relate their situations and quandaries to me, a shift takes place, where somehow the impasse with its feelings gets passed over to me. I start to feel their impasses and immobility; it is always a very uncomfortable feeling. *Now I too am stuck.* I find myself instantly thinking there must be an easier way to make a living. I have learned at such junctures to pray, "God, what is going on here?" or "OK, I'm listening to you, Lord." As I do this, I relax, I am not alone, and I know help will be forthcoming. The tenor of the interview then softens, and where before there was awkward, stilted conversation, now there is increasing spontaneity. Ideas pop into my mind, but often the patient also volunteers thoughts, ideas, or memories. The interview becomes alive!

Here is an example, taken from my book, *Christianity and Change*: A 34-year-old woman brought her 11-year-old daughter for the first visit on an emergency basis. The child had just returned to school after summer vacation. On the first day, she had become frightened after seeing a movie at school in which the ghosts of two pilots who had died in a plane crash visited the passengers of other planes. She subsequently hysterically refused to attend school, becoming physically ill if made to do so. The urgency of the situation and the panic of both parties strongly reminded me to begin to pray without ceasing. The mother had left her husband, the child's stepfather, three months previously. My attention was called to the pair's body language. First, the mother appeared harassed, tired, and a bit unkempt, so it was the more surprising that I suddenly found her sexually attractive. Rather than denounce the old Adam, I prayed, "What's going on here?" The prayer and the subsequent answer spanned only an instant. The thought flashed into my mind that she was having an affair, or was at least sexually active. I wondered in prayer if her daughter had seen her with a lover. With the daughter out of the room, the mother revealed that she was confused, defiant, and involved sexually away from home. I asked her if she had any kind of relationship with God, and she defiantly replied, "I don't want anybody telling me what to do!" I next saw the daughter alone, her demeanor giving me an impression of considerable strength. Now I prayed for help putting together the observations of a chaotic, rebellious mother and a fundamentally strong child. I asked the girl, "Are you worried about your mother and afraid to leave her alone?" Her emphatic "Yes!" told me that this was the crux of the situation.

Here is another example, a man I saw just the other day: A 56-year-old man came to me complaining of depression. In addition to being deeply depressed, he looked ill. He was very overweight and disheveled, his face plethoric, his eyes puffy and bloodshot. He projected a sense of being under siege, and the feeling instantly became mine. I quickly dispensed with the wish to be on a vacation somewhere and shot an arrow prayer to God. A feeling of calm and confidence swept through me.

In the previous intake session, he told me he was a Christian man who had worked faithfully for a company for many years before being laid off early in the recession, after which he developed diabetes, hypertension, and depression. He described a childhood in which his mother beat him and favored his older brother. "He got the breast; I got the wing." He had struggled with alcoholism, but was six months sober.

He volunteered that he was not sleeping well and was plagued with repeated nightmares of being at work. I prayed, listened with my third ear, and asked him about his work. He described repeated run-ins with a much younger and insensitive supervisor. He volunteered another dream, of violence having to do with knives. His eyes narrowed, and I had an impression of anger. The word *resentment* occurred to me. I went with the thought, saying, "Anger, getting laid off, an insensitive boss, going back to work over and over again, sounds like you don't have any closure." He nodded and gave me emotional agreement that he was resentful. His statement about the breast and wing popped into my mind, so I said, "This sounds like a repeat, no breast, but a wing in the face." He nodded again and leaned forward. I used the word resentment again, tying it to his childhood. He responded by pouring out details of his mother's harsh treatment and his brother's subsequent abandonment of him.

I thought again of the dream of knives and violence. Knowing that in general alcoholism can be symptomatic of resentment and thinking of knives and violence as suggesting retaliation, I hazarded the interpretation that there were a number of people in his life with whom he had unfinished business. He again agreed wholeheartedly. Knowing that he was a man of prayer, I asked him if he had ever prayed for help to forgive these people who had hurt him. He was astonished! He replied that it had never occurred to him!

I tied together everything he had said, telling him that his reactions were entirely understandable. I suggested that, of the several people that he had issues with, he pick one, perhaps the easiest, and write a letter, not to mail, but to share with me, to try to get some closure. Again, he assented with his whole being. He made a return appointment. Prayer in this situation greased the skids. Both of us were plummeted into a zone of spontaneity, rapport, thought, and behavior.

He returned for follow-up and reported that he had written a letter to a supervisor who most recently had aggrieved him. He read it to me. It was packed with resentment, but he related a change. As he wrote the letter, he realized that he was not alone in his grievance, that this supervisor had rubbed many of his co-workers the wrong way, as well. It wasn't just him. His perspective was expanding. He eagerly agreed to write another letter for our next appointment. He went on in subsequent weeks to find closure with the people who had hurt him. His depression lifted.

A TIME FOR HEALING

In this section I tell of role prayer played in my own recovery from some very painful self-conflict.

The incisiveness of praying without ceasing cuts more than one way. There came a point in my life when I became the patient. It occurred when my father died. He had suffered a vascular dementia (numerous little strokes had taken away much of his intellect) and had been in a nursing home for eight years, where I visited him monthly. Since he was 92 and had zero quality of life, one would think I would have taken his death in stride. Instead, I found myself against a wall. I wasn't depressed, grieving, or distraught; rather, I simply knew that in some inexplicable fashion a time had come. My father was prone to rages, and about 12 times in my childhood he had beaten me with a belt. Such beatings can instantly drive a child inside himself and set up a lifetime of inner isolation. But I was totally unaware of this at the time. Unbeknownst to me, I had my own unfinished business.

There was a psychiatrist down the hall whose work I respected, so I made an appointment with him. His appearance was remarkable; he suffered from post-polio syndrome, and he walked with braces, with great difficulty. As time for the appointment neared, I increasingly worried that he would not know what he was doing, and I had no idea what was wrong with me. I started praying that the Lord would inspire us both, and I continued to so throughout our encounters.

I told him how I felt up against a wall, and he inquired as to any other times I had sought help. I replied that I had once consulted Milton Erickson (a world famous psychiatrist, well known in psychiatric circles, who, coincidentally, also suffered from post-polio syndrome). He leaned forward, impressed, and asked how that had gone. I blurted out, "He beat the hell out of me!" He raised his eyebrows, nodded, grinned, and strained forward, like a bloodhound picking up a scent. Within five minutes he had elicited my story of my father's beatings. He fixed me with his stare, and declared, "You are a victim of child physical abuse." Hot tears filled my eyes as I protested that such treatment of children was routine in those days, I had deserved it, etc., etc. He would hear none of my rationalizations.

I returned for our next session and reported a dream. In the dream, I and others had unearthed the corpses of Indians. Remarkably, as I brushed off the dirt and clay, they stirred. The doctor said that I had been numb and now was starting to feel. I replied that my mother regularly referred to me as a wild little Indian. (I do apologize to any Native American readers.) I continued to pray for the doctor's and my inspiration. I told him of night terrors that I had suffered for many years, which over time had merged into nightmares where I was confronted by a malignant presence; I often tried to stay in these dreams to see what the presence was, but the anxiety was always unbearable. In addition, I suffered a fear of the dark. He wondered if these pointed to a posttraumatic stress disorder. I could recall the whippings later in life, but I had no early memories of trauma. But my mother's younger sister was still alive; she had lived with us when I was a boy. I would ask her. Aunt Edna now lived three hours away. I leapt into my car.

Aunt Edna was a reclusive alcoholic, but she was sober for our visit and welcomed me. She was fully aware of my father's rages and beatings and described a number of instances when she was present. She recalled a time when I was about three or four and visiting her and my grandparents. They overheard me swearing at another child, using an adult invective. My grandfather, a perceptive man, said, "He must have heard it somewhere." Edna and I decided that I must have been acting out or reenacting a trauma. Our reconstruction had a powerful resonance with me. That must have been it! In a rage he apparently took the belt to a very small child.

Edna supplied me with other information. My father's mother was a devout Christian who believed that if you spare the rod, you spoil the child. My father's father would travel, and upon returning home she would tell of my dad's misdeeds, upon which his father would get out the belt. My dad, when he left home at 18, never returned; he had emotionally and physically completely cut them off. I recall meeting them only once. The night after my visit with Aunt Edna I had a dream of being in the dark, *but the darkness was pleasant, and I was perfectly comfortable.*

My nightmares had resolved, but I still slept poorly. I awakened frequently, my mind racing. The doctor thought that feelings were trying to come up and that my mind raced to keep them down. I decided that when I awakened, I would get up, sit at the window, and pray, asking the Lord to help me bring the feelings on. I focused on feelings welling up in my chest and throat and prayed that they would become more intense. I could feel them intensifying and something in me fighting to quell them. I kept praying. Finally they gushed forth, once rage, once tears of grief, once a scream. Then I was done and began to sleep calmly and deeply.

Our work together progressed. The doctor showed me how I had adapted to my childhood environment by being tough (remember trying to prove myself a man), hiding the essential parts of myself, and amputating my normal needs for attention, love, and affection. I had turned myself into a stone. Maybe it worked when I was little, but it certainly didn't work as a husband, dad, and friend to others. I began to enjoy a brand-new openness and spontaneity in my daily life; I could embrace and take pleasure in my inner child.

This entire episode in my life closed with a dream, an experience more vivid, real, and tangible than ordinary waking. I dreamed I was in some kind of medieval cathedral, and a tall, unsmiling, pockmarked face man confronted me. He put across a sense of cruel indifference. He told me he was disgusted with me, disappointed in me. He was through with me and was leaving. As he turned his back and walked away, I said, "Aren't you going to say good-bye?" I realized he had absolutely no affective connection to me. I awakened in utter awe and wonder. I was free at last!

THE PRAYERS
OF THE CHURCH

I hope that I have shown though my experiences that God—animating us with his breath and voice yet leaving us radically free—is profoundly available to us in prayer. Yet this availability depends on, indeed exists within, a context. We have seen that all Life exists in community, that all Life *is* community. The guidance, enlightenment, and healing I have described all took place within a historical, social, cultural, and religious framework. Anything I have achieved, or that has been achieved in me, has been built upon the network of the community of believers called "Church." I love the verse in Psalm 122:1, which says, "I was glad when they said to me, 'Let us go to the house of the Lord.'"

The practices of communal prayer and worship, the embracing of *that which is,* and the much more personal and immediate practices of meditation and praying without ceasing have evolved and continue to evolve through the efforts of countless devoted persons in widely disparate disciplines: in Christian communities and writings, in 12-step programs, in Buddhist communities, among psychiatrists, and psychologists, and in secular communities such as the arts and sciences, including physics, biology, and evolutionary biology. *Christianity, to continue to creatively evolve, needs to constantly be in dialogue with all these other disciplines. To do otherwise is to declare it has nothing to learn and hence blind itself and ultimately become sclerotic.*

CHAPTER TEN

GOD ON TRIAL

Many stumble over the existence of evil and suffering and give up
their faith in the process. I review the experience of three writers and
then present a true story of my own struggle with the subject.

The existence of evil and suffering in the world has been a stumbling block to faith and belief for many people, and the seeming contradiction between suffering and the omnipotence and omnibenevolence of God the subject of endless theological and philosophical debate. Nick Spencer, in his book *Darwin and God*, writes that Darwin (fig. 10.1) started out his voyage on the *Beagle* as an Anglican Christian

Courtesy Wikimedia Commons[1]

FIGURE 10.1
Charles Robert Darwin. By John Collier.
National Portrait Gallery, London.

who had at one point considered becoming a clergyman.[2] He had been steeped in church doctrine, but he had never had any particular personal experience with God. Darwin's heart was in his naturalist pursuits. On the other hand, his wife Emma was devoutly religious. Though the couple disagreed on spiritual issues, they supported each other, Emma even critiquing Darwin's ideas and editing his writings. She urged him to think about God with his heart, not his head. Nonetheless, he gradually gave up his intellectualized belief in God as the direct creator of life as he developed his theory of evolution by natural selection. Spencer argues, however, that it was the age-old problem of suffering—first in theory, then through the dreadful loss of his favorite child Anne—that did in his faith. Affective experience trumps dogma, doctrine, and intellectual theology every time.

Stories of loss of faith are everywhere: In his book *Losing My Religion,* William Lobdell, a former religion reporter for the *Los Angeles Times,* writes about his conversion to Christianity and later his loss of faith.[3] An investigative reporter, he took on the Catholic sexual abuse debacle as his beat. In the process of interviewing countless victims and witnessing the past cover-ups and present stonewalling by church officials, he became increasingly skeptical of the very existence of God. He then faltered over a baby born premature, who rallied, then died: Was this not cruel? Of the 2004 South Asia tsunami, he noted that it made no sense. What kind of God would allow so many people to die and create so much heartbreak and so much misery? He concluded that the reason that prayers for an amputee's limb to be regenerated don't work is because either God doesn't care or he doesn't exist. He ceased attending church and asked to be reassigned away from the *Times* religion beat. A very frank and honest person, he described how, during a bout of stomach flu, he caught himself praying to God. However, this glimmer of belief did not last, and at the book's conclusion, he was firmly agnostic.

That there is enormous suffering and rampant evil in the world is self-evident. I pick up the April 29, 2009, edition of the *Los Angeles*

Times, and I note a bombing in Iraq, swine flu in Mexico and world-wide, the killing of seven Tijuana police officers by a drug cartel, the death of four in the crash of a tour bus, and the death of a young lab assistant in a fire at UCLA. Recently, the daughter-in-law of a college friend was struck and killed by lightening as she tended flowers in her garden. Closer to home, my youngest grandson is afflicted with autism, an utterly life-changing situation for our oldest son and his wife. Where is God when bad things happen to good people? I am no stranger to this question, as you will see in the following true story. The story amounts to a *theodicy,* a defense of God and his goodness in the face of suffering and evil throughout the creation.

PRESENCE

BY RALPH H. ARMSTRONG

Camarillo State Hospital sat in that little valley, surrounded by rock-studded, cactus-covered hills, about two miles from the Pacific Ocean, for 60 years. At its peak, it cared for 7,500 of California's most mentally tortured souls. In 1998, the California legislature closed it, and its picturesque location and Spanish architecture were designated to become California State University, Channel Islands. Though when I was there it was no institution of higher learning, in its own unique way it gave me a dramatic lesson on the nature of God.

The hospital was a sprawling web of wards consisting of large dayrooms and equally large dormitories sleeping 40 to 80 patients. Muttering, grimacing people carrying on conversations with nobody in view milled about in smoke-filled rooms, watched over by psychiatric technicians dispensing medications, breaking up altercations, and placing in seclusion and restraints the overly troubled. A separate building housed the medically ill; it had an ICU, a surgery suite, a dental office, outpatient clinics, and several teeming wards filled with demented persons, people with Alzheimer's and Huntington's, and dozens with posttraumatic dementias who in attempting to hang, gas, or shoot themselves had only succeeded in destroying their brains, not their cardiovascular systems. A visiting neurosurgeon, reeling from the sight and stench of such large numbers of wrecks of time, dubbed one of these units "Limbo Number Nine."

I was the hospital's neurologist. For 10 years, every Wednesday I ran the neurology clinic, then stayed the next 16 hours in a shift covering the hospital overnight. Crowds of epileptics, retarded patients with terrible seizure disorders wearing football helmets, confused patients whose doctors were equally bewildered by the intellectual impairments of otherwise apparently healthy young people, and a host of persons suffering exotic disorders such as von Recklinghausen's disease, benign intracranial hypertension, Sturge Weber disease, and other conditions waited in a huge dayroom to be seen. I never saw people with migraine, multiple sclerosis, or myasthenia gravis. Apparently, they belonged to another category of misery altogether.

The most common disorders I treated were seizures. A frequent sign of many brain diseases is the epileptic seizure, the seizures themselves varying from brief blank stares to complex automatisms such as touching hair, face, clothing, and so on to precipitous falls with a few movements of limbs to full-scale fits consisting of a sudden cry, the fall, the body then rigidly extending itself out for perhaps 30 seconds, forcibly expelling urine and feces, then a violent convulsion, arms and legs thrashing rhythmically, with biting of tongue, all lasting up to

3 minutes, followed by a postictal coma looking like death. The latter, called grand mal seizures, are very dramatic and very frightening to see, even for the most experienced observer. Modern neurology has at its disposal an array of anti-epileptic medicines to treat seizures, and I used them all. For this population, they were often of scant help.

One morning, a particular schizophrenic woman came for management of her seizure disorder. Haggard, with missing teeth, wrinkled skin, nicotine-stained fingers, and stringy, tangled, yellow-gray hair, she looked 30 years older than the 40 years stated in the chart. She wore a frayed, threadbare chemise with a print of faded blue flowers. Her eyes darted right and left, responding, I suppose, to voices that she perceived coming from who knows where. I would have dismissed her as one of thousands, but our eyes met, and I was shocked to see in them a presence, a sentience, a pro-found sadness, and an unbearable awareness of her existence. Then, as if to make the communication unequivocal, she had a grand mal seizure, right in front of us. We all reacted wildly, though there was really little to do but put a gauze-wrapped tongue depressor, prepared for just such an eventuality, between her teeth and pillows under her head and elbows to keep them from banging on the concrete floor. I made a note and wrote orders adjusting her anticonvulsants, and when she came to, technicians took her back to her psychiatric unit.

I was struck by this woman's suffering. Physicians become accustomed to dealing with suffering, perhaps even callous, distant, or jaded. Of course, there are varieties and degrees of suffering. It is painful to lose loved ones or health or experience failure or face death, but these events are bearable when love and support are available. To suffer alone is unbearable. It was the woman's isolation and alienation that most impressed me.

Photo by the author

FIGURE 10.2

The Bell Tower at California State University–Channel Islands.

I have always remained in awe of suffering. To me, pain, the first cry of a newborn, and the last agonal gasp of someone dying all carry a supernatural quality. I have a spiritual bent. I am a Christian, and I worship and pray regularly. I have long confronted and argued with God about the problem of pain. When I was a third-year medical student, one of the first patients I cared for was a 21-year-old woman dying of renal failure, there being no dialyses or kidney transplants in those days. I recall standing in a closet weeping and raging at God. Perhaps for many this is an excuse for unbelief: If there were a loving God, he wouldn't allow 21-year-olds to die or older women to be schizophrenic epileptics and so on. I am not immune to such reasoning.

I reported that evening for my night shift of covering the hospital. I took call from a sleeping room in the bell tower, a landmark at the university (fig. 10.2) even today. The room

had a red concrete floor, the screens on the windows were full
of holes, and the walls were dotted with squashed mosquitoes.
I ate in a patient dining room, sitting at a table by myself in the
back of the kitchen, eating big dollops of mashed sweet potatoes
and pale ham slices, and reading about Di, Charles, and O. J.
Simpson in tabloids someone always left there. My wife would
derisively tease me about my lack of taste, but I am easy to
please, so the accommodations and food were endurable.

When I was back in my room shortly after supper, the
phone rang, and an excited nurse shouted that I must come
to unit 32 immediately. The unit was nearby, so I raced over,
through a courtyard with a crumbling, empty fountain, and up
a dark stairway with old wrought iron railings, to the upstairs
ward. A breathless tech took me to a woman's bathroom, where
the woman I'd just seen in the neurology clinic lay on the
floor. Her worn and faded dress had huge holes in it, charred
at the edges, exposing red, blistered, weeping skin, covering
maybe half her body. I gagged at the lingering stench of burnt
flesh and the sight of her wounds. A tech produced a book of
matches, all burned; the poor soul had set herself on fire!

After returning from the neurology clinic, she had with-
drawn to her bed in the women's dorm and had refused to go
to the evening meal at the cafeteria. Alone in the dorm, she
stuffed wads of paper under her dress, torching herself shortly
before everybody returned from supper. What a graphic way to
communicate to us the agony of her internal hell! We did
what little we could for her. We put a clean sheet over her,
saturated the sheet with normal saline, and awaited an ambu-
lance to take her to the burn center. I never saw her again.

That is, I never saw her again in person. However, in my
mind's eye, I saw her constantly for weeks. That one's inner
pain could be so intense haunted me. The scene depressed me

deeply, and it reawakened the question with which human-kind struggles, the problem of pain and suffering. Driving to or from work, I would argue with God about why he allows any suffering, let alone the pitiful and extreme hurt this person endured—the conflict and paradox of it all, my omniscient, all-powerful, all-loving God and the alienation and despair of his creation.

These thoughts and images became quite intrusive, less so when I was occupied with one task or another but particularly so when I was back at the neurology clinic or on call in the evening at the hospital. About four weeks after the incident and in my room in the bell tower for my night shift, I was lying on my bed staring at the ceiling and mulling over all of this when the images coalesced into a literal fantasy that rendered the conflict in picture form, a vivid and almost tangible image: All of us were being swept downstream in a river of pain and blood, helpless and foundering in the torrent. Out loud I shouted, "God, why don't you pluck us out of this!"

In the next instant, a thought, distinct and well formed, plunged into my mind, "I don't pluck you out; I jump in!"

I immediately felt a sense of relief. In a flash, I saw that this life—that which is, life with all its tragedy, loss, violence, and death, its brevity, its fragility, its beauty, its ugliness, its joy, its grief, its uncertainties—is sacred. It is what is, not what I think it should be, and God has declared all of it lovable and worthwhile by joining us and living, suffering, and dying with us.

A window, a hint of an explanation of the mystery of his incarnation and crucifixion.

I was about 30 years younger at the time of this lesson, and the answer I received has stood the test of time. But there was, and is, much more.

WHY DO PEOPLE SUFFER?
BIBLICAL VIEWS

Professor of Religious Studies Bart Ehrman
lost his faith over the problem of suffering.
A profoundly biblically literate man,
he breaks down the Scriptures' explanations of the
whys of suffering into five categories.

Bart Ehrman, the James A. Gray Professor and Chair of the Department of Religious Studies at the University of North Carolina, is the
author of *God's Problem: How the Bible Fails to Answer Our Most Important
Question—Why We Suffer.* Professor Ehrman was a born-again Christian;
a graduate of Moody Bible Institute in Chicago, Wheaton College, and
Princeton Theological Seminary; and pastor at a Baptist church before
losing his faith over the issue of suffering. He states, "I could no longer
reconcile the claims of faith with the facts of life. . . . The problem of
suffering became for me the problem of faith." He goes on to ask,

> *If God had come into the darkness with the advent of the Christ child,
> bringing salvation to the world, why is the world in such a state? . . .
> . . . If he came into the darkness and made a difference,
> why is there still no difference* [Italics mine]? Why are the sick still
> wracked with unspeakable pain? Why are babies born with birth
> defects? Why are there droughts that leave millions starving?[4]

Throughout the book, he returns again and again to the whys of
the perpetration of unspeakable evils such as the Holocaust; the hor-
rors of war and genocides; global plagues and pandemics such as AIDS,
influenza, and bubonic plague; and the massive deaths and dislocations
from natural disasters such as tsunamis, earthquakes, volcanic eruptions,
and hurricanes.

While writing his PhD dissertation, he was asked to teach a course titled "The Problem of Suffering in the Biblical Traditions," and this launched a lifelong interest in humankind's suffering and initiated his doubts and eventual agnosticism. What makes his book so interesting is not only his documentation and description of human suffering but also a prodigious biblical scholarship that enables him to explore various views of suffering put forth in the books of the Scriptures and to expose numerous contradictions that believers fall prey to as they relate their beliefs to the Bible. For example, noting that millions suffer alienation and condemnation from believers because of sexual orientation, he points out that the same books that proscribe same-sex relations "require people to stone their children to death if they are disobedient, execute anyone who works on Saturday or . . . eats pork chops, and to condemn anyone who wears a shirt made of two kinds of fabric."[5] I particularly liked his interpretations of considerable segments of the Old Testament, Psalms, and New Testament writings that never get read on Sundays in church, because of their violent, vengeful, wrathful, frightening, apocalyptic, and/or otherwise incomprehensible content, his argument being that they are attempts to rationalize and explain the sufferings of Israel by speculating on the causes of suffering in theological terms. He breaks down the Scriptures' explanations of suffering into five categories: (1) the classical view of suffering, that God punishes the sins of the people by inflicting various calamities; (2) suffering at the hands of others; (3) redemptive suffering; (4) suffering as a test from God; and (5) Jewish-Christian apocalypticism.

PEOPLE SUFFER BECAUSE GOD IS PUNISHING THEIR SINS

The prophets of the Old Testament were particularly prone to interpret the misfortunes of Israel as God's punishment for their misdeeds. For example, Amos links Israel's oppressing the poor and breaking God's laws with the threat of invasion by the Assyrians as God's sentence, the sins of the people leading to military defeat. In a passage that never gets read in Church on Sunday mornings, Amos says,

I gave you cleanness of teeth [famine] in all your cities,
  and lack of bread in all your places,
    yet you did not return to me, says the Lord.
And I also withheld the rain from you when there were still
    three months to the harvest . . .
    yet you did not return to me, says the Lord . . .
I sent among you a pestilence after the manner of Egypt;
  I killed your young men with the sword . . .
    yet you did not return to me, says the Lord . . .
Therefore thus I will do to you, O Israel;
  because I will do this to you, prepare to meet your God,
O Israel![6]

According to Ehrman, Amos's message is clear: He sees famine, drought, plague, and military defeat as retribution from God for social injustice, worshiping other gods (spiritual apostasy), and failure to keep the Law. Alternatively, Amos offers his prescription for constructive living with words that you *will* hear in Church, and in the sermons of Martin Luther King, Jr.:

I hate, I despise your festivals, and I take no delight
  in your solemn assemblies.
Even though you offer me your burnt-offerings and
  grain-offerings, I will not accept them; . . .
Take away from me the noise of your songs;
  I will not listen to the melody of your harps.
But let justice roll down like waters,
  and righteousness like an everflowing stream.[7]

Ehrman goes on to argue that the view of God punishing sin with suffering predominates the thinking of the majority of authors who produced the biblical texts but that this view came to be seen as dissatisfying to later authors of ancient Israel, including Job, Ecclesiastes, and Daniel, who took implicitly or explicitly contrary views. But I can't help thinking that writers such as Amos, quoted above, were not so locked into a simplistic, linear explanation of suffering as Ehrman surmises. Rather, could it be that they perceived the numerous subtle seeds of Life's internecine and self-conflict and were trying to say that suffering was their inevitable yield, denoting such outcomes as the wrath of the Lord? For example, I certainly see in my psychiatric practice that peoples' hidden self-hate, resentments, rigidities, fears, and unbelief may lead to widespread painful outcomes downstream, maybe way downstream, amounting to a kind of judgment. And could it be that Job, Ecclesiastes, and Daniel, along with others, were not contradicting such perceptions but instead were attempting to add to and refine our understanding of suffering?

PEOPLE SUFFER AT THE HANDS OF OTHERS

Ehrman next turns to suffering induced by the actions of others, first citing Hitler and the Holocaust and Pol Pot and the Khmer Rouge, then turning to the Old Testament prophets, who inveighed against the injustices caused by the rich's exploitation of the poor. In the historical books, he notes the enslavement of the Israelites in Egypt,[8] Joshua's slaughter of the population after the fall of Jericho,[9] and in the New Testament, Herod's slaughter of the innocents.[10] Then there is David, Bathsheba, and the murder of Uriah,[11] and Solomon's enslavement of indigenous peoples to build the Temple.[12] In the New Testament, he cites the Roman's use of crucifixion, the stoning of Stephen,[13] and the siege of Jerusalem in 70 CE. And what are peoples' reaction to such cruelty and brutality? Rage, grief, helplessness. Ehrman quotes Jeremiah's poem of depression,[14] his prayer for God's vengeance,[15] and Psalms that express grief and the wish for revenge.[16] He summarizes that God (if he exists) is not to blame for man's inhumanity to man and closes by asking, "How can we possibly believe that an all-powerful and all-loving God exists given the state of the world?"[17] *For my part, I notice a common denominator in his examples:*

domination and submission and the abuse of power by the strong over the weak,
all examples of Life as self-conflictual. Ehrman is basically blaming God for the
existence of Life's self-conflict.

SUFFERING AS REDEMPTIVE

The third biblical category of suffering that Ehrman addresses is
redemptive suffering, the story of Joseph being a prime example. Recall
that Joseph was sold into slavery by his brothers to a passing caravan
and taken to Egypt, where, in a twist of history, he rose to become
Pharaoh's prime minister. Many years later, fleeing a terrible drought,
the brothers and their father, Jacob, arrive in Egypt, only to eventually
be confronted by Joseph. Terrified, the brothers expect retribution, but
Joseph forgives them with the famous words, "Do not be afraid! Am
I in the place of God? Even though you intended to do harm to me,
God intended it for good."[18] Ehrman writes that this idea, that what human beings "intend for evil" God can "intend for good" can be found
implicitly behind a large number of the biblical narratives of suffering,
the concept reaching its apogee in the sufferings of Jesus on the cross for
our salvation. He goes on to state that the idea that God can bring good
out of evil is behind much of what the book of Acts has to say about the
missionary activities of the early Christian church. After citing numerous other examples of suffering leading to redemption, he concludes that
this is in some ways the core message of the Bible—that it is not simply
despite suffering but precisely through suffering that God manifests his
power of salvation. We'll return to this point as well below.

SUFFERING AS A TEST FROM GOD

In the fourth category of suffering, the Scriptures suggest that suffering can be a test sent by God. Certainly, Job's suffering was a test of
his commitment to God, but the biggest test was God's demand that
Abraham sacrifice his son Isaac. Recall that Abraham and Sarah bore
Isaac in their previously childless advanced years, the result of a promise

from God that they were to be the source of a great people. But then while Isaac was still a boy, God commands Abraham to sacrifice him. Just as Abraham compliantly raises his knife over the boy bound to the altar, an angel intervenes, saying, "Abraham, Abraham! . . . Do not lay your hand on the boy . . . for now I know that you fear God, since you have not withheld your son, your only son, from me"[19] (fig. 10.3).

It is difficult to put a positive spin on the stories of God permitting the testing of Job and his test of Abraham, except to say that the

FIGURE 10.3
Abraham and Isaac, and the angel stopping the sacrifice.
Rembrandt 1634.

Courtesy libre GNU autor fallecido, and Wikimedia Commons[20]

ancients, as with the idea of God's sending suffering as punishment of sin, were trying to make the point that suffering is indeed a test, and if you see God as causing everything, as they did, then the test comes from God. As I mentalize the story of Abraham's sacrifice of his son, I notice that *God changed his mind!* This story is not the only passage where God changes his mind. What are the biblical writers trying to tell us?

I see testing all the time in my practice of addiction medicine. Newly clean-and-sober addicts are invariably tested by some adverse event that challenges them not to resort to their fix. Addicts regularly tell me, "I was doing good; I had a week or two of sobriety, then my cat died or my wife got mad at me or the police stopped me and searched my car, so I said 'fuck it' and went out and used." (Pardon my language, but I've heard these exact words hundreds of times). I use these relapses to mentalize with the patient: What does "f-it" mean? What is underneath the sentiment? We learn that f-it is the tip of the iceberg, the adverse event having tapped into a deep sense of pessimism and hopelessness within the addict, the discussion of which can be a salutary learning experience. So I can see how this could be construed as a test from God, though I would not use such explanations with my patients.

SUFFERING BECAUSE OF DEVOTION TO GOD: APOCALYPTIC THINKING

Ehrman's fifth category of the Scripture's treatment of suffering is apocalyptic writing. Jewish writers, expanding beyond the idea that suffering came to God's people because of their sins, noted that at times the people of God suffered *because* they were trying to do God's will. Instead of suffering for their sins, they were suffering for their righteousness. Consequently, writers set out to explain this and came up with *apocalypse,* a Greek word that denotes revelation. For them, cosmic forces of evil were aligned against the people of God, causing them pain and suffering, but soon, they insisted, God would intervene and set up his own kingdom, the kingdom of God.

Apocalyptic thought originated around 150 to 170 years BCE, during the Maccabean revolt. Israel, at the crossroads of civilization, had repeatedly suffered invasion, first from the Assyrians (722 BCE); the Babylonians (586 BCE); the Persians (539 BCE); Alexander the Great (356–323 BCE); after his death, the Egyptians; then the Syrians in 198 BCE.[21] A particularly odious Syrian ruler, Antiochus IV, despoiled the Temple and attempted to crush the Jewish religion, hence constituting a case of suffering not because of God's judgment of Israel but because God's enemies decreed it. The apocalyptic Book of Daniel was written during the reign of Antiochus IV to assure the people that, despite

Courtesy Wikimedia Commons[22]

FIGURE 10.4

Belshazzar's Feast (see Daniel 5). Rembrandt. National Gallery London.

their terrible suffering, God would have the last word. In Figure 10.4, Rembrandt depicts Daniel 5:1-31, where King Belshazzar of Babylon (symbolizing Antiochus IV and Syria), taking the sacred golden and silver vessels stolen from the Temple in Jerusalem, toasts the gods of gold and silver, bronze, iron, wood, and stone. Immediately, the disembodied finger of a human hand appears and writes on the wall: MENE, MENE, TEKEL, PARSIN, which Daniel, the court seer, interprets as "God has numbered the days of your kingdom and brought it to an end, you have been weighed on the scales and found wanting, your kingdom is divided and given to the Medes and Persians."[23] That night Belshazzar is killed. His sin? Arrogance. (Thus we know where the phrase "the writing on the wall" comes from.) Daniel's stories, visions, and dreams are depicted as taking place during the Babylonian exile, several hundred years earlier, but various aspects of the book's symbolism place it during the reign of Antiochus IV, who in the book is the final beast to be put to death by God. The Son of Man in one of Daniel's dreams symbolizes the people of Israel, previously persecuted and slaughtered, now exalted. And how will their suffering end? Ehrman states that for Amos, suffering ceases when the people of God repent and return to God's ways. In contrast, for Daniel, it will end when God destroys the evil forces that oppose him in the world, when he sets up his kingdom for his people.

Ehrman notes that apocalyptic literature such as Daniel and the New Testament Book of Revelation (fig. 10.5) has given rise to a worldview that he terms "apocalypticism," following the four major tenets subscribed to by Jewish apocalypticists: dualism, pessimism, vindication, and imminence. *Dualism* says that there are two fundamental forces at work in the world, good and evil—controlled by God and Satan, angels and demons, and righteousness and sin and death. In this cosmic conflict, humans are relatively powerless against evil and, consequently, suffer. This age is given over to the devil, and because the powers of evil are in control, there are earthquakes, famines, epidemics, wars, and death. But eventually God will intervene and set up a new kingdom on

FIGURE 10.5

The Four Horsemen of the Apocalypse (see Revelation 6:1-8). Notice the color of the horses. Viktor Vasnetsov, 1887.

earth. *Pessimism* says that because we are caught in a cosmic battle and the forces of evil are in control in this evil age, there is nothing we can do to make things better. No sense planting trees or changing lightbulbs, let alone putting money into the educational system for our kids. In *vindication,* God will intervene in a cataclysmic act of judgment on the world, with those on God's side rewarded and those who have sided with the devil punished. The end is *imminent* and will come soon; get ready for the Rapture.

Several New Testament writers note that Jesus' work on earth was to destroy the works of the devil, to counter the devil's appeal to our grandiosity, self-interest, and wishes to get even. But Jesus did not have an apocalyptic worldview in the sense described above. He was a realist who couched everything he said and did in the present. When he said repeatedly, "The kingdom of God is at hand," he was making a statement about the present and his activity in it. *I have serious problems with the apocalyptic worldview, to which many Christians even today subscribe.*

First, *dualism* applied to people just does not work. This can be a religion's biggest failing. Although there is a small subset of people who are truly malevolent (antisocial personality disorder), the vast majority of people are well-intentioned and at worst misguided. I would fail miserably at my job as a psychiatrist and addictionist if I saw my patients in black and white. (There is one other caveat: Malignantly narcissistic people have a penchant for the political process and, if in power, can wreak havoc on nations and continents. Our American founding fathers recognized this and designed a constitution that has discouraged the assent and limited the influence of antisocial and severely narcissistic people.) *Pessimism, vindication,* and the *imminent end,* in addition to being founded on the false premise of dualism, are future oriented, have no real currency in the present, fuel judgmental attitudes, and lead to failures in mentalization—that is, appreciating the mental positions and states of our neighbors. Mentalization will be addressed in detail in the next chapter.

A THEODICY

A theodicy is a defense of God's justice in the face of suffering.
Is God to blame because there are in the universe shifting continental
plates and huge gravitational forces? Can we accuse him for
infectious diseases, when in fact we and all of Life are caught up in
predator/prey cycles? Is it his fault that we, with our big brains, can wage
atomic war or prey on others with the sophistication of Bernie Madoff?
We rejoice that, though the world can be a dangerous place,
the universe is fine-tuned for Life, which spreads out to fill every cranny.
God is not a puppeteer but is in fact the master gardener.

In considering a defense of God's justice in the face of Life's suffering, I have reviewed the experience of three Christians, Charles Darwin,

William Lobdell, and Bart Ehrman, each of whom lost his faith over the experience and issues of suffering and evil. I offered a preliminary theodicy with a personal story in "Presence." I have particularly focused on the work of Bart Ehrman—a profoundly articulate man with an extraordinary grasp of the Scriptures; he has raised a variety of challenging questions about the nature of suffering and God's link to it. I hope to address his various assertions about suffering.

Both Ehrman and Lobdell protest the death and suffering caused by natural disasters such as drought, tsunamis, earthquakes, and volcanoes. Lobdell asks what kind of God would allow so many people to die. My answer? Since its inception 13 billion years ago, the universe has been in a state of flux, galaxies colliding, comets smashing into planets (our moon is thought to be the result of a gigantic collision), exploding supernovas, all objects pulled about by cosmic gravitational forces. Anywhere in the universe where there is a planet, there will be the shifting of continental plates, resulting in volcanoes, earthquakes, and if there are oceans, tsunamis. At the same time, this violent universe is fine-tuned for Life, which burgeons out, if conditions are right, to fill every nook and cranny, yet it is always vulnerable to being crushed, resulting in pain and sorrow. So where is God in this universe? Is he the master puppeteer, pulling the strings, or is he the master gardener, tending a plot where the plants have lives of their own, often letting the weeds grow alongside the wheat so as to increase the harvest?

And why disease, plagues, pestilence, pandemics, AIDS, and worldwide influenzas? Again, since the beginning of Life, there has been conflict, viruses attacking bacteria, bacteria consuming each other, each developing better weaponry and defense, always struggling to survive. Why, then, do people treat other people with such blatant disregard and predation? I have shown that since Life's inception, any creature that can move has been both predator and prey, scratching out an existence, forced to adapt to an ever changing land- or seascape, developing ingenious morphological and social structures in the process. Humankind is

the reductio ad absurdum of everything living, the biggest brains allowing extremes of social structure (attachments, love, families, political in-
volvements, or the opposite—alienation and isolation), means of waging
combat (atomic warfare), sophistication of predation (Bernie Madoff),
and the methods and mentality of dominance (arrogance and pride), to
name a few. But I insist that, the news to the contrary, humankind is
getting better. In the next chapter, "The Future of Christianity," I will
show how we can apply the art of mentalization to improve our ability
to love others and ourselves.

MALEVOLENCE

Animals can be extremely violent,
but only humans can act malevolently.

A s I have argued, self-conflict is an intrinsic facet of Life; it all traces
back to the Darwinian struggle for survival but even further to Life's
and humankind's move against God. The natural world disasters, such
as earthquakes and tsunamis and the collisions of galaxies are indifferent
phenomena responding to natural forces. Animal predators and selfish
genes can be lethal, but the sickness and death they can unleash are
by-products of their desire and intent to make a living or mount a defense. A flesh-eating bacteria may be thought of as evil—that is, destructive—but it is only behaving as flesh-eating bacteria do. Only humans seem capable of acting malevolently, where the infliction of pain
(fig. 10.6) and/or death of the object of attack are the pure primary
aims. *Malevolence stems in part from the acting out of the wish for revenge and
to get even.* No wonder Jesus so emphasized the crucial importance of
forgiveness!

For example, the Holocaust is traceable to one man, Adolf Hitler.
Why did this man and his Nazi henchmen wreak such destruction on

FIGURE 10.6

Guernica, a tile replica of the mural by Pablo Picasso, commemorating the bombing of Guernica, Basque country, Spain, by German and Italian warplanes during the Spanish Civil War. It dramatizes the sufferings of innocent people caught in the madness of war.

the Jews and other peoples? As a psychiatrist, I partly subscribe to the views of Alice Miller, a German psychologist who included a biography of Hitler in her book *For Your Own Good*.[26] In it she notes that Hitler, as well as many other prominent Nazis, were victims of childhood physical and emotional abuse, and they were full of vengeance. Throughout his childhood, Hitler was whipped daily by his father. In my experience, such treatment heightens baseline hubris and engenders a wish for revenge and the desire to get even, the child perceiving that to survive, he or she must regain control and maintain his or her brittle pride by destroying the other. But I think that is only part of the explanation for malevolence: The Nazis were psychopaths and antisocial personalities.

Hitler was world-class in his criminality, arrogance, and exercise of retribution, the extent of which was delusional and psychotic. Could it be that the majority of malevolence visited on others in the world is by brutalized and antisocial children grown up, megalomaniacal, and bent on settling scores?

Why do people become antisocial? Research into the etiology of psychopathy has generated another ocean of literature. Areas of investigation include genetics, family history, neurobiology, comorbid psychiatric disorders, issues of attachment, and abuse/neglect histories. For example, Gao et al. examined the connections between bonding with mother and father, childhood physical abuse, separation from parents in the first three years of life, and psychopathic personality in adults aged 28.[27] In this study, these different components of bonding were significantly correlated with the incidence of antisociality. It is clear to me that deficiencies in attachment relationships early in life are most significant. We'll consider aspects of in detail in the next chapter. What about the devil as the source of psychopathy? I believe in the existence of the devil and his power to deceive, but to invoke him in causality is to pose a "devil-of-the-gaps" argument.

Ehrman omitted one aspect of suffering that is mentioned but not dwelt on in the Joseph story and is implicitly present throughout the Old and New Testaments: slavery, certainly malevolent in nature. In the Scriptures, the Exodus of the Hebrews from Egypt explicitly involved slavery, but generally the phenomenon is taken for granted, and there are few references to the massive injustice, humiliation, violence, and enormous pain of slavery. In our own time, it has been a clearly religious issue, with the faith in God of Abraham Lincoln (fig. 10.7), Martin Luther King, Jr., and a vast army of others resolutely moving our nation forward to diminish this horror. But even as I write this sentence, the monstrosity of slavery continues, now in the trafficking of young women in Thailand and Ukraine to function as sex slaves. I recently watched a *Frontline* (PBS television) special on the sex trade

FIGURE 10.7

First Reading of the Emancipation Proclamation of President Lincoln, by Francis
Bicknell Carpenter, 1864. From left to right: Edwin Stanton, Secretary of War; Salmon
Chase, Secretary of Treasury; President Lincoln; Gideon Welles, Secretary of Navy;
Caleb Blood Smith, Secretary of Interior; William Seward, Secretary of State;
Montgomery Blair, Postmaster; Edward Bates, Attorney General.

in Ukraine, where young women were kidnapped or spirited away to
work as slaves in Turkey. For the *Frontline* video, investigative journalists exposed a sex-trafficking ring with the help of a pimp named
Vlad, who had a change of heart about his actions. So to answer Ehrman's first question, "If he came into the darkness to make a difference, why is there no difference?" I reply that there *is* a difference,
that by their faith and actions Lincoln, King, and many others, including the investigative journalists in the *Frontline* special, have helped and
are helping many in the world to wake up and repent (from the Latin,
re = again, *pent* = think), to reconsider destructive attitudes and actions,
as the pimp Vlad did. Still, we have a long way to go.

FREE WILL AND SUFFERING

It is easy to underestimate how utterly free we are.

One might then ask, "Well, why does God allow chance and self-conflict, and why should he permit any child to be beaten, let alone allow Holocausts? Why do people become psychotic, delusional, or so malevolently bent on revenge?" Bart Ehrman discounts free will as an adequate answer to the whys of such evils, but I don't think we Christians realize or accept the radical extent to which God respects Life's intelligence, creativity, independence, and autonomy. Our freedom, and indeed all of Life's freedom, is much more far-reaching and total than we realize or even want to admit; rather, we have needed, I fear, to see God pulling the strings. Maybe, at the heart of it all, we humans fear responsibility and have trouble thinking for ourselves. Could it be that we dislike making decisions and therefore gravitate to cults, political parties, religions, or marriages where we get others to decide for us and take care of us? Humankind suffers from "decido-phobia." Most of all, we loathe loneliness and uncertainty, and too often we are more than willing to cede our autonomy to those who purport to have the answers. *What a contradiction, hubris and dependency.* But does a universe that runs on its own or an earth that shifts, buckles, and crumples or Life that is corrupted by violence and self-conflict mean that God has left us alone?

KEEPING MY RELIGION

Got faith? Hold fast to it and persevere.

The arguments of Darwin, Lobdell, and Ehrman are interesting and compelling, but in fact they are reflections of a larger phenomenon—the question of belief, how persons come to believe and how their beliefs play out. Each of these men in their early years received instruction in the faith, and each in time processed belief and adapted it to suit himself. It is as though a cosmic Sower cast seeds of belief and they took root— Darwin as a scientist, Lobdell as a writer and seeker of truth, Ehrman as a scholar. But Jesus cautioned that belief can be evanescent, some seeds falling on rocky ground, others eaten by birds.[29] I too can be wracked by thoughts of unbelief, and I have always identified with the man who ran up to Jesus and exclaimed, "I believe; help my unbelief."[30] But I have no intentions of losing my religion. And how am I going to prevent its slipping away, as it did for Darwin, Lobdell, and Ehrman? *Perseverance:* "But as for that [seeds] in good soil, these are the ones who, when they hear the word, hold it fast with an honest and good heart, and bear fruit with patient endurance."[31] Nonetheless, Darwin, Lobdell, and Ehrman raise legitimate questions that must be answered.

THE CRUCIFIED GOD

We rejoice in the resurrection,
but the Cross is the crux of Christianity.

Life has always had to adapt, to eat, and to avoid being eaten. Even molecules struggle to make a living. Life's Breath, instructed by the Word, evolved and elaborated on the two best instruments of all for survival—intelligence and community. The family of humankind was the final achievement. But intelligence, particularly in our hands, has proven to be a two-edged sword capable of being used for harmony and cooperation or domination, subjugation, and destruction. *Homo sapiens* can take legitimate pride in its brain power, but sadly, puffery is always at hand. As a consequence, alongside our vulnerability, suffering, and subjection to evil and death there exists hubris—a sense that we have all the answers or that we don't need anybody. Or worst of all, the mind of the perpetrator. It seems that only humans can quietly and consistently nurture and nourish the wish for revenge. All of us are quite capable at any moment in time of being either victim or victimizer. We are masters of manipulativeness. None of these bodes well for community. Unfortunately, rising above our isolation, self-conflict, suffering, and capacity to do evil is not easy. This is where we need a guide to lead us to safety, healing, and restoration and to empower us to become the persons and people whom God calls us to be.

The people of Jesus' time expected the kind of messiah and savior that evolution would predict: a conqueror, a mighty warrior, a person of temporal power who would crush God's and Israel's enemies. How disappointed in Jesus they were when he rode into Jerusalem on the colt of an ass! Not exactly living up to expectations. Isn't it from the lofty, the weighty, or the important that I draw my power? And furthermore to be abandoned by his followers and friends and treated and executed as a common criminal! And all of this by humankind, Life's crowning achievement and its steward and representative before God.

So where is God when it hurts? Jürgen Moltmann, a professor of systematic theology at the University of Tübingen in Germany, in his book *The Crucified God,* writes how it is in the crucifixion of Jesus that we, and I would add all of Life, are led out of our suffering to salvation.[32] Referring to objections like those of Ehrman, Lobdell, and Darwin as "protest atheism," Moltmann states that it is God himself who suffers and dies as Jesus, and having endured rejection, abandonment, and humiliation, finally loses his connection with God before he dies on the cross. "My God, my God, why have your forsaken me?"[33] In doing so, he joins us and all of Life in our separation from God. Moltmann notes that in this theology, *God and suffering are no longer contradictions,* for God's being is in suffering, and the suffering is in God's being itself. God himself loves and suffers the death of Jesus in his love. God, then, is no cold heavenly power, nor does he tread his way over corpses, but he is known as the human God in the crucified Son of Man.

In my own life, for too long I clothed myself in a tough exterior, denied my need for God and others, and deluded myself with grandiose plans of wealth. I hid behind my intellect, position, and accomplishments. I hypertrophied such accoutrements to avoid and conceal old childhood hurts. What was I hiding from? My own sense that I am unlovable. Why did Cain kill Abel? Could it have been out of fear? Could it be that Cain feared that God had, in his criticism of his sacrifice, rejected and forsaken him, meaning he was unlovable? *Humankind's sense of being unlovable is the ultimate source of rage.* And why do we feel unlovable? Because we don't love. *Sadly, none of us has inherited Abel's genes.* But Jesus, rejected and forsaken, joins us in our alienation. He became the epitome of God-forsakenness for us to show us that we and all Life *are* loveable. He subjected himself to our self-conflict and became self-conflicted himself, to initiate our deliverance from it. The cross is God's ultimate revelation of himself. God himself suffers.

Humankind, Life's representative before God, now can see God in a new and intimate way. God is now approachable, not as a lofty sovereign but as one of us, as a fellow sufferer. Jesus shows forth the full extent of love, by laying down his life for his friends. He knows our suffering, but love is more than that. Love is the four-letter word for a relationship that transforms and gives meaning to Life's pattern and possibilities. He makes sacred our struggles to survive, not by transporting us beyond suffering but by suffering with us. Moltmann refers to Luther, who stated that whereas medieval mysticism understood the cross as a divinization of man, the reverse is true—humankind is de-divinized and given new humanity in the community of the crucified Christ. To be de-divinized is to become real, to become reality based.

The "de-divinization" is crucial. Moltmann, continuing with Luther, points out that we humans, having some knowledge of God through the things he has made, tend to use that knowledge for our own aggrandizement. Just as we constantly justify ourselves through our accomplishments, we may use our knowledge of God to pad our own hubris. Such a knowledge of God merely enables us to fool ourselves about the truth of our situation. *In other words, I can with religiosity quite deftly blind myself to my intrinsic self-conflict.* But to know God in the suffering and death of Jesus allows me to take my self-conflict seriously. Moltmann states:

> In revealing himself in the crucified Christ he [God] contradicts the God-man who exalts himself, shatters his hubris, kills his gods and brings back to him his despised and abandoned humanness. . . . God reveals himself in the contradiction and the protest of Christ's passion to be against all that is exalted and beautiful and good, all that the dehumanized man seeks for himself and therefore perverts.
>
> . . . To know God in the cross of Christ is a crucifying form of knowledge, because it shatters everything to which a man can hold and on which he can build . . . and precisely in so doing sets him free.[34]

It was grace, God's empowerment, but also his encouragement, love, putting me in the right place at the right time, and giving me the right people that helped me to set aside my pride and embrace my flawed humanity. Thus have I been drawn along the path to safety and restoration that is salvation. I have contributed to the process with an insatiable desire to learn, but I got that from him as well. The Breath that animates me, and all of us, has always wanted to learn.

THE FUTURE
OF CHRISTIANITY

"Let the same mind be in you that was in Christ Jesus." [1]

Jesus is unique in putting aside self-interest for our
well-being. The future of Christianity and all of us is to be
found in the goal Jesus set for us, to love and
to serve. But what is love?
Science offers valuable new insights.

A close study and synthesis of the facts of biological science and evolution and Judeo-Christian Holy Writ has yielded a number of interesting and novel insights. Biological and evolutionary sciences have shown us a Life exuberant in its diversity, stunning in its intelligence, and bewildering in its geologic time-scale flexibility. Most important, these sciences lend themselves to the interpretation that Life is an agent in its adaptations. As Life has learned, central nervous systems have grown, until finally, in the last seconds of geologic time, hominid evolution has perfected the big brain of *Homo sapiens*.

Yet for all its intelligence, and perhaps because of it, Life is intrinsically in conflict with itself. An appreciation of self-conflict compels us to reconsider what the Church has called "sin." Sin in Life and in each of us begins with a disregard for, discounting of, and opposition to God, leading to a number of consequences. The Church has focused on the consequence of moral misbehavior, but it now appears that moral misconduct is a downstream and secondary effect of self-conflict's deleterious impact on Life as community, akin to fever and cough in an underlying bacterial pneumonia.

To enable Life's supreme achievement, humankind, to return to God and to begin to overcome our conflicts with self and others, God entered our world in the person of Jesus. We have seen that the goal of all creatures in biological evolution has been to survive; even living in community has been a strategy for survival. Recall the words of Jeff Bezos, CEO of Amazon, quoted in the Introduction to this book: "What is very dangerous is not to evolve." Invention for businesspeople like Bezos is about beating the competition. *But Jesus presents us with a complete departure from that paradigm;* astonishingly, he completely put aside self-interest, even to the point of death, to reconcile us to God. Indeed, He laid down his life for his friends. The future of Christianity and all of us is to be found in the goal Jesus set for us, to love and to serve.

We progress toward Christianity's goal in evolution, to love and to serve, by learning to know God, facing and overcoming our conflicts, and restoring community, for ourselves and for all of Life. We are not alone in this endeavor, as the previous paragraph makes clear. In addition, God has developed within us through evolution the power and ability to love, and it is our task to cultivate this power. The ability to emotionally comprehend the first two commandments is found within us.

The ultimate resource that lies within us is the peculiar intelligence that our brains and minds possess. Stuart Kauffman, a philosopher of mind, writes that our minds are "meaning-doing" systems, uniquely able to perceive or construct meaning out of our perceptions. Kauffman asks where "meaning" comes from. He answers, "Meaning derives from agency . . . without agency, as far as I can tell, there can be no meaning . . . . The mind makes meaning. It makes understandings."[2] *I will argue that it is in the capacity to discern meaning that love takes place.*

But what is love? Can science shed light on a subject that has its own ocean of literature? In this book, I have shown how an ocean of scientific discovery in biology has contributed to our understanding of how God is working in his creation. Now, I'd like to show how findings in behavior science research can move us along in attaining healing of our conflicts with self and others and coming to love *by unleashing and harnessing the meaning-making power within us.* To this end, I'll introduce the of John Bowlby and his subsequent contributors; the work of Catholic Christian psychiatrist W. Earl Biddle; the post research on mentalization by Jon Allen, Anthony Bateman, and Peter Fonagy; and James Masterson's work on forgiveness.

ATTACHMENT THEORY

John Bowlby found that failures in consistent parenting amplify our conflictual nature. His was experimentally validated by researchers, who described two specific kinds of attachment styles, secure and insecure.

Conflict within ourselves infects all of us, down to the molecules, and it amounts to something analogous to an addiction. Like an addiction, it is endemic, treatable, but always in danger of rearing its perplexing choices. Recall that self-conflict is the antithesis of community. We get serious about community in the months before childbirth, the time when a family unit and hence community spring to life and the bonds of attachment are forged. These are emotional times for us as new parents, because the memories of the quality of our own nurture are activated. It is a dangerous time when new parents can readily pass on to their offspring the traumas and conflicts of their own childhoods. In other words, generic self-conflict is easily amplified by childhood suffering and/or faulty parenting. What follows is what some very elegant scientific research can tell us about this period in life.

John Bowlby (fig. 11.1), a British psychiatrist and psychoanalyst, clashed with the ideological Freudian biases of the psychoanalytic community of his time. Rejecting the Oedipus complex as fundamental to human nature,[3] he sought instead experimental evidence for what

Image copyright of Sir Richard Bowlby, with permission

FIGURE 11.1

Dr. John Bowlby (1907–1990).

motivated children's behavior. Through his observations on nonhuman primates, he developed the idea of an attachment behavioral system existing to regulate infant safety. The primate offspring, with their long periods of dependency on the mother, rely on maintenance of proximity to attachment figures for survival. Bowlby began his work with humans by examining the responses of children who were separated from their parents and placed in unfamiliar environments such as hospitals and residential nurseries. He noted that such major and traumatic separations led to the emergence of anxiety and ambivalence with respect to previous loved persons and eventually to a state of detachment in which both affectionate and hostile feelings were repressed. His ideas about the primary importance of attachment over Oedipal longings were considered heretical by the British Psychoanalytic Society. Bowlby later quipped, "It has been extremely unfashionable to attribute psychopathology to real-life experiences."[4] Notice the word *ambivalence*: It is synonymous with self-conflict. *In other words, failures in consistent parenting amplify endemic self-conflict.*

Following Bowlby's formulations, researcher Mary Ainsworth went on to quantify attachment reactions through the development of the laboratory-based Strange Situation procedure.[5] This research tool made use of an infant's responses to very brief separations from, and reunions with, a given parent to classify the organization of its attachment to the parent as secure, avoidant, or resistant/ambivalent. *Secure organization was found to be predictable from the mother's sensitivity to her baby's signals and communications in the home.* The two insecure forms of attachment organization—detached avoidant (distancing) and overtly anxious resistant/ambivalent (clinging)—were related respectively to maternal rejection and unpredictability. Researchers extending Ainsworth's work found that children who had been secure with their mothers in the Strange Situation during infancy were found subsequently to enjoy more favorable relations with their peers and teachers.

At the same time, parents of the subject children were assessed using the Adult Attachment Interview (AAI). The combination of the Strange Situation assessing children and the AAI assessing their parents has led to the recognition of three organized categories or *states of mind* with respect to attachment. The children's responses to separation and reunion have been described as *secure, avoidant,* and *resistant-ambivalent.* The corresponding states of mind within caretaking adults have been named *secure-autonomous, dismissing,* and *preoccupied.* Remarkably, each AAI category has repeatedly been found to predict the infant Strange Situation response to that parent.[6] Table 11.1 (see next page) illustrates the relationship between AAI in parents and Strange Situation responses in the babies.

Mary Main writes that researchers worldwide have replicated the relationship explicated above. "Studies in four countries conducted in four different laboratories, and including a poverty sample of very young mothers, have indicated that the same average parent-to-child, secure/insecure match of 75% holds *even when the interview is conducted before the birth of the first child*" [Italics mine].[7]

ADULT ATTACHMENT INTERVIEW	INFANT STRANGE SITUATION RESPONSE
SECURE-AUTONOMOUS: These parents valued and were objective about their own attachment relationships. Their descriptions intimated forgiveness, compassion, and subtle humor. They tried to be accurate in their recollections. Their speech tended to be fresh, original, coherent, and flexible. They were comfortable discussing both good and bad. They had a balanced sense of their needs.	**SECURE:** In the playroom at the outset, is happy with mother and explorations. Cries when mother leaves, greets her upon return. Distressed when she leaves again, moves quickly toward her on her return. Again calms down and resumes exploration of the playroom. Striking was the immediate calming. Noted was the mother's sensitivity and response to the baby's signals.
DISMISSING: These parents tended to dismiss the importance and effects of early relationships. They made brief positive statements about a parent that were contradicted by their anecdotes. Their memories were sparse, and they often said "I don't remember." They avoided discussing anger and distress. They implicitly denied that they had needs.	**AVOIDANT:** Infant doesn't seem to notice when the mother first leaves and continues playing with the toys. Upon mother's return, seems to stiffen, bends slightly away from her, and continues with the toys. When she leaves again, baby shows no emotions and focuses on the toys. Upon her second return, baby pays no attention to her. Monitoring of baby's vital signs indicated physiological distress, however. These children had learned to be scornful of their needs.
PREOCCUPIED: In contrast to the distancing of dismissive parents, these parents were preoccupied with attachment issues. They actively complained of parents' faults and their early experiences. They talked a lot and went off on tangents. Speech was confused, vague, or full of jargon. They were very needy.	**RESISTANT-AMBIVALENT:** Infant is immediately distressed in the playroom, even with mother present. When mother leaves, is more distressed, and continues to cry loudly after mother returns. Refuses to explore. Is again very upset when mother leaves the second time, may tantrum upon mother's return, finally clinging petulantly to mother's leg. They appeared very immature and needy.

TABLE 11.1

Infant, Child, and Adult Attachment and the Strange Situation[8]

Hesse and Main went on to describe a fourth category of attachment style, one seen where gross histories of childhood trauma, abuse, and/or neglect were present in the parent, as might be found in psychiatric and criminal populations.[9] These parents may present with overtly or subtly frightening behavior and on the AAI show marked lapses in reasoning and discourse, particularly when they are discussing abuse or loss; they are termed *unresolved-disorganized*. The infant is termed *disorganized-disoriented* on the basis of exhibiting a diverse array of inexplicable, odd, disorganized, disoriented, or overtly conflicted behaviors in the parent's presence. One infant, for example, cried loudly while attempting to gain her mother's lap, then suddenly fell silent and stopped moving for several seconds. Others rocked on hands and knees following an abortive approach. Others screamed by the door upon separation from the parent and then moved silently away upon reunion. A constant theme was contradictory movement patterns. The researchers concluded that certain forms of frightening parental behavior will arouse contradictory propensities to approach and to take flight from the parent. Such patterns in infants predict disruptive-aggressive and dissociative disorders in childhood and adolescence.

So what do we have here? We have remarkable evidence for the communication of our states of being, particularly our ambivalent mental states as they pertain to our attachments to our children! Furthermore, subsequent research has shown that the results of the AAIs of pregnant women predict *in advance* the attachment styles of the future infant. Attachment research vividly characterizes the anatomy of maternal love or hostility or indifference and how it affects the baby. The lasting behavior patterns laid down in the infant in response to the mother-infant relationship are termed the "internal working model." Last, in the secure attachment bond of a mother and her infant, we have the prototype for communion, one of the two basic drives of the self![10] Notice that frustration of the drive for communion leads to ambivalent and contradictory behavior—that is, worsening self-conflict.

THE INTERNAL
WORKING MODEL (IWM)

*We carry around within us portraits or models of our
important attachment relationships.
How we love is strongly influenced by them.*

The study of attachment then moved toward investigating the "level of representation." An informative film series by James and Joyce Robertson (1967–1972) looked at infant and children's separations from their parents and found that toddlers who in all likelihood had never previously been significantly rejected could also come to avoid their mothers on the basis of changes in mental or emotional processes taking place in the absence of interaction.[11] Striking was the film *Thomas*, in which a two-year-old who had previously enjoyed a harmonious relationship with his mother was placed in an extended foster care placement. In the film, he was several times presented with her photograph. At first Thomas kissed and fondled the photograph. Several days later, however, he backed away from it, looking down and fiddling with the toy he was holding. In response to a final presentation of his mother's photograph, Thomas actively turned his back on it with an anxious expression. Since a photograph cannot "behave," it cannot be said that it elicited Thomas's changing reactions. Since he had not seen his mother during this period, the gradual development of avoidance of the photograph must have included aspects of changes in their *imagined* relationship.

The Strange Situation is a laboratory test of the representational processes within the children. Following up with the infants who had been through the Strange Situation, differences in infant Strange Situation behavior predicted corresponding differences in retested six-year-old children. For example, drawings that follow-up children made of their families were found to be highly predictable from first-year attachment to the mother. In addition, children's separation-related narratives were predictable from infant Strange Situation behavior with the mother, leading to the conclusion that different patterns of infant-mother interaction must have led to the development not only of different behavior but also of *different representational processes*. Ainsworth's findings about inner representations supported Bowlby's concept of the IWM. Ainsworth describes Bowlby's IWM as she states, *"We have been concerned with nothing less than the nature of love in its origin and origins in the attachment of a baby to [its] mother"* [italics mine].[12] Attachment is manifested through specific patterns of behavior, but the patterns themselves do not constitute the attachment. Attachment is internal. This internalized something that we call "attachment" is communicated as feelings, memories, wishes, expectancies, and intentions, all of which serve as a kind of filter for the reception and interpretation of interpersonal experience. The IWM is a kind of template shaping the nature of outwardly observable response.

W. EARL BIDDLE
AND THE REALITY OF THE IMAGE

Images are our portraits of those who cared for us.
These images appear indirectly or directly in our dreams.

In Chapter 9, I related a personal generational history of physical abuse of my father in the name of Christianity, resulting in his emotional cutoff from his family of origin and his ill-controlled rage. I described my own history of attachment trauma (we'll explore this term below), with its resulting sleep disturbances, nightmares, anger, and chronic fear. I told of downstream effects such as struggles with getting myself up and going, feelings of powerlessness, and trying to prove myself a man. Finally, I portrayed grandiose but vague plans that couldn't conceal confusion and indecision regarding a career. Mentioned elsewhere were womanizing and an inability to commit myself to a woman; the bottom line was that I was unable to love.

Prior to and early in medical school I sought on two occasions counsel with priests. Both made it quickly known through their advice that they were uncomfortable with my complaints and had no ability or expertise to help me. At the beginning of my second year in medical school, I heard of a Bible study where I might meet eligible women; instead, I met an Episcopal priest, the Rev. S. Dunham Wilson. He was completely different; he listened thoughtfully to me, thoroughly heard out my complaints, gave an appraisal of what he thought was wrong, and offered a way out. I trusted his assessment and entered counseling with him. My personal evolution received a rocket boost forward. I found the results of the relationship so salutary that I have made it a life's goal to pass along what I have received.

Fr. Wilson was a protégé of W. Earl Biddle, MD, a psychiatrist, Roman Catholic layman, and author of books and articles integrating religion and psychiatry.[13] His insights prefigured modern attachment theory, with its IWM and its extremely useful method of mentalization, which we will cover in detail below. Biddle was clinical director of Philadelphia State Hospital. Like Bowlby, he practiced in a climate of allegiance to Freud's Oedipus Complex. And like Bowlby, he understood that relationships, not sexual drive, determined a person's mental health. For example, he sought experimental validation or falsification of the Oedipus Complex by the use of age regression of adults under hypnosis. He found that rather than wishing for intercourse with the opposite-sexed parent, his experimental subjects desired a *communion* with both parents.

Biddle posited that children from early on construct inner portraits of those charged with their care. If the child's quest for communion with a parent figure is chronically frustrated, the child's *mother image* will reflect that deprivation. The mother image of a securely attached person will appear in dreams, feelings, unguarded comments, and imaginings as conveying a sense of nurture and support. Conversely, the internal mother image of a child of an unresolved/disorganized mother, as listed above, would be nightmarish. Biddle would then literally assume the concrete presence of the bad mother image and approach it for dialogue. Biddle's mother and father images are the pictorial representations that populate the IWM.

Dreams are a particularly transparent window for viewing the images of the IWM. For example, addicts in recovery often complain of "using" dreams in which they are tempted to use or in the dream do indeed use. Inquiry leads to an understanding of the addict's attachment frustrations, the siren call of the substance constituting a fantasized assurance that the drug will lead to soothing and nurture. Of course, it is a lie. In other words, drugs are "food" that fill the gap in attachment of an inadequate mother. I thus interpret using dreams as a reaction to the emergence of the depriving mother image. At this point, we can discuss patients' frustration and pessimism that their needs will ever be legitimately met. I may point out that in fact they are receiving nurture from their AA group, sponsor, residential treatment center, or church. I may add that if God is their father and mother, they can be more optimistic that they will be cared for. It is no accident that many stories in the Scriptures, such as Jesus feeding the multitudes and the Last Supper, are about food, symbolizing God's persistent intent to nurture his creation.

In my counseling with Fr. Wilson, I was instructed to pray nightly to have a dream of eating good food, to which my dreams would then reply. The "good food" would symbolize an optimism that I could indeed find what I needed in life—that is, a secure attachment. I then kept track of my dreams. The instruction to dream of good food was a powerful challenge to me to update my IWM. *And the dreams do respond, often by raising objections.* Much of therapy has to do with dealing with the pessimism that nothing really will ever change. People can hardly believe that they will ever be well, that their attachment needs will be honored. Does this approach work? In a study I did using this method with 64 women in a substance abuse residential treatment center, 70% were clean and sober at the end of one year, and 20% had cut back their substance use considerably. Their using dreams ceased, and their anxieties and depressions resolved as they more confidently opened up to me about their pain and struggles. These women were healed by their faith—that is, they came to believe that their attachment needs could indeed be met. This confidence started with me as I conveyed that God as their father and mother was present for them. It spread to comfort with the community of their residential treatment center peers and outward to their AA groups.

ATTACHMENT TRAUMA

Traumatic experiences with the attachment figures of young children can radically alter life outcomes. Can you imagine how much attachment trauma there is in the world?

Many kinds of traumas impact us. Humankind is beset by natural disasters, the traumas of war, famine, pestilence. Political oppression, racial biases, and innumerable other injustices prevail. But the studies of attachment theorists show us that the traumas within families are foundational, with the quality and style of the mother-infant relationship the absolute core. Here are the origins of the hurricanes of violence that sweep the earth. We have seen that all life is beset by self-conflict, but among the animals, conflict coexists with cooperation in a kind of balance. Although living is brutal and death is commonplace, Life is intrinsically interconnected, cooperative, and harmonious.

But humankind's attachment needs are unique, and their frustrations massively amplify life's intrinsic self-conflict. Furthermore, traumas associated with attachments lead inevitably to the uniquely human desire and capacity for revenge. I referred to the work of the German psychologist Alice Miller in Chapter 10.[14] Miller argued that in Germany after World War I, punitive child-rearing practices led to a generation of men and women bent on getting even. Particularly, Adolf Hitler's father whipped young Adolf daily and in the process created a person filled with psychotic rage and resentment. At the heart of the philosophy of German child rearing was the demand for obedience. Miller offers in great detail the childhood history of Rudolph Hoss, the commandant of Auschwitz. Ironically, the elder Hoss had hoped that through the meticulous inculcation of obedience his son would become a priest.

Let us consider more closely attachment trauma. Who are the perpetrators of attachment trauma? Although a fraction of sins visited on children come from parents who are indeed criminals, the vast majority of traumas come from well-meaning parents who would insist, if asked, that they love their children. I have no doubt that my father—though trapped within himself, uncommunicative, arbitrary, and rageful—loved me. My father's mother would have insisted that he was whipped for his own good. Rudolph Hoss's father zealously wanted the best for his son. What all these parents missed in their push to raise obedient children was to be in touch with and empathetic with the mental and feeling states of their children. They failed to mentalize.

MENTALIZATION:
THE LANGUAGE OF COMMUNION

Mentalization is the art of accurately reading other people,
grasping their intentions, doing so with compassion and the valuing
of the other. It is the language of communion with another.

Bowlby, Ainsworth, Main, Biddle, and others established that small children above all thrive on relationships with caregivers who can understand and grasp their needful mental states and respond compassionately. Children so treated develop secure attachments. The mental state surrounding and characterizing a secure attachment is shared by mother and child and constitutes a state of *communion*. The next generation of attachment researchers, particularly Anthony Bateman and Peter Fonagy, take us further into the true range and significance of the communications leading to secure attachments. In the study of mothers and their infants in the Strange Situation, it became apparent to these researchers that the mothers of securely attached babies tuned into their babies more effectively; that is, they *mentalized*. They intuitively understood their babies' immediate communications, and their replies were accurate and met with relaxation. On the other hand, the mothers of insecurely attached babies mentalized poorly. As the research quoted above shows, securely attached children six years later were better mentalizers. It appears that mentalization begets mentalization; furthermore, the better the mentalization, the more resilient and capable of self-regulation the person. I will go on to argue that mentalization is the language of all communion between persons or between persons and God.

I refer in previous chapters to mentalization as the mental endeavor to grasp the mind of another, to understand and have empathy for that person's mental states in order to appreciate his or her needs and intents. I described the art of praying (I call it "praying without ceasing") to more accurately mentalize. I use the cognitive-emotional operation of mentalization to better comprehend the minds and hearts of biblical characters and the writers who penned them. I make the audacious suggestion that we can mentalize with God. I acknowledge that clergy are usually trying to mentalize as they teach a Bible study or prepare a sermon. Indeed, we all more or less attempt to mentalize all the time, though we have by no means exhausted the rich potentials of the exercise.

Effective mentalization, then, is the key to secure attachments. To begin to get a handle on this crucial concept, let us return to its origins. A secure attachment is necessary for the optimal development of mentalization. Recall that the secure attachment is a position of safety and strength, a base from which a toddler can explore various aspects of the environment. By analogy, if I as a psychiatrist provide patients with a secure base, then they can explore the various unhappy and painful aspects of their lives, past and present, many of which they find difficult or perhaps impossible to think about and reconsider without a trusted companion to provide support, encouragement, sympathy, and on occasion, guidance.

Allen, Fonagy, and Bateman write that maternal mirroring plays the pivotal role in the development of a mentalized sense of self.[15] Research shows that mind is not developed solely from within but rather largely from the outside. Infants, in effect, find their minds in the mind of their caregivers. The best mentalizing in the developing child depends on the mentalizer—that is, on the caregiver's mentalizing. If mentalizing capacity develops through relationships, the quality of those relationships will be pivotal, starting with the complex interplay between parental mentalizing, secure attachment in the child, and the child's mentalizing capacities.[16] Out of the child's growing abilities to mentalize will grow the ability to self-regulate. Attachment research is demonstrating that a child's affect regulation stems from being accurately mentalized, *not from warmth or benevolence alone*.[17] As we also have implied, mind-minded mothers are good trauma therapists. When their child has been through a frightening experience, they help the child to express his or her fear and make sense of it in a reassuring way, restoring a sense of safety.

Allen et al. give some handy definitions of mentalizing: holding mind in mind, attending to mental states in self and others, understanding misunderstandings, seeing oneself from the outside and others from the inside, or cultivating mentally a sense of the mental functioning of self or another. The authors state that mentalizing is first a constructing or picturing in the mind, imagining, or giving a mental quality to the actions of the self or another person. They emphasize that mentalizing pertains to the mental states of ourselves and/or others. Not all mental activity is mentalizing; rather, mentalizing is concerned with mental states. The authors define mentalizing as imaginatively perceiving or interpreting a person's specific intents.[18]

So what is a mental state? We have established that Life is an agent in its fate, and nowhere is agency more apparent than in humankind. At any given moment, each of our thoughts and feelings adds up to a particular intent. Every mental state is built around an intent. There can be several or many intents, and they can be very layered and simultaneous, ranging, for example, from wishing for a drink of water to seeking out the face of God. In addition, intents can be multiple and contradictory, as in the disorganized/disoriented infants referenced above, who moved toward and away from the abusive caretaker at the same time. Ultimately, mental states have an existential basis. The narrowest scope of mentalizing would be to focus on the state of mind at a given moment.[19] Yet as we discuss the mental states of others, we expand on mental states by articulating reasons for beliefs, feelings, and actions. Furthermore, these emotions and stories are taking place in brains that might be damaged and hence might be psychopathological. Ultimately, mentalizing is the attempt to make sense of a person's communication, what he or she is saying, what he or she wants, and what he or she is up to. Clearly, the more chaotic and traumatic a person's history, the more difficult it can be to discern that person's intents.

So far, we have considered mentalizing from a parent–child perspective. But this modern concept evolved initially from psychotherapy research. Generalizing the mentalizing stance beyond that of a good psychotherapist, Allen et al. argue that mentalizing is a fundamental human capacity that all but those in the autism spectrum generally take for granted; mentalizing is our capacity to relate to each other as persons.[20] But mentalizing is anything but simple. The authors describe a mentalizing stance as any inquisitive, curious, open-minded, and even playful interest in the mental states of self and others.[21] Writing again about psychotherapy, they consider the focus on mentalizing to be a refinement rather than an innovation, merely sharpening attention to a common factor inherent in psychotherapeutic treatments. Therapy contexts teach us that mentalizing also includes a comfort with uncertainty and not knowing, an interest in understanding better, consistent focus on the mind of the other, adaptation of interventions to the other's mentalizing capacity, orientation toward generating alternative perspectives, and authenticity. In mentalizing, the effective psychotherapist demonstrates a willingness to find out about patients, what makes them tick, how they feel, and the reasons for their underlying problems. *The mentalizing stance is respectful and devoid of assumptions. In my social and personal life and in the life of my church, I have people who treat me this way. From them I get the undeniable sense that I am authentically loved.*

Mentalization taken to its logical extreme leads to a mental state of *communion* between persons. We all have likely experienced moments when we are in a rhythm, "in a zone," with a loved one.

> Communion is best understood as an event. Everyone
> can recall specific, special moments of closeness, intimacy,
> and attachment to a parent, spouse, friend, or child.
> Mary's moment with Jesus (Luke 10:38-43) is an example.
> Communion is thus a feeding of the soul. Fantasies of
> communion, which may have a sexual aspect, are metaphors
> for these moments. The Song of Solomon is another
> biblical example.
> . . . Particularly, such nourishment benefits all that is
> crucial to children, particularly those under three, since it is
> in early childhood that the foundations of the self are laid.[22]

Psychotherapy, at its best, often leads to an openness, trust, and give-and-take that create moments of communion. This is the most gratifying feature of the work. I've written earlier that it is facilitated by "praying without ceasing." But I find it very difficult to re-create such incidents on paper, because I typically cannot remember what took place. Allen et al. quote Daniel Stern, a gifted psychotherapist who has written about the phenomenon. Stern's "work attests to the role of spontaneity and creativity in the therapeutic process." He emphasizes "'present moments' and 'moments of meeting,'" which are, in effect, the articulation of the phenomenon of "mentalizing in the therapeutic process."[23]

The authors note that Stern's present-centered focus on the here and now contrasts with most psychodynamic treatments, in which there is a rush toward meaning, leaving the present moment behind. In the psychotherapeutic process, the task for patient and therapist is to continually *move along* the process in a therapeutic way. Stern states that this moving along, while it is happening, is largely a spontaneous, locally unpredictable process. He states that the therapist cannot know exactly what the patient is going to say next, until he or she says it or does it. He adds that if the therapist thinks she knows, she is treating a theory and not a person. The authors note that consistent with the mentalizing stance, Stern advocates holding theory at a further distance during the session so that the immediate relationship can be lived more fully. They note that Stern highlights *present moments,* typically spanning several seconds, as warranting special attention. These moments have special therapeutic value in being novel, engaging, unpredictable, and also potentially problematic so as to require some sort of mental action and psychological work. He particularly focuses on the present moment, or the moment of meeting. He states that the present moments that interest us most are those that arise when two people make a special kind of mental contact. Stern is describing mentalizing at its best in characterizing psychotherapy as having the main implicit task of regulating the immediate intersubjective field, carrying out the regulation by probing, testing, and correcting the reading of the other's mental state in light of one's own. *Here, I believe, is the essence of the outgrowth of praying without ceasing, that outgrowth being an instant of communion. This paragraph captures for me the relationship between praying without ceasing and mentalizing.*

JESUS, THE ULTIMATE MENTALIZER

The Gospels are a treasure trove of descriptions
of Jesus' ability to read our minds with compassion and
valuation. We can learn to do the same.

If Jesus' powers of observation about people existed because he was
God incarnate, we learn something about God, but little about ourselves. But the doctrines of the Church declare unequivocally that he
was a man. It follows that he had the brain of a man and hence possessed
the abilities and limitations of cognition common to all of us. I will argue that, contrary to the idea that his cognitive processes came from his
divinity, Jesus was a profound mentalizer, with capacities that we can all
learn from and aspire to. We can have a mind like his: *Let this mind be in
you that was in Christ Jesus.* [24]

Mentalization encompasses a range of functions having in common
the awareness of others' mental states. Jesus' default mentalizing stance
was *compassion*. The word occurs numerous times in the Gospels and is
defined in the Merriam Webster dictionary as "sympathetic consciousness of others' distress together with a desire to alleviate it." But one must
be ready to exercise compassion, and implicit in the Gospel accounts was
Jesus' readiness to do so. Such availability of compassion is in contrast to
our mentalizing stances, where our default settings are egocentric.

Jesus' ministry began with his temptation by the devil in the wilderness. The exclusively mental experience involved the self-conflict around
the intent of his ministry: to pursue an agenda of temporal power or to
remain open to the guidance of God. And the purposes of the Gospel
writers? To portray Jesus as the next Adam, subjected once again at the
beginning to the temptations of the serpent, but this time in a wilderness
rather than a garden and with a reversal in outcomes.

After his ordeal in the wilderness, Jesus' first action was to call his
disciples. In parallel accounts in Mark and Matthew,[25] he called James

and John, and they responded instantly to be fishers of men. It is presumed that their reaction was one of obedience to the voice of the Mighty God. But the calling of the disciples in John 1:29-51 suggests a different dynamic—that of knowing and being known, of recognizing and being recognized, with the help of the Almighty. First, there is John the Baptist's witness:

> "I myself did not know him; but I came baptizing with water for this reason, that he might be revealed to Israel." And John testified, "I saw the Spirit descending from heaven like a dove, and it remained on him. I myself did not know him; but the one who sent me to baptize with water said to me, 'He on whom you see the Spirit descend and remain is the one who baptizes with the Holy Spirit.'"[26]

On the word of John the Baptist, Andrew and Peter, two of his disciples, decide to follow Jesus, but a third, Nathaniel, is skeptical: "Can anything good come out of Nazareth?" Philip says to him, "Come and see."

> When Jesus saw Nathaniel coming toward him, he said of him, "Here is truly an Israelite in whom there is no deceit!" Nathaniel asked him, "Where did you come to know me?" Jesus answered, "I saw you under the fig tree before Philip called you." Nathaniel replied, "Rabbi, you are the Son of God! You are the King of Israel!" Jesus answered, "Do you believe because I told you that I saw you under the fig tree? You will see greater things than these."[27]

We can infer from these men's almost instantaneous reactions to Jesus that they were moved by a most powerful and gratifying emotion, that of being recognized, known, and valued in a profound and fundamental way (fig. 11.2). Jesus' mentalization, his accurate characterization

FIGURE 11.2

Courtesy Wikimedia Commons[28]

The Calling of St. Matthew. Caravaggio.

of Nathaniel, strikes a chord in Nathaniel, leading to an exuberant confession of belief. These interactions suggest a strong connection between mentalization—being known, recognized, and valued—and belief. John's Gospel makes explicit Jesus' ability to mentalize: "He knew all people and needed no one to testify about anyone; for he himself knew what was in everyone."[29]

The link between mentalization—the gratifying emotional response of being known, recognized, valued, and accepted—and the experience of moments of communion is richly illustrated in Jesus' discourse with the Samaritan woman by the well.[30] His mentalizations led the woman to declare to the others in the village, "Come, see a man who told me everything I have ever done." The Samaritans engaged in their own intense mentalizations, and after spending two days with Jesus, exclaimed to the woman, "It is no longer because of what you said that we believe, for we have heard for ourselves, and we know that this is truly the Savior of the world." Note again the relationship of mentalization to knowing and belief.

Jesus mentalized both what he took in and what he put out to others. On the input side, the Gospels constantly characterized him as aware within himself of the thoughts and motives of those around him. He was equally prolific on the output side, his parables always implicitly speaking to the mental states of those in his audience. I particularly like Eugene Peterson's paraphrase of Matthew 13:10-14.[31] Jesus had just told the crowd the Parable of the Sower:

> The disciples came up and asked, "Why do you tell
> stories?" He replied, "You've been given insight into
> God's kingdom. You know how it works. Not everybody
> has this gift, this insight; it hasn't been given to them.
> Whenever someone has a ready heart for this, the
> insights and understandings flow freely. But if there is
> no readiness, any trace of receptivity soon disappears.
> That's why I tell stories: to create readiness, to nudge
> the people toward receptive insight. In their present state
> they can stare till doomsday and not see it, listen till
> they're blue in the face and not get it."

In Matthew 5:22-26, Jesus counsels us not to insult another or call anyone a fool. To what end? To condemn a person, to demean someone in any way, is to fail to mentalize, to grasp that person's being accurately.

These vignettes hardly scratch the surface of how Jesus implicitly and explicitly mentalized himself and others. I would suggest that we as Christians have particularly benefited because he taught us, and continues to teach us, how to be aware of, understand, control, and use our mental states.

A study of mentalization in the Gospels illustrates the levels to perceiving the mental states of others. First, attention must be paid to the mental or physical states of others. Then, the willingness to make the effort to mentalize follows. Certainly, a young mother, freshly bonded with her baby, is intensely motivated to mentalize. Jesus' equivalent motivation sprang from his prayer life. Third is the acquisition of the skills to accurately read others. Jesus was so good at this that it was deemed supernatural. *I think that he was skilled in reading the body language and voice inflections of those around him, integrated his observations with praying without ceasing, and hence came to very accurate conclusions.* The fourth part of mentalizing concerns its being defined and explored as a therapeutic tool. In other words, Jesus had compassion. This is exactly how he deals with our alienation from God, to bring us back and to remove some of the obstacles to mentalizing, the primary one being lack of forgiveness. We are capable of refining all of the above skills.

FAILURES OF AND OBSTACLES TO MENTALIZATION

When we fail to pay attention, when we are absorbed in our own opinions, ideologies, presumptions, or lusts, we are not mentalizing.

It takes effort to look at oneself from the outside and to look at another person from the inside. The default mode of our thinking is egocentrism. In numerous ways and from different angles, Jesus encouraged us to transcend egocentrism, and his goal was to get us to mentalize as he did. He vigorously confronted the various faces of egocentrism that he encountered in the Pharisees and the disciples, and his acts of healing, feeding, and humble service were all based on compassion.

The broadest failure to mentalize is to not pay attention, to persist in some absorption that excludes another. Active avoidance of mentalization can take place: Those who preceded the Good Samaritan studiously avoided getting involved. More severe is psychological unavailability; child neglect originates here. Also overtly damaging is child physical or sexual abuse; a raging or lustful adult devalues the child and hence can destroy his or her mentalizing ability, ensuring transgenerational transmission of inadequate mentalization. Allen et al. state,

> Yet not only neglect but also abuse and traumatizing actions . . .
> entailed mentalizing failure. . . . Abusive behavior represents
> egocentrism at the extreme; in the face of passionate rage
> or lust, the abusive parent is oblivious to the child's mental
> states or emotional needs. . . .
> . . . Ironically, the most traumatizing impact of the
> mentalizing failures evident in attachment trauma might
> be their undermining of the development of mentalizing
> capacities in the child, one outcome of which is the
> intergenerational perpetuation of trauma.[32]

Many Christians, particularly those in the United States, have a particularly strong ideological, religious, or political bent; if allowed to become fixed, rigid, and to dominate one's thinking, these biases may result in a judgmental and antimentalizing stance. In other words, being opinionated neutralizes mentalization. My hope is that Christians of all persuasions will become more sensitive, patient, tolerant, and willing to listen to the positions and viewpoints of others. And I hope that we are forgiving each other more.

FORGIVENESS

Resentment is a prime obstacle to mentalizing.
Forgiveness is the antidote.

Forgiveness was central to Jesus' teaching and actions; it entails and reinforces a profound mentalizing stance. The word *forgiveness* occurs 61 times in the Revised Standard Version of the Bible, according to my pocket concordance. Resentment is very corrosive and severely narrows attention and scope. Attachment trauma can result in the wish to get even, an extremely antimentalizing posture that can be acted out through drug or alcohol use or in violence toward the self or other. The wish can be quite buried and out of the conscious awareness of the one who holds it. I use myself as an example:

James Masterson was a psychoanalyst who wrote and lectured widely.[33] He spoke specifically about how necessary it was for recovery from personality disorders to "master the Talionic Impulse." In his work with persons whose personalities were distorted by histories of attachment trauma, he would often say at critical moments in the therapy, "Do you want to get well, or get even?" I subsequently found in my work that many substance users were using "at" someone, drinking or using to tell that person or the world to go to hell. I wasn't expecting to find such impulses in myself, but a vivid and bizarre dream changed my mind. I dreamed that a disembodied Cuisinart blade, spinning at high speed and suspended like a helicopter in midair, moved toward me, and finally moved around my leg. It spoke that it would inflict little nicks on me until I bled to death.

Dreams too can be mentalized, and here I offer a simple method to quickly capture a dream's message. Believe it or not, I learned this in the eighth grade, where I had a teacher who taught and drilled us to write little one-line précis' of stories, articles, and paragraphs. Can you write such a sentence for the above dream? The good thing about the method

is that it doesn't have to be right but, rather, something that can be modified until it emotionally fits. In other words, the method is an exercise
in active mentalization. My précis might say, "I have something inside
me that outside my volition repeatedly nicks me, to do me harm." One
might quickly respond, "Well, that sounds like a self-critical attitude!"
I was to realize subsequently just how self-critical and resentful I was;
I was turning my anger against myself. It took time and assistance to
work through my resentments and forgive.

As we repeat the phrase in the Lord's Prayer, "as we forgive those
who trespass against us," we need to ask in addition that we become
aware of those deeply held resentments that may date back a lifetime.
Then we can ask that we be enabled to want to forgive. Of course, this
applies to us as trespassers, as well.

CHRISTIANITY AND THE FUTURE

I describe four places in the life of Christianity where
mentalization is or can be crucial. There are many more.

How can we further employ the art of mentalization, which was after
all the communication stance of choice of Jesus? It is my opinion that
Christianity's 2,000-year history of growing into Jesus' mentalizing stance
has benefited us immensely, and Christians in many different settings
have learned this compassionate, therapeutic, and deeply respectful
style. As we learn the language of communion and put aside opinionated, egocentric, judgmental, dismissing, ideological, and punitive
communication styles that are antimentalizing, we come to love each
other and our neighbors in unsurpassed ways. I believe that in our future
we will discover more and more how to communicate accurately and
therapeutically. I quickly see four specific applications of mentalization.
There are undoubtedly many more.

The first is pastoral counseling, an art that goes back to the beginnings of Christianity. Salvation is at heart the healing of our minds and souls; I can attest personally with gratitude the path of inquiry and pursuit of mental health on which the pastoral counselor Fr. Wilson set me. Although he himself proved to suffer from his own demons, he nonetheless gave to me passions that I long to pass on to others. In addition to pastors and priests who counsel effectively, there are an array of Christians in secular venues practicing medicine, psychiatry, psychology, nursing, social work, and marriage and family therapy. I pray that we all continue to grow in the art and specifically perfect the discipline of mentalization, as Jesus did.

The second is of more recent origin. Marriage Encounter originated in the Roman Catholic Church in Spain in 1952 and has spread worldwide to many denominations and other religions. In a weekend group retreat setting, participant couples are taught to "dialogue" by writing letters expressing feelings and then plumbing these feelings. The method is intensely mentalistic and can demand considerable effort and patience to get the communication right. The milieu greatly magnifies any attachment issues participant couples may have. In other words, the question "Does he or she really care?" looms large. The good news is that the vast majority of those who elect to go to Marriage Encounter do indeed care, but many may be very unskilled at saying so, causing the early going to be quite rocky. Counselors are on hand if needed. The result, learning to dialogue, is typical of accurate mentalization; there is a breakthrough to communication, yielding a marvelous sense of relief and bonding. The skill of dialogue is then practiced and modeled at follow-up sessions. The practice can become part of a mentalizing stance, providing resilience to the marriage. You can access the websites of the Marriage Encounters of various congregations by googling "Marriage Encounter."

The third is an altogether new application of mentalization. Michael Rhodes is a Hollywood film director and producer who has created a character education program for school children called Film Clips.[34] Brief segments of currently popular motion pictures are selected that portray any of a number of moral or personal dilemmas familiar to children. A group or class of children are shown the clips and are then invited to share their thoughts, feelings, and reactions. The response and participation of the children are electric, and they volunteer easily and speak profoundly about an array of issues. In other words, Film Clips enables children to mentalize beautifully, and the children love it and learn.

Minding the Baby (MTB)[35] is a fourth application of mentalization that churches might consider adopting or emulating. It is a home-visiting program directed at inner-city young mothers who are isolated and likely traumatized themselves. In the MTB program, a visiting team provides services for physical and mental health, parenting, and child development. Teaching and modeling mentalization skills are emphasized. Early research is showing several key improvements in parenting and family skills, with significant impact on the health, welfare, and quality of life of the mother-infant dyads. *Given that the quality of this dyad lays the foundations for the mental and interpersonal health of the next generation, it seems to me that churches could play a major role by focusing their resources on programs like MTB.*

Opportunities for pastors, physicians, other health workers, and family friends to mentalize with young parents abound; one need not wait to set up a program. For example, I have been caring for a 23-year-old woman, a heroin addict. She was clean and sober for a year when she became pregnant. She and her boyfriend moved in with her mother, where she delivered. She came in to see me complaining of anxiety, panic attacks, and cravings for heroin. Each time she brought her infant son, Ben, with her. I observed her with Ben; she looked stressed and at times desperate. Ben looked agitated, cried, and his mother responded by stuffing a bottle in his mouth or standing and jostling him up and down. He would briefly settle down but then start to cry again. My patient had no idea why she was so anxious. I pointed out my observations and ventured that she was bewildered by Ben's irritability and reacted with anxiety, which made Ben anxious, a vicious circle. She started to cry; my interpretations were correct. I coached her on calmly trying to read her son. At one point, she frankly looked Ben in the eye, smiled, and said, "Ben, I don't know how to read you." Their eyes met, and Ben relaxed. Both felt the moment of communion. We talked of how this was a zone that the two could attain with some practice.

I asked her if her mother might be able to help her mentalize with her son. Not surprisingly, she replied that her mother was consistently highly critical of her. Mother, it appeared, was part of the problem. By the time the session ended, my patient and I had found a zone of our own. I suggested she ask some of the older women in her church about grasping the mind of infants. She returned a month later and wheeled Ben and his stroller into my office; she looked positively joyous. I asked if she was now more tuned into Ben. She grinned broadly as she gave a resounding yes! She had indeed asked for assistance, and her mother and other women had warmed to the task of explaining their experiences with their babies. She exclaimed that things were so much better with Ben. "He is such a good baby!" she exclaimed. The two had found the zone.

At our most recent follow-up, she appeared calm, confident, and reassured. She reported that she was tapering down on a medication that was helping her stay away from heroin. I asked for her thinking on the work we had done together, and she replied quickly and forcefully, "I realized it wasn't about me. It was about him! He is just a baby, and he has needed me to make sense of what he is feeling and thinking."

SUMMARY

Life, animated and propelled forward by the breath of Life and the Word of the Lord, has reached its evolutionary goal in *Homo Sapiens*. The intelligence and community aspects of Life come together in humankind to create the focus of our attachments to one another. The glue, the chemistry of the bonds of attachments, is the communicative stance called mentalization. Mother and infant give birth to a secure attachment as the mother values the mind of her baby and the baby discovers his or her mind in response to the mother's accurate ministrations. In exactly the same manner, Jesus calls our spiritual minds into being through his profound mentalization skills. As we come to abide in him, and he in us, we learn his compassion and skills and set aside egocentrism, resentment, and isolation. *Our evolutionary self- and internecine conflicts and their amplifications fade as we appreciate how much he values us.* The end result of effective mentalization is communion with one another and with God. This is salvation.

ENDNOTES

INTRODUCTION

1 Penenberg AL. "Amazon Taps Its Inner Apple," *Fast Company*, July/August 2009.

2 Fowler TB and Kuebler D. *The Evolution Controversy: A Survey of Competing Theories* (Grand Rapids, MI: Baker Academic, 2007).

3 President Obama has appointed Francis Collins, the former director of the Human Genome Project, to be director of the National Institutes of Health. Dr. Collins's book *The Language of God* (New York: Free Press, 2006) is an excellent exploration of evidence for belief.

4 Darrel Falk is a geneticist and professor of biology at Point Loma Nazarene University. His friendship, guidance, and book *Coming to Peace with Science: Bridging the Worlds between Faith and Biology* (Madison, WI: InterVarsity Press, 2004) have been great sources of inspiration for this present work.

5 Miller KR. *Only a Theory: Evolution and the Battle for America's Soul* (New York: Viking Press, 2008).

6 Pallen MJ and Gophna U. "Bacterial Flagella and Type III Secretion: Case Studies in the Evolution of Complexity," *Genome Dyn* 3 (2007):30–47.

7 In the lawsuit *Kitzmiller v. Dover*, parents of children in the Dover Pennsylvania School District filed suit disputing the teaching of ID in classrooms.

8 Miller, *Only a Theory*, p. 211.

9 Image at http://commons.wikimedia.org/wiki/File:Flagellum_base_diagram_en.svg.

10 Kandel E. *In Search of Memory: The Emergence of a New Science of Mind* (New York: WW Norton, 2006).

11 Coyne JA. *Why Evolution Is True* (New York: Penguin Books Worldwide, 2009).

12 Image at http://commons.wikimedia.org/wiki/File:Ctenomorpha_chronus.jpg.

13 Carroll SB. *The Making of the Fittest: DNA and the Ultimate Forensic Record of Evolution* (New York: WW Norton, 2006).

14 Colling RG. *Random Designer: Created from Chaos to Connect with the Creator* (Bourbonnais, IL: Browning Press, 2004).

15 I reify "Life" because it is in essence a unitary whole. All Life is intimately interconnected and has in common a genetic and molecular makeup. All Life shares the Breath of Life provided by God. More on this later in the chapter.

16 Colling, *Random Designer*, p. 1.

17 Bloom JD and Arnold FH. "In the Light of Directed Evolution: Pathways of Adaptive Protein Evolution." *PNAS* 106 (June 16, 2009):9995–10000.

18 Dougherty MJ and Arnold FH. "Directed Evolution: New Parts and Optimized Function," *Curr Opin Biotechnol* 20, no. 4 (Aug. 2009):486–91.

19 Fowler and Kuebler, *The Evolution Controversy*, pp. 227–326.

20 Franklin Harold is emeritus professor of biochemistry and molecular biology at Colorado State University and author of *The Way of the Cell: Molecules, Organisms, and the Order of Life* (London: Oxford University Press, 2001).

21 Eva Jablonka is professor at the Cohn Institute for the History and Philosophy of Science and Ideas at Tel Aviv University. She is a microbiologist. Marion Lamb was senior lecturer at Birkbeck College, University of London, before her retirement. They have authored *Evolution in Four Dimensions: Genetic, Epigenetic, Behavioral, and Symbolic Variation in the History of Life* (Cambridge, MA: MIT Press, 2005).

22 Lynn Caporale is a molecular biologist who has taught and done research at several American universities. Currently, she is an independent consultant in drug discovery and functional genomics. The book reviewed here is *Darwin in the Genome: Molecular Strategies in Biological Evolution* (New York: McGraw-Hill, 2003).

23 Lynn Margulis is a biologist and professor in the Department of Geosciences at the University of Massachusetts. Dorion Sagan is a science writer who frequently coauthors with his mother, Dr. Margulis.

24 Anthony Trewavas is a plant biologist and professor at the University of Edinburgh. He is pre-eminent in his field, having published over 220 papers and two books on plant-cell signal transduction and plant behavior.

25 Another way of saying this is that Life is *plastic;* its active plasticity is
 on a timescale of hundreds of thousands to millions of years.
26 Caporale, *Darwin in the Genome,* pp. 4–5.
27 Reader beware, however. This is a god-of-the-gaps declaration! It can
 be proved false if science can create Life in the laboratory. See the
 discussion of origin-of-life experiments and their implications at
 the end of Chapter 1.
28 Sin, too, is capitalized; it inflicts all of Life.

CHAPTER ONE

1 Schrödinger E. *What Is Life? The Physical Aspect of the Living Cell; with
 "Mind and Matter," and "Autobiographical Sketches"* (Cambridge,
 UK: Cambridge University Press, 1967).
2 Image at http://commons.wikimedia.org/wiki/File:Erwin_
 Schrödinger.jpg.
3 Wikipedia. *What Is Life?* Retrieved January 2009, from http://
 en.wikipedia.org/wiki/What_Is_Life%3F.
4 Harold F. *The Way of the Cell: Molecules, Organisms and the Order
 of Life* (New York: Oxford Univ. Press, 2001).
5 Margulis L and Sagan M. *What Is Life?* (Berkeley and Los Angeles:
 Univ. of Calif. Press, 1995).
6 Image at http://commons.wikimedia.org/wiki/File:Proterozoic_
 Stromatolites.jpg.
7 Palmer D. *Prehistoric Past Revealed: The Four Billion Year History of
 Life on Earth* (Berkeley and Los Angeles: University of California
 Press, 2003).
8 Palmer, *Prehistoric Past Revealed,* p. 135.
9 Shen B et al. "The Avalon Explosion: Evolution of Ediacara Morphospace,"
 Science 319, no. 5859 (Jan. 4 2008): pp. 81–84.
10 Palmer, *Prehistoric Past Revealed,* pp. 136–37.
11 Valentine et al. "Fossils, Molecules and Embryos: New Perspectives
 on the Cambrian Explosion," *Development* 126 (1999):851–59.
12 Koonin EV. "The Biological Big Bang Model for the Major Transitions in
 Evolution," *Biol Direct* 20, no. 1 (2007):21.
13 Maugh T II. "Fossils Shed Light on Human Lineage," *Los Angeles Times*
 (Aug. 9, 2007).

14 Gibbons A. "Breakthrough of the Year: *Ardipithecus Ramidus,*" *Science* 326 (Dec. 18, 2009):1598.

15 Image at http://commons.wikimedia.org/wiki/File:Humanevolution chart. png. From Reed DL et al. "Genetic Analysis of Lice Suggests Direct Contact between Modern and Archaic Humans," *PLoS Biol* 2, no. 11 (Oct 5, 2004).

16 Patton P. "One World, Many Minds," *Sci Am Mind* (Dec. 2008).

17 Morris SC. *Life's Solution: Inevitable Humans in a Lonely Universe* (Cambridge, UK: Cambridge Univ. Press, 2003).

18 Harold, *The Way of the Cell*, p. 18.

19 Harold, *The Way of the Cell*, pp. 87–90.

20 Harold, *The Way of the Cell*, pp. 96–97.

22 Is all adaptation learning, or is it the result of blind random processes? Is Life an agent or merely clay? Are blind random processes in reality the trial-and-error strategy of agentive Life?

23 Margulis and Sagan, *What Is Life?* pp. 89–90.

21 Image at http://commons.wikimedia.org/wiki/File:E-coli-in-color.jpg.

24 Perkins S. "Microbes Thrive in Seafloor Rock," *Science News* (June 21, 2008) p. 7; Santelli CM et al. "Abundance and Diversity of Microbial Life in Ocean Crust," *Nature* 453, no. 7195 (May 29, 2008):653–56.

25 Roussel EG et al. "Extending the Sub-Sea-Floor Biosphere," *Science* 320, no. 5870 (May 23, 2008):1046.

26 Quoted in Angier N. "Pursuing Synthetic Life, Dazzled by Reality." *New York Times,* Feb. 5, 2008.

27 Harold, *The Way of the Cell*, pp. 121–22.

28 Image at http://commons.wikimedia.org/wiki/File:Cell_structure.png

29 Harold, *The Way of the Cell*, chap. 8.

30 Image at http://commons.wikimedia.org/wiki/File:Protist_collage.jpg

31 Harold, *The Way of the Cell*, p. 24.

32 Davidov Y and Jurkevitch E. "Predation between Prokaryotes and the Origin of Eukaryotes," *Bioessays* 31, no. 7 (July 2009):748–57; Cavalier-Smith T. "Predation and Eukaryote Cell Origins: A Coevolutionary Perspective," *Int J Biochem Cell Biol* 41, no. 2 (Feb. 2009):307–22; Lake JA. "Evidence for an Early Prokaryotic Endosymbiosis," *Nature* 460, no. 7258 (Aug. 20, 2009):967–71.

33 Image at http://commons.wikimedia.org/w/index.php?title=Special%3A Search&search=Antisense+DNA+oligonucleotide.

34 Clark D and Russell L. *Molecular Biology Made Simple and Fun* (St. Louis, MO: Cache River Press, 2005).

35 Caporale L. *Darwin in the Genome* (New York: McGraw-Hill, 2003), p. 127.

36 Image at http://commons.wikimedia.org/wiki/File:DNA-structure-and-bases.png.

37 Many kinds of RNA carry out a variety of cell and nucleus functions. The RNA that transcribes from DNA to create amino acids for the fabrication of proteins is called messenger RNA (mRNA).

38 Image at http://commons.wikimedia.org/wiki/File:Codontable1.PNG.

39 Freeland SJ and Hurst LD. "The Genetic Code Is One in a Million," *J Mol Evol* 47, no. 3 (Sept. 1998):238–48.

40 Freeland SJ, Knight RD, and Landweber LF. "Measuring Adaptation within the Genetic Code," *Trends in Biochemical Science* 25, no. 2 (Feb. 2000):44–45.

41 Morris, *Life's Solution*, p. 18.

42 Freeland SJ et al. "Early Fixation of an Optimal Genetic Code," *Mol. Biol. Evol* 17, no. 4 (April 2000):511–18.

43 Caporale, *Darwin in the Genome*, pp. 22, 17. See 19–25.

44 Saey T. "Epigenetics: From Islands to the Shores: Tissue-Specific DNA Tagging Found in Unexpected Regions," *Science News*, Feb. 14, 2009.

45 Dawkins R. *The Extended Phenotype* (New York: Oxford Univ. Press, 1982), pp. 156, 158.

46 Jablonka E and Lamb M. *Evolution in Four Dimensions: Genetic, Epigenetic, Behavioral, and Symbolic Variation in the History of Life* (Cambridge, MA: MIT Press, 2005), p. 86; see pp. 85–88.

47 Image at http://commons.wikimedia.org/wiki/File:Protein-structure.png.

48 Image at http://commons.wikimedia.org/wiki/File:Synapse_diag1.png.

49 Clark and Russell, *Molecular Biology Made Simple and Fun*, p. 28. Also see p. 35.

50 Harold, *The Way of the Cell*, p. 45.

52 Robinson R. "Ciliate Genome Sequence Reveals Unique Features of a Model Eukaryote," *PLoS Biology* 4, no. 9 (2006), e304. Article available at http://dx.doi.org/10.1371/journal.pbio.0040304. Image at http://commons.wikimedia.org/wiki/File:Tetrahymena_thermophila.png.

51 Harold, *The Way of the Cell*, pp. 142–57.

53 Harold, *The Way of the Cell*, pp. 144–45.

54 Harold, *The Way of the Cell*, p. 146.

55 Lynch M. "The Frailty of Adaptive Hypotheses for the Origins of Organismal Complexity," *PNAS* 104 (May 15, 2007): 8597–8604.

56 Harold, *The Way of the Cell*, pp. 51–54.

57 Barbara McClintock was a gifted researcher. A cytogenetist, she led in understanding chromosomes, gene recombination, transposition, regulation, and meiosis. Her work was long resisted, but she finally was recognized with a Nobel Prize in 1982.

58 Jablonka and Lamb, *Evolution in Four Dimensions*, p. 88.

59 Jablonka and Lamb, *Evolution in Four Dimensions*, pp. 88–89.

60 Jablonka and Lamb, *Evolution in Four Dimensions*, p. 98.

61 Wright B. "A Biochemical Mechanism for Nonrandom Mutations and Evolution," *J. Bacteriology* 182, no. 11 (June 2000):2993–3001.

62 Jablonka and Lamb, *Evolution in Four Dimensions*, p. 98.

63 Freeland and Hurst, "The Genetic Code Is One in a Million"; Freeland et al. "Measuring Adaptation within the Genetic Code"; Freeland et al. "Early Fixation of an Optimal Genetic Code,"

64 Psalm 139:14.

65 Homo = alike. Chirality = the handedness of an asymmetrical molecule. Life uses only left-handed amino acids and only right-handed sugars. How and why in the world did Life come up with these choices? Creationists who argue that homochirality points to a creator are posing a god-of-the-gaps argument.

66 Jack W. Szostak is professor of molecular biology at the Department of Molecular Biology and Center for Computational and Integrative Biology, Massachusetts General Hospital, Boston. His Nobel Prize was for his work on the protective function of telomeres, the tips of genes.

67 Schrum JP, Zhu TF, Szostak JW. "The Origins of Cellular Life," *Cold Spring Harb Perspect Biol* (May 19, 2010): doi: 10.1101/cshperspect.a002212.

CHAPTER TWO

1 Image at http://commons.wikimedia.org/wiki/File:Ammonia_tepida.jpg.

2 Sam Bowser's website is at www.bowserlab.org/foraminifera/forampage2.htm/.

3 *Encounters at the End of the World*. A Werner Herzog Film. Discovery Films, Image Entertainment, Los Angeles, CA.

4 Edward Heron-Allen's (1861–1943) work on foraminifera at Sussex led to his election as a Fellow of the Royal Society.

5 Shapiro JA. "Bacteria Are Small But Not Stupid: Cognition, Natural Genetic Engineering and Socio-Bacteriology," *Stud Hist Philos Biol Biomed Sci* 38, no. 4 (Dec. 2007): 807–19. Epub 2007 Nov 19.

6 Goldsmith E. "Intelligence Is Universal in Life," *Riv Biol* 93, no. 3 (Sept.–Dec. 2000):399–411.

7 Dere E et al., "The Case for Episodic Memory in Animals," *Neurosci Biobehav Rev* 30, no. 8(2006):1206–24. Epub 2006 Oct 31.

8 Dere et al., "The Case for Episodic Memory in Animals," p. 1206.

9 Bailey CH and Kandel ER. "Synaptic Remodeling, Synaptic Growth and the Storage of Long-Term Memory in Aplysia," *Prog Brain Res* 169 (2008):179–98. Quotation from p. 179.

10 Image at http://commons.wikimedia.org/wiki/File:Aplysia_californica.jpg.

11 Bailey and Kandel, "Synaptic Remodeling, Synaptic Growth and the Storage of Long-Term Memory in Aplysia," p. 179.

12 Glanzman DL. "New Tricks for an Old Slug: The Critical Role of Postsynaptic Mechanisms in Learning and Memory in *Aplysia*," *Prog Brain Res* 169 (2008):277–92.

13 Tero A et al. "Rules for Biologically Inspired Adaptive Network Design," *Science* 327, no. 5964 (Jan. 22, 2010):439–42; Sanders L. "Slime Mold as Master Engineer," *Science News*, Feb. 13, 2010.

14 Image from Tero et al. "Rules for Biologically Inspired Adaptive Network Design."

15 Reprinted from Current Biology, vol. 17, no. 18, Alexandros Papachristoforou et al., "Smothered to Death: Hornets Asphyxiated by Honeybees," pages R795–R796. Copyright September 18, 2007, with permission from Elsevier.

16 Reprinted from *Animal Behaviour*, vol. 73, no. 6, Scott Powell and Nigel R. Franks, "How a Few Help All: Living Pothole Plugs Speed Prey Delivery in the Army Ant Eciton Burchellii," pages 1067–76. Copyright June 2007, with permission from Elsevier.

17 Papachristoforou A et al. "Smothered to Death: Hornets Asphyxiated by Honeybees."

18 Milius S. "Pothole Pals: Ants Pave Roads for Fellow Raiders," *Science News*, June 2, 2007; See also Powell S and Franks NR. "How a Few Help All."

19 Prior H, Schwarz A, and Gunturkun O. "Mirror-Induced Behavior in the Magpie (Pica pica): Evidence of Self-Recognition," *PLoS Biol* 6, no. 8 (Aug. 19, 2008):e202.

20 Image from Bird CD and Emery NJ. "Rooks Use Stones to Raise the Water Level to Reach a Floating Worm," *Curr Biol* 19, no. 16 (Aug. 6, 2009):1410–14

21 Image at http://commons.wikimedia.org/wiki/File:Georgia-Aquarium-Cuttlefish-RZ.jpg.

22 Bird CD and Emery NJ. "Rooks Use Stones to Raise the Water Level to Reach a Floating Worm"; Bower B. "Crows Use Sticks, Stones to Show Skills at Manipulating Tools in Lab," *Science News*, Aug. 29, 2009.

23 Margulis L and Sagan D. *What Is Life?* (Berkeley and Los Angeles: Univ. of Calif. Press, 1995), p. 218.

24 Image at http://commons.wikimedia.org/wiki/File:Amoeba_(PSF).png.

25 Margulis and Sagan, *What Is Life?* Fig. 18 caption, p. 220.

26 Margulis and Sagan, *What Is Life?* pp. 93–96.

27 Margulis and Sagan, *What Is Life?* pp. 96, 97.

28 Harold, *The Way of the Cell*, pp. 65, 66.

29 Harold, *The Way of the Cell*, p. 82.

30 Image at www.sciencenewsforkids.org/articles/20080409/Note3.asp.

31 Sakurai M et al. "Vitrification Is Essential for Anhydrobiosis in an African Chiromomid, *Polypedilum vanderplanki*," *PNAS* 105 no. 13 (April 1, 2008): 5093–98; Castelvecccchi D. "Live Another Day: African Insect Survives Drought in Glassy State," *Science News*, March 29, 2008.

32 Iturriaga G, Suárez R, and Nova-Franco B. "Trehalose Metabolism: From Osmoprotection to Signaling," *Int J Mol Sci* 10 (2009):3793–3810.

33 Jablonka E and Lamb M. *Evolution in Four Dimensions: Genetic, Epigenetic, Behavioral, and Symbolic Variation in the History of Life* (Cambridge, MA: MIT Press, 2005), pp. 66–67.

34 Joint Genome Institute authored documents are sponsored by the U.S. Department of Energy under Contracts W-7405-Eng-48, DE-AC02-05 CH11231, and W-7405-ENG-36. Accordingly, the U.S. government retains a non-exclusive, royalty-free license to publish or reproduce these documents, or allow others to do so, for U.S. government purposes. All documents available from this server may be protected under the U.S. and Foreign Copyright Laws and permission to reproduce them may be required. The public may copy and use this information without charge, provided that this Notice and

any statement of authorship are reproduced on all copies. JGI is not responsible for the contents of any off-site pages referenced.

35 Putnam NH et al. "Sea Anemone Genome Reveals Ancestral Eumetazoan Gene Repertoire and Genomic Organization," *Science* 317, no. 5834 (July 6, 2007):86–94.

36 Sullivan JC, Reitzel AM, and Finnerty JC. "A High Percentage of Introns in Human Genes Were Present Early in Animal Evolution: Evidence from the Basal Metazoan *Nematostella vectensis*," *Genome Inform* 17 no. 1 (2006):219–29.

37 David Haig is an Australian evolutionary biologist and geneticist and professor at Harvard. He is interested in intragenomic conflict, genomic imprinting and parent–offspring conflict. See Wikipedia "David Haig (biologist)."

38 Jablonka and Lamb, *Evolution in Four Dimensions*, p. 276.

39 Jablonka and Lamb, *Evolution in Four Dimensions*, p. 135.

40 Caporale L. *Darwin in the Genome: Molecular Strategies in Biological Evolution* (New York: McGraw-Hill, 2003), pp. 191, 193.

41 Morris SC. *Life's Solution: Inevitable Humans in a Lonely Universe* (Cambridge, UK: Cambridge Univ. Press, 2003), p. 327.

42 Image at http://commons.wikimedia.org/wiki/File:Opabinia_smithsonian.JPG.

43 Image at http://commons.wikimedia.org/wiki/File:Evolution_eye.png.

44 The eye on the left is the human eye. It has a blind spot, whereas the octopus eye does not.

45 Morris, *Life's Solution*, p. xiii.

46 Denes AS et al. "Molecular Architecture of Annelid Nerve Cord Supports Common Origin of Nervous System Centralizationin Bilateria," *Cell* 129 (April 20, 2007):277.

47 Telford MJ. "A Single Origin of the Central Nervous System?" *Cell* 129, no. 2 (April 20, 2007):237–39.

48 Koch C and Greenfield S. "How Does Consciousness Happen?" *Scientific American*, Oct. 2007, p. 83.

49 Robinson D. *Consciousness and Mental Life* (New York: Columbia University Press, 2008).

50 Margulis and Sagan, *What Is Life?* p. 30.

51 Margulis and Sagan, *What Is Life?* p. 222.

52 Image is at http://commons.wikimedia.org/wiki/File:Caravaggio_-_I_bari.jpg.

CHAPTER THREE

1 Patton P. "One World, Many Minds," *Sci Am Mind*, Dec. 2008/Jan. 2009, pp. 72–77.
2 Eisenberg J. *A Collector's Guide to SeaShells of the World* (New York: McGraw-Hill, 1981).
3 Jablonka E and Lamb M. *Evolution in Four Dimensions: Genetic, Epigenetic, Behavioral, and Symbolic Variation in the History of Life* (Cambridge: MIT Press, 2005):311–13.
4 Caporale LH. *Darwin in the Genome: Molecular Strategies in Biological Evolution* (New York: McGraw-Hill, 2003), pp. 72–76.
5 Caporale, *Darwin in the Genome*, p. 78.
6 Image at http://commons.wikimedia.org/wiki/File:BartailedGodwit24.jpg.
7 Jablonka and Lamb, *Evolution in Four Dimensions*, p. 176.
8 Sanders L. "Nonstop Godwit Flights," *Sci News*, Nov. 22, 2008.
9 Siepka SM et al. "Genetics and Neurobiology of Circadian Clocks in Mammals," *Cold Spring Harb Symp Quant Biol* 72 (2007):251–59.
10 Zhu H et al. "Chasing Migration Genes: A Brain Expressed Sequence Tag Resource for Summer and Migratory Monarch Butterflies (Danaus plexippus)," *PLoS ONE* 3, no. 1 (Jan. 9, 2008):e1345.
11 Zhu H et al. "Defining Behavioral and Molecular Differences between Summer and Migratory Monarch Butterflies," *BMC Biol* 7 (March 31, 2009):14.
12 Sahagun L. "Crashing Grunion's Beach Party: Researchers Collect Eggs, Sperm in an Effort to Establish a Stable Captive Population," *Los Angeles Times*, April 15, 2008, p. B. 1; Wikipedia "Grunion."
13 The inverted and transposed vision film can be accessed at http://www.mindhacks.com/blog/2009/07/vision_shift_glasses.html. Toward the bottom of the page click on the archived film *Living in a Reversed World: Some Experiments on How We See the Directions of Things*.
14 Image at http://commons.wikimedia.org/wiki/File:Eric_Kandel_by_aquaris3.jpg.
15 Schwartz J and Begley S. *The Mind and the Brain* (New York: ReganBooks, 2002).
16 Caporale, *Darwin in the Genome*, pp. 4–5.
17 Caporale, *Darwin in the Genome*, pp. 31, 32.
18 Sompayrac L. *How the Immune System Works* (Malden, MA: Blackwell, 2003).
19 Caporale, *Darwin in the Genome*, p. 45.
20 Image at http://commons.wikimedia.org/wiki/File:Macrophage.jpg.

21 Phillips B and Shine R. "When Dinner Is Dangerous: Toxic Frogs Elicit Species-Specific Responses from a Generalist Snake Predator," *Am Nat* 170, no. 6 (Dec. 2007):936–42.

22 Richard G. Colling's website can be accessed at www.randomdesigner.com. Look for the link to *A Random Universe*.

23 Jablonka and Lamb, *Evolution in Four Dimensions*, p. 101.

24 Kirschner MW and Gerhart JC. *The Plausibility of Life* (New Haven, CT: Yale University Press, 2005), pp. 35, 36, 39.

25 Image at http://www.pseudogene.org/definition.html.

26 Gerstein M and Zheng D. "The Real Life of Pseudogenes," *Scientific American*, Aug. 2006, p. 55.

27 Harrison PM and Gerstein M. "Studying Genomes Through the Aeons: Protein Families, Pseudogenes and Proteomic Evolution," *J Mol Evol* 318, no. 5 (May 17, 2002):1155–74.

28 Harrison and Gerstein, "Studying Genomes Through the Aeons," p. 1155.

29 Sakai H et al. "Frequent Emergence and Functional Resurrection of Processed Pseudogenes in the Human and Mouse Genomes," *Gene* 389, no. 2 (March 15, 2007):196–203.

30 Sakai H et al. "Frequent Emergence and Functional Resurrection of Processed Pseudogenes in the Human and Mouse Genomes," p. 196.

31 Bamford DH et al. "What does Structure Tell Us about Virus Evolution?" *Curr Opin Struct Biol* 15, no. 6 (Dec. 2005):655–63.

32 Forterre P. "The Origin of Viruses and Their Possible Roles in Major Evolutionary Transitions," *Virus Res* 117, no. 1 (April 2006):5–16.

33 Image at http://commons.wikimedia.org/wiki/File:3D_Influenza_virus.png.

34 Sompayrac L. *How Pathogenic Viruses Work* (Sudbury, MA: Jones & Bartlett, 2002).

35 Image at http://commons.wikimedia.org/wiki/File:Virus_Replication.svg.

36 Sompayrac, *How Pathogenic Viruses Work*, p. 21.

37 From *Scheme of Influenza A Virus Replication*, "Influenza A Virus," Wikimedia Commons.

38 Ryan F. *Darwin's Blind Spot* (Boston, New York: Houghton Mifflin, 2002).

39 Jablonka and Lamb, *Evolution in Four Dimensions*, pp. 144–45.

40 Fowler TB and Kuebler D. *The Evolution Controversy: A Survey of Competing Theories* (Grand Rapids, MI: Baker Academic, 2007).

41 Evans PD et al., "Microcephalin, a Gene Regulating Brain Size, Continues to Evolve Adaptively in Humans," *Science* 309, no. 5741 (Sept. 9, 2005):1717.

42 Mekel-Bobrov N et al. "Ongoing Adaptive Evolution of ASPM, a Brain Size Determinant in *Homo sapiens*," *Science* 309, no. 5741 (Sept. 9, 2005):1720.

43 Jablonka and Lamb, *Evolution in Four Dimensions*, p. 155.

44 Caporale, *Darwin in the Genome*, p. 7.

45 Image at http://commons.wikimedia.org/wiki/File:Milton-Erickson.jpg.

CHAPTER FOUR

1 Miller KR. *Only a Theory: Evolution and the Battle for America's Soul* (New York: Viking Press, 2008).

2 Colling RG. *Random Designer: Created from Chaos to Connect with the Creator* (Bourbonnnais, IL: Browning Press, 2004).

3 The ultimate safecracker strategist is the human immunodeficiency virus (HIV), which changes 30,000 base pairs of its outer coat every replication, making it an overwhelmingly moving target for the human immune system.

4 Miller, *Only a Theory*, p. 124.

5 See Cunningham A. "Taken for a Spin: Scientists Look to Spiders for the Goods on Silk," *Science News*, April 14, 2007, p. 231.

6 Image at http://commons.wikimedia.org/wiki/File:Spider_web_with_dew_drops.jpg.

7 Jablonka E and Lamb M. *Evolution in Four Dimensions: Genetic, Epigenetic, Behavioral, and Symbolic Variation in the History of Life* (Cambridge, MA: MIT Press, 2005), p. 69.

8 Somatic cells are the cells of muscle, kidney, brain, and so on, while germline cells reside in the testes or ovaries, to create the next generation.

9 Shapiro, JA. "A 21st Century View of Evolution: Genome System Architecture, Repetitive DNA, and Natural Genetic Engineering," *Gene* 345 (2005):91–100.

10 Dawkins R. *The Extended Phenotype* (New York: Oxford Univ. Press, 1982), p. 158.

11 Harold F. *The Way of the Cell: Molecules, Organisms, and the Order of Life* (London: Oxford University Press, 2001), p. 61.

12 Telomeres are the tips of genes, protecting the genes much as a plastic tip protects the end of a shoelace.

13 Miller, *Only a Theory*, pp. 105–07.

14 Tattersall, I. "How Did Modern Human Cognition Evolve?" In H. Cohen and B. Stemmer (eds), *Consciousness and Cognition: Fragments of Mind and Brain* (San Diego, CA: Elsevier, 2007).

15 Image at http://commons.wikimedia.org/wiki/File:Chromosome2_merge.png.

16 Image at http://commons.wikimedia.org/wiki/File:Ihmisten_sukupuu3_vuosi2004.jpg.

17 Tattersall, "How Did Modern Human Cognition Evolve?" p. 2.

18 Image at http://commons.wikimedia.org/wiki/File:Neanderthal_child.jpg.

19 Tattersall, "How Did Modern Human Cognition Evolve?" pp. 5–6.

20 Shapiro, JA. "A 21st Century View of Evolution."

21 Colling RG, written personal communication, January 2010.

22 Image at www.ncbi.nlm.nih.gov/bookshelf/br.fcgi?book=mcb& part=A2187&rendertype=figure&id=A2189.

23 Shapiro, "A 21st Century View of Evolution," p. 93.

24 Image at http://commons.wikimedia.org/wiki/File:Cells_of_the_immune_system.jpg.

25 Sompayrac L. *How Pathogenic Viruses Work* (Sudbury, MA: Jones & Bartlett, 2002).

26 Caporale, *Darwin in the Genome* (New York: McGraw-Hill, 2003), pp. 4–5.

27 Prabhakar S et al. "Human-Specific Gain of Function in a Developmental Enhancer," *Science* 321, no. 5894 (Sept. 5, 2008):1346–50.

28 Image on p. 7 at www.ncbi.nlm.nih.gov/pmc/articles/PMC2658639/pdf/nihms-64250.pdf.

29 Prabhakar S et al. "Human-Specific Gain of Function in a Developmental Enhancer," p. 3. See article at www.ncbi.nlm.nih.gov/pmc/articles/PMC2658639/pdf/nihms-64250.pdf.

30 Image at http://commons.wikimedia.org/wiki/File:Choanoflagellata_Kent.JPG.

31 Maxmen A. "Animal Origins: Genome Reveals Early Complexity," *Science News*, Feb. 16, 2008, pp. 99–100.

32 Miller, *Only a Theory,* chap. 3.

33 Jablonka and Lamb, *Evolution in Four Dimensions*, p. 320.

34 Caporale, *Darwin in the Genome,* p. 124. Also see chaps. 12 and 13.

35 Quoted in Angier N. "Pursuing Synthetic Life, Dazzled by Reality," *New York Times*, Feb. 5, 2008.

36 Jablonka E and Lamb MJ. "Précis of Evolution in Four Dimensions," *Behav Brain Sci.* 30, no. 4 (Aug. 2007):353–65.

37 Image at http://commons.wikimedia.org/wiki/File:Chromatin_Structures.png.

38 Quina AS, Buschbeck M, and Di Croce L. "Chromatin Structure and Epigenetics," *Biochem Pharmacol* 72, no. 11 (Nov. 30, 2006):1563–69.

39 Jablonka and Lamb, "Précis of Evolution in Four Dimensions," p. 353.

40 Jablonka and Lamb, *Evolution in Four Dimensions,* pp. 144–45.

41 Jablonka and Lamb, *Evolution in Four Dimensions,* p. 348.

42 Jablonka and Lamb, *Evolution in Four Dimensions,* p. 105.

43 Jablonka and Lamb, *Evolution in Four Dimensions,* p. 355

44 Jablonka and Lamb, *Evolution in Four Dimensions,* pp. 355, 356, 361.

45 Rett syndrome is an X-linked neurodevelopmental disorder characterized by severe motor and cognitive impairment as well as autistic symptoms. It affects females primarily and is lethal in males.

46 Jiang Y et al. "Epigenetics in the Nervous System," *J Neurosci* 28, no. 46 (Nov. 12, 2008):11753–59.

47 Morris SC. *Life's Solution: Inevitable Humans in a Lonely Universe* UK: Cambridge Univ. Press, 2003).

48 Caporale, *Darwin in the Genome,* pp. 119, 120.

49 Caporale, *Darwin in the Genome,* p. 121.

50 Fernald RD. "Evolving Eyes," *Int J Dev Biol* 48 (2004):701–05.

51 Fernald, "Evolving Eyes," p. 701.

52 Gehring WJ. "New Perspectives on Eye Development and the Evolution of Eyes and Photoreceptors," *J Heredity* 96, no. 3 (2005):171–84.

53 Image at http://commons.wikimedia.org/wiki/File:Drosophilidae_compound_eye_.jpg.

54 Image at http://commons.wikimedia.org/wiki/File:Planariafull.jpg.

55 Margulis L and Sagan D. *What Is Life?* (Berkeley and Los Angeles: Univ. of Calif. Press, 1995), p. 231.

56 Margulis and Sagan, *What Is Life?* p. 231.

57 Margulis and Sagan, *What Is Life?* pp. 224, 226.

58 Margulis and Sagan, *What Is Life?* pp. 232, 233.

CHAPTER FIVE

1 Image at http://commons.wikimedia.org/wiki/File:Pelican_diving_4969.jpg.

2 Roughgarden J. *The Genial Gene* (Berkeley: Univ. of Calif. Press, 2009).

3 Roughgarden, *The Genial Gene,* pp. 135, 136.

4 John Nash, a brilliant economist, became psychotic and remained so for many years before recovering. The book and motion picture *A Beautiful Mind* portray his life.

5 Harold F. *The Way of the Cell: Molecules, Organisms, and the Order of Life* (London: Oxford University Press, 2001), p. 94.

6 Harold, *The Way of the Cell,* pp. 90–94.

7 Harold, *The Way of the Cell,* pp. 111–12.

8 Jablonka E and Lamb M. *Evolution in Four Dimensions: Genetic, Epigenetic, Behavioral, and Symbolic Variation in the History of Life* (Cambridge, MA: MIT Press, 2005), pp. 6, 7; also see chaps. 2 and 3.

9 Wagner GP, Pavlicev M, and Cheverud JM. "The Road to Modularity," *Nat Rev Genet* 8, no. 12 (Dec. 2007):921–31.

10 Wilkins AS. "Genetic Networks as Transmitting and Amplifying Devices for Natural Genetic Tinkering," *Novartis Found Symp* 284 2007):71–86.

11 Lieberman DE and Hall BK. "The Evolutionary Developmental Biology of Tinkering: An Introduction to the Challenge," *Novartis Found Symp* 284 (2007):1–19.

12 Feschotte C. "The Contribution of Transposable Elements to the Evolution of Regulatory Networks," *Nat Rev Genet* 9, no. 5 (May 2008): 397–405.

13 Shapiro, JA. "A 21st Century View of Evolution: Genome System Architecture, Repetitive DNA, and Natural Genetic Engineering," *Gene* 345 (2005):91–100.

14 Feschotte, "The Contribution of Transposable Elements to the Evolution of Regulatory Networks," p. 397.

15 Image at http://commons.wikimedia.org/wiki/File:Runzelmarken.jpg.

16 Margulis L et al. "Community Living Long Before Man: Fossil and Living Microbial Mats and Early Life," *Sci Total Environ* 56 (1986):379–97.

17 Margulis L and Sagan D. *What Is Life?* (Berkeley and Los Angeles: Univ. of Calif. Press, 1995), pp. 93–96.

18 Image at http://commons.wikimedia.org/wiki/File:Conjugation.svg.

19 Margulis and Sagan, *What Is Life?* pp. 96, 97.

20 Bassler BL and Losick R. "Bacterially Speaking," *Cell* 125 (April 21, 2006):237–46.

21 Nadell CD et al. "The Evolution of Quorum Sensing in Bacterial Biofilms," *PLoS Biol* 6, no. 1 (January 2008):e14.

22 Image at http://commons.wikimedia.org/wiki/File:Biofilm.jpg.

23 Dietrich LEP et al. "Redox-Active Antibiotics Control Gene Expression and Community Behavior in Divergent Bacteria," Science 321, no. 5893 (Aug. 29, 2008):1203–06.

24 Castelvecchi D. "Biowarfare: Engineered Virus Can Invade Bacterial Film," *Science News,* June 20, 2007, p. 404.

25 Saey TH. "Bacteria Make Molecular Snorkels for Surviving in Crowded Spaces," *Science News,* January 17, 2009, p. 8.

26 Chivian D et al. "Environmental Genomics Reveals a Single Species
    Ecosystem Deep within Earth," *Science* 322, no. 5899 (Oct. 10,
    2008):275–78; also see Saey TH. "Gold Mine Houses Community
    of One," *Science News*, November 8, 2008, p. 20.
27 "The Origins of Immunity?" *Science News*, August 25, 2007.
28 Image at http://commons.wikimedia.org/wiki/File:PloverCrocodile
    Symbiosis.jpg.
29 Margulis and Sagan, *What Is Life?*
30 Roughgarden, *The Genial Gene*, p. 153.
31 Martinez-Romero E. "Coevolution in Rhizobium-Legume Symbiosis?"
    DNA Cell Biol 28, no. 8 (Aug. 2009):361–70.
32 Margulis and Sagan, *What Is Life?* p. 121.
33 Image at http://commons.wikimedia.org/wiki/File:Animal_mitochondrion_
    diagram_en.svg.
34 Roughgarden J. *Evolution and Christian Faith* (Washington, DC: Island
    Press, 2006), p. 78.
35 Roughgarden, *Evolution and Christian Faith*, p. 77.
36 Margulis and Sagan, *What Is Life?* pp. 126–28.
37 Image at http://commons.wikimedia.org/wiki/File:Stylophora_
    pistillata.jpg.
38 Margulis L. "The Conscious Cell," *Ann NY Acad Sci* 929 (April 2001):55–70.
39 Image at http://commons.wikimedia.org/wiki/File:Flagella.png.
40 Image at http://commons.wikimedia.org/wiki/File:Complete_neuron
    _cell_diagram_en.svg.
41 Azevedo FA et al. "Equal Numbers of Neuronal and Nonneronal Cells Make
    the Human Brain an Isometrically Scaled-Up Primate Brain," *J Comp
    Neurology* 513, no. 5 (April 2009):532–37.
42 Koch C and Greenfield S. "How Does Consciousness Happen?" *Scientific
    American*, October 2007, pp. 76–83.
43 Koch and Greenfield, "How Does Consciousness Happen?" p. 80.
44 Koch and Greenfield, "How Does Consciousness Happen?" p. 81.
45 Ryan F. *Darwin's Blind Spot* (Boston, New York: Houghton Mifflin, 2002).
46 Gage F. "Neuronal Plasticity and Neuronal Diversity." Plenary address at the
    World Congress of Psychiatric Genetics, San Diego, November 2009.
47 Roughgarden, *Evolution and Christian Faith*, p. 75.
48 Image at http://commons.wikimedia.org/wiki/File:Portuguese_Man-O-
    War_%28Physalia_physalis%29.jpg

49 Image at http://commons.wikimedia.org/wiki/File:Leaf_cutter_ants_arp.jpg.

50 Roces F. "Individual Complexity and Self-Organization in Foraging by Leaf-Cutting Ants," *Biol Bull* 202, no. 3 (June 2002):306–13.

51 Anthony Trewavas is a professor at the University of Edinburgh. He has special interests in plant-cell signal transduction and plant behavior. He has published over 220 papers and two books. He is a fellow in a number of professional societies.

52 Trewavas A. "Aspects of Plant Intelligence." In S. C. Morris (ed), *The Deep Structure of Biology: Is Convergence Sufficiently Ubiquitous to Give a Directional Signal?* (West Conshohocken, PA: Templeton, Press 2008).

53 Trewavas, "Aspects of Plant Intelligence," p. 70.

54 Trewavas, "Aspects of Plant Intelligence," p. 71.

55 Trewavas, "Aspects of Plant Intelligence," p. 72.

56 Trewavas, "Aspects of Plant Intelligence," p. 73.

57 Trewavas, "Aspects of Plant Intelligence," p. 79.

58 Trewavas, "Aspects of Plant Intelligence," pp. 80, 81.

59 Trewavas, "Aspects of Plant Intelligence," p. 82.

60 Trewavas, "Aspects of Plant Intelligence," p. 83.

61 Trewavas, "Aspects of Plant Intelligence," p. 93.

62 Trewavas, "Aspects of Plant Intelligence," pp. 89–90.

63 Trewavas, "Aspects of Plant Intelligence," p. 95.

64 Trewavas, "Aspects of Plant Intelligence," pp. 97–98.

65 Trewavas, "Aspects of Plant Intelligence," pp. 98, 102.

66 Trewavas, "Aspects of Plant Intelligence," p. 102.

CHAPTER SIX

1 Persico, J. *Eleventh Month, Eleventh Day, Eleventh Hour: Armistice Day, 1918,* (New York: Random House, 2005), p. 392.

2 Image at http://commons.wikimedia.org/wiki/File:Bartolomeo_Manfredi_-_Cain_Kills_Abel,_c._1600,_Kunsthistorisches_Museum_(Vienna).jpg.

3 Genesis 3:7.

4 Genesis 4: 2-16.

5 Menninger, K. *Man against Himself* (San Diego, CA: Harcourt Brace Jovanovich, 1985).

6 Mark Kurlansky is a widely traveled and versatile author, journalist, and playwright.

7   E. O. Wilson is a renowned biologist, naturalist, conservationist, author, and emeritus professor at Harvard.

8   Milius S. "Slave Ants Rebel," *Science News*, Sept. 13, 2008, p. 6.

9   Clark D and Russell L. *Molecular Biology Made Simple and Fun* (St. Louis, MO: Cache River Press, 2005), p. 10.

10   Burt A and Trivers R. *Genes in Conflict* (Cambridge, MA: Harvard University Press, 2006), pp. 1, 2, 3.

11   Burt and Trivers, *Genes in Conflict*, p. 1.

12   Burt and Trivers, *Genes in Conflict*, p. 1.

13   Burt and Trivers, *Genes in Conflict*, p. 2.

14   Burt and Trivers, *Genes in Conflict*, p. 3.

15   Burt and Trivers, *Genes in Conflict*, p. 4.

16   Burt and Trivers, *Genes in Conflict*, p. 4.

17   Burt and Trivers, *Genes in Conflict*, p. 7.

18   Burt and Trivers, *Genes in Conflict*, pp. 448, 449.

19   Burt and Trivers, *Genes in Conflict*, p. 448.

20   Burt and Trivers, *Genes in Conflict*, p. 47.

21   An Australian Evolutionary Biologist, David Haig is famous for his work in genomic conflict and imprinting.

22   Jablonka E and Lamb M. *Evolution in Four Dimensions: Genetic, Epigenetic, Behavioral, and Symbolic Variation in the History of Life* (Cambridge, MA: MIT Press, 2005), pp. 257, 278–89.

23   Burt and Trivers, *Genes in Conflict*, p. 125.

24   Burt and Trivers, *Genes in Conflict*, p. 9.

25   Van Schaik CP and Kappeler PM. "Infanticide Risk and the Evolution of Male-Female Association in Primates," *Proc R Soc Lond B* 264 1997):1687–94.

26   Van Schaik and Kappeler, "Infanticide Risk and the Evolution of Male-Female Association in Primates," p. 1688.

27   Van Schaik and Kappeler, "Infanticide Risk and the Evolution of Male-Female Association in Primates," p. 1691.

28   Van Schaik and Kappeler, "Infanticide Risk and the Evolution of Male-Female Association in Primates," p. 1688.

29   Collins F. *The Language of God* (New York: Free Press, 2006).

30   Jablonka and Lamb, *Evolution in Four Dimensions*, p. 88.

31   Jablonka and Lamb, *Evolution in Four Dimensions*, p. 85.

32   Burt and Trivers, *Genes in Conflict*, pp. 228, 229.

33   Burt and Trivers, *Genes in Conflict*, p. 6.

34 Burt and Trivers, *Genes in Conflict*, p. 229.

35 Image at http://www.sci.sdsu.edu/~smaloy/MicrobialGenetics/topics/
    transposons/Tn10-transposase.gif.

36 Burt and Trivers, *Genes in Conflict*, p. 290.

37 Burt and Trivers, *Genes in Conflict*, p. 281.

38 Burt and Trivers, *Genes in Conflict*, p. 475.

39 Hedges DJ and Deininger PL. "Inviting Instability: Transposable
    Elements, Double-Strand Breaks, and the Maintenance of Genome
    Integrity, *Mutat Res* 616, nos. 1–2 (March 1, 2007):46–59.

40 Moyes D, Griffiths DJ, and Venables PJ. "Insertional Polymorphisms:
    A New Lease of Life for Endogenous Retroviruses in Human
    Disease," *Trends in Genetics* 23, no. 7 (2007):326–33.

41 Ruprecht K et al. "Endogenous Retroviruses and Cancer," *Cell Col Life
    Sci* 65 (2008):3366–82.

42 Kwon DN et al. "Identification of Putative Endogenous Retroviruses
    Actively Transcribed in the Brain," *Virus Genes* 36, no. 3 (June 2008):
    439–47. Quotation from p. 439.

43 Kwon et al. "Identification of Putative Endogenous Retroviruses
    Actively Transcribed in the Brain."

44 Girard A and Hannon GJ. "Conserved Themes in Small-RNA-Mediated
    Transposon Control," *Trends Cell Biol* 18, no. 3 (March 2008):136–48.

45 Jablonka and Lamb, *Evolution in Four Dimensions*, p. 134.

46 Jablonka and Lamb, *Evolution in Four Dimensions*, pp. 132–37.

47 Volff JN. "Turning Junk into Gold: Domestication of Transposable
    Elements and the Creation of New Genes in Eukaryotes," *Bioessays* 28
    (Sept. 2006):913–22. Quotation from p. 913.

48 Muotri AR et al. "The Necessary Junk: New Functions for Transposable
    Elements," *Hum Mol Gen* 16 (2007): R159–R167. Quotation from p. R159.

49 Jablonka and Lamb, *Evolution in Four Dimensions*, p. 250.

50 Romans 8:20-23.

51 Genesis 1.

52 Image at http://commons.wikimedia.org/wiki/File:Lost_Son-Auguste_
    Rodin-Victoria_and_Albert_Museum-2.jpg.

53 Genesis 3:19.

54 See "Seven Deadly Sins" at http://en.wikipedia.org/wiki/Seven_deadly_sins.

55 Manning B. *A Glimpse of Jesus: The Stranger to Self-Hatred* (New York:
    HarperCollins, 2004).

56 Mentalization is the human ability to read other persons, to perceive their needs and intents, and to be in empathy with their feelings. Mentalization carries with it a sense of compassion for others and a valuing of others. This mental capacity is the glue of all human bonding. It is a skill waiting to be developed.

57 Image at http://en.wikipedia.org/wiki/File:Edward_Hicks_-_Peaceable_Kingdom.jpg.

CHAPTER SEVEN

1 *Kairos* is an ancient Greek word meaning the right or opportune moment, the supreme moment, like a window of opportunity, the moment a pregnant woman delivers. Also, kairos is in a sense timeless, as it reflects God's creativity, his propensity to call Life out of the unformed elements. Courtesy Wikipedia and Reference.com.

2 More on "that which is" in Chapters 9 and 10.

3 Clock time.

4 Image at http://commons.wikimedia.org/wiki/File:Uspenski_Cathedral_iconostasis.jpg.

5 A few of the biblical references are as follows (New Revised Standard Version): Genesis 1:30, 2:7, 6:17, 7:15, 7:22; Job 4:9, 12:10, 27:3, 32:8, 33:4, 34:14, 37:10; Psalms 33:6, 104:29, 146:4; Ecclesiastes 3:19; Isaiah 57:16, 40:7, 42:5; Ezekiel 37:9; Daniel 5:23; Wisdom 7:25; Acts 17:25; Revelation 11:11.

6 Image at http://heritage.stsci.edu/2006/13/index.html.

7 Genesis 1:3.

8 Psalm 33:6.

9 John 1:1, 3.

10 Genesis 12:1.

11 Genesis 2:17.

12 Image at http://commons.wikimedia.org/wiki/File:Jordaens_Fall_of_man.jpg.

13 Genesis 3.

14 Genesis 4.

15 In the Old Testament, look at the Book of Daniel, particularly Daniel 4, where Daniel interprets King Nebuchadnezzar's dream of a great tree being chopped down. Also consider Luke 9:46, where the disciples argue about who among them is greatest, and any passage in the New Testament pertaining to the Pharisees. In fact, the entire Scriptures repeatedly deal with various aspects of hubris.

16 Gordon C and Rendsburg G. *The Bible and the Ancient Near East* (New York: W. W. Norton, 1997).

17 Image at http://commons.wikimedia.org/wiki/File:GilgameshTablet.jpg.

18 Gordon and Rendsburg, *The Bible and the Ancient Near East,* p. 47.

19 Gordon and Rendsburg, *The Bible and the Ancient Near East,* p. 48.

20 Gordon and Rendsburg, *The Bible and the Ancient Near East,* p. 48.

21 Image at http://commons.wikimedia.org/wiki/File:Chicxulub.jpg. Author: Shuttle Radar Topography Mission. Source: http://photojournal.jpl.nasa.gov/catalog/PIa03381.

22 Genesis 8:21.

23 I am indebted to the Rev. S. Dunham Wilson, Episcopal priest and esteemed mentor, now deceased, for this interpretation.

24 Genesis Chapter 1.

25 Bateman A and Fonagy P. *Mentalization-Based Treatment for Borderline Personality Disorder* (Oxford UK: Oxford University Press, 2006).

26 John 17:3.

27 Genesis Chapters 12–25.

28 The Book of Exodus.

29 Image at http://commons.wikimedia.org/wiki/File:MosesMosaic.jpg.

30 Image at http://commons.wikimedia.org/wiki/File:David_and_Goliath_by_Caravaggio.jpg.

31 Self-conflict is *treatable!* Humankind might be torn by conflict, but change is possible for those with the motivation to change. The stages of change are (1) *Precontemplation:* "Nothing wrong with me"; (2) *contemplation:* "I'm realizing I have some issues"; (3) *preparation:* "I've got to do something about this"; (4) *action:* "I have a plan and am taking steps"; (5) *maintenance:* "It's working, keep doing what I'm doing"; and (6) *termination:* "The issues I had are resolved, and I'm moving on." From Prochaska JO, Norcross J, and DiClemente C. *Changing for Good* (New York: Avon Books, 1994).

32 Image at http://commons.wikimedia.org/wiki/File:Marcks_Hiob_Nürnberg.jpg.

33 Job 38:1–7.

34 Image at http://commons.wikimedia.org/wiki/File:Bible_Ezechielovo_vidění.JPG.

35 Hosea 1: 4–8.

36 Image at http://commons.wikimedia.org/wiki/File:127.Ezekiel's_Vision_of_the_Valley_of_Dry_Bones.jpg.

CHAPTER EIGHT

1 Image at http://commons.wikimedia.org/wiki/File:El_Greco_021.jpg.

2 John 10:10.

3 Image at http://commons.wikimedia.org/wiki/File:St_Mark_Lamberto_OPA_Florence.jpg.

4 Johnson LT. *The Apostle Paul* (Chantilly, VA: The Teaching Company, 2001).

5 Image at www.traceyclarke.org/christinthewilderness.html.

6 Image at http://commons.wikimedia.org/wiki/File:Valentin_de_boulogne,_John_and_Jesus.jpg.

7 Luke 22:42.

8 Image at http://commons.wikimedia.org/wiki/File:Giambattista_Tiepolo_-_The_Crucifixion.jpg.

9 Image at http://commons.wikimedia.org/wiki/File:Wga_12c_illuminated_manuscripts_Mary_Magdalen_announcing_the_resurrection.jpg.

10 Luke 23:34.

11 Mark 15:39.

12 McKenzie, JL. *Dictionary of the Bible* (Milwaukee, WI: Bruce Publishing, 1965).

13 The 11 disciples drew lots to choose someone to take Judas's place; Matthias became the new 12th disciple. See Acts 1:26.

14 1 Corinthians 15:6.

15 McKenzie, *Dictionary of the Bible,* p. 733.

16 Acts 7:58.

17 Image at http://commons.wikimedia.org/wiki/File:ConversionStPaul.JPG.

18 Image at http://commons.wikimedia.org/wiki/File:El_Greco_-_Saint_Paul.JPG.

19 Johnson, *The Apostle Paul,* "Romans."

20 Peterson, E. *The Message* (Colorado Springs, CO: NavPress, 2002).

21 According to Dictionary.com, a digression in the form of an address to someone not present or to a personified object or idea, as "O Death, where is thy sting?"

22 *Alcoholics Anonymous: The Big Book* (New York: Alcoholics Anonymous World Services, 1978).

23 Romans 3:21-24 reads: "But now, apart from law, the righteousness of God has been disclosed, and is attested by the law and the prophets, the

righteousness of God through faith in [or *through the faith of*] Jesus
Christ for all who believe. For there is no distinction, since all have
sinned and fall short of the glory of God; they are now justified by his
grace as a gift, through the redemption that is in Christ Jesus."

24 Johnson, *The Apostle Paul.*
25 I experienced a partial "salvation," the word coming from the Greek
soteria, which means "safety, soundness."
26 Other passages emphasize God's initiative in our salvation: Ephesians
2:8, 9 and Philippians 2:13.
27 John 1:4.
28 Deuteronomy 21:23.
29 Romans 8:2–3, 6, 10.
30 Image at http://commons.wikimedia.org/wiki/File:Paulus_St_Gallen.jpg.
31 Romans 8:18-25.
32 I worked for a time as a psychiatrist at the Ventura County Jail. The
inmates were mostly self-defeating types or drug addicts, with a
smattering of child molesters, but there were also a few who sent
chills down my spine. These were truly evil people who deserved
the label of Antisocial Personality Disorder.
33 Armstrong RH. *Christianity and Change* (Kansas City, MO: Sheed and
Ward, 1990).
34 Lapierre D. *The City of Joy* (New York: Warner Books, 1985).
35 Pillard RC and Bailey JM. "Human Sexual Orientation Has a Heritable
Component," *Hum Biol* 70, no. 2 (April 1998):347–65.
36 Kendler KS, Thornton LM, Silman SE, and Kessler RC. "Sexual Orientation in
a U.S. National Sample of Twin and Nontwin Sibling Pairs,"
Am J Psychiatry 157 (2000):1843–46.
37 Rahman Q. "The Neurodevelopment of Human Sexual Orientation," *Neurosci
Biobehav Rev* 299, no. 7 (2005):1057–66.
38 Roughgarden, J. *Evolution's Rainbow* (Berkeley: Univ. of Calif. Press, 2004, 2009).
39 Image at http://apod.nasa.gov/apod/ap100513.html

CHAPTER NINE

1 Image at http://commons.wikimedia.org/wiki/File:CuyamaValley
Springtime.jpg.
2 Image at http://commons.wikimedia.org/wiki/File:Erdöl_Bohrturm.jpg.

3 Image at http://commons.wikimedia.org/wiki/File:Castro_Street_SF.jpg.

4 Parker WR and St Johns E. *Prayer Can Change Your Life* (New York: Prentice Hall Press, 1957).

5 Luke 11:13.

6 Job 38-39.

7 Matthew 6:34.

8 Image at http://commons.wikimedia.org/wiki/File:Grotte_Massabielle.jpg.

9 Mt. Calvary retreat house was destroyed in a huge fire in 2009.

10 Psalm 40:1.

11 Psalm 42:1.

12 Psalm 55:1.

13 Psalm 62:1.

14 Johnston W. *Mystical Theology: The Science of Love* (Maryknoll, NY: Orbis, 1995).

15 Kornfield J. *A Path with Heart: A Guide through the Perils and Promises of Spiritual Life* (New York: Bantam, 1993).

16 Armstrong RH. *Christianity and Change: Steps to Growth and Healing in Christian Counseling* (Kansas City, MO: Sheed & Ward, 1990).

17 Genesis 12:1-3.

18 Genesis 32:24-30.

19 Exodus 7.

20 1 Samuel 3.

21 1 Samuel 23:2.

22 1 Kings 3.

23 Reik T. *Listening with the Third Ear* (New York: Farrar & Straus, 1949).

CHAPTER TEN

1 Image at http://commons.wikimedia.org/wiki/File:Charles_Robert_Darwin_by_John_Collier_cropped.jpg.

2 Spencer N. *Darwin and God* (London: Society for Promoting Christian Knowledge, 2009).

3 Lobdell W. *Losing My Religion: How I Lost My Faith Reporting on Religion in America and Found Unexpected Peace* (New York: HarperCollins, 2009).

4 Ehrman B. *God's Problem: How the Bible Fails to Answer Our Most Important Question—Why We Suffer* (New York: HarperCollins, 2008), pp. 3, 5.

5 Ehrman B. *God's Problem*, p. 17.

6 Amos 4:6-12.

7 Amos 5:21-24.

8 Exodus 1:8-10.

9 Joshua 6:21.

10 Matthew 2:16.

11 2 Samuel 11.

12 1 Kings 9:15-22.

13 Acts 7:54-60.

14 Jeremiah 20:14-18.

15 Jeremiah 11:19-20.

16 Psalm 6:2-4, 6-10 and Psalm 83.

17 Ehrman, *God's Problem*, p. 121.

18 Genesis 50:19-20.

19 Genesis 22.

20 Image at http://commons.wikimedia.org/wiki/File:Rembrandt_Harmensz._van_Rijn_035.jpg.

21 Ehrman, *God's Problem*, 205–206.

22 Image at http://commons.wikimedia.org/wiki/File:Rembrandt_-_Das_gastmal_des_Belsazar.jpeg.

23 Daniel 5: 26-28.

24 Image at http://commons.wikimedia.org/wiki/File:Apocalypse_vasnetsov.jpg.

25 Image at http://commons.wikimedia.org/wiki/File:Mural_del_Gernika.jpg.

26 Miller A. *For Your Own Good: Hidden Cruelty in Child-Rearing and the Roots of Violence* (New York: Farrar, Straus & Giroux, 1983).

27 Gao Y et al. "Early Maternal and Paternal Bonding, Childhood Physical Abuse and Adult Psychopathic Personality," *Psychol Med* 40, no. 6 (June 2010): 1007–16.

28 Image at http://commons.wikimedia.org/wiki/File:Emancipation_proclamation.jpg.

29 The Parable of the Sower, Luke 8:4-15.

30 Mark 9:24.

31 Luke 8:15.

32 Moltmann J. *The Crucified God: The Cross of Christ as the Foundation and Criticism of Christian Theology* (New York: HarperCollins, 1991).

33 Matthew 27:46.

34 Moltmann, *The Crucified God*, p. 212.

CHAPTER ELEVEN

1 Philippians 2:5.

2 Kauffman S. *Reinventing the Sacred: A New View of Science, Reason, and Religion* (New York: Basic Books, 2008), pp. 192–93.

3 Freud postulated that children wished to displace the same-sexed parents and sexually possess the opposite-sexed parent. This came to be known as the Oedipus complex.

4 Bowlby R. "The Trouble with Attachment Theory." From an address at UCLA March 9–10, 2002.

5 Mary D. Salter Ainsworth (December 1913–1999) was an American developmental psychologist who extended Bowlby's attachment theory. Specifically, she developed an experimental method called "The Strange Situation," to quantify and characterize the attachments of mothers and their babies (Courtesy Wikipedia).

6 Main, M. "The Organized Categories of Infant, Child, and Adult Attachment: Flexible versus Inflexible Attention under Attachment-Related Stress," *J Am Psychoanal Assoc* 48, no. 4 (December 2000):1055–96.

7 Main, "The Organized Categories of Infant, Child, and Adult Attachment: Flexible versus Inflexible Attention under Attachment-Related Stress," p. 1091.

8 Adapted from Main, "The Organized Categories of Infant, Child, and Adult Attachment," p. 1091.

9 Hesse E. and Main M. "Disorganized Infant, Child, and Adult Attachment: Collapse in Behavioral and Attentional Strategies," *J Amer Psychoanalytic Assn* 48, No. 4 (December 2000):1097–1127.

10 I argue in a previous work that the self has two basic drives—the drive for communion and the drive for separation-individuation (Armstrong, RH. *Christianity and Change: Steps to Growth and Healing in Pastoral Counseling,* Kansas City, MO: Sheed & Ward, 1990).

11 The Robertsons greatly helped Bowlby advance his work through their film documentaries of the reactions of young children separated from their parents. Their films can be accessed at www.robertsonfilms.info.

12 Quoted in Main, "The Organized Categories of Infant, Child, and Adult Attachment," p. 1064.

13 Biddle WE. *Hypnosis in the Psychoses* (Springfield, IL: Charles C Thomas, 1967); Biddle WE. "Images, the Objects Psychiatrists Treat," *Archives of General*

Psychiatry 9, no. 5 (1963):464–70; Biddle WE. *Integration of Religion and Psychiatry* (New York: Macmillan, 1955).

14 Miller A. *For Your Own Good: Hidden Cruelty in Child-Rearing and the Roots of Violence* (New York: Farrar, Straus & Giroux, 1983).

15 Allen JG, Fonagy P, and Bateman AW. *Mentalizing in Clinical Practice* (Washington, DC: American Psychiatric Press, 2008), p. 9.

16 Allen et al., *Mentalizing in Clinical Practice*, p. 93.

17 Allen et al., *Mentalizing in Clinical Practice*, p. 19.

18 Allen et al., *Mentalizing in Clinical Practice*, pp. 3–4.

19 Allen et al., *Mentalizing in Clinical Practice*, p. 35.

20 Allen et al., *Mentalizing in Clinical Practice*, p. 69.

21 Allen et al., *Mentalizing in Clinical Practice*, p. 7.

22 Armstrong, *Christianity and Change*, p. 90.

23 Allen et al., *Mentalizing in Clinical Practice*, p. 155.

24 Philippians 2:5.

25 Matthew 4:18; Mark 1:16.

26 John 1: 31-33.

27 John 1:47-51.

28 Image at http://commons.wikimedia.org/wiki/File:Calling-of-st-matthew.jpg.

29 John 2:24-25.

30 John 4:7-42.

31 Peterson E. *The Message* (Colorado Springs, CO: NavPress, 2002).

32 Allen et al., *Mentalizing in Clinical Practice*, pp. 216–17.

33 Masterson JF. *The Narcissistic and Borderline Disorders: An Integrated Developmental Approach* (New York: Brunner/Mazel, 1981).

34 Website is at www.filmclipsonline.com/.

35 Allen JG and Fonagy P, eds. *Handbook of Mentalization-Based Treatment* (Chichester, UK: John Wiley, 2006), pp. 271–88.

BIBLIOGRAPHY

Alcoholics Anonymous: The Big Book (New York: Alcoholics Anonymous World Services, 1978).

Allen JG and Fonagy P, eds. *Handbook of Mentalization-Based Treatment* (Chichester, UK: John Wiley, 2006).

Allen JG, Fonagy P, and Bateman AW. *Mentalizing in Clinical Practice* (Washington, DC: American Psychiatric Press, 2008).

Angier N. "Pursuing Synthetic Life, Dazzled by Reality," *New York Times*, Feb. 5, 2008.

Armstrong RH. *Christianity and Change: Steps to Growth and Healing in Christian Counseling* (Kansas City, MO: Sheed & Ward, 1990).

Azevedo FA et al. "Equal Numbers of Neuronal and Nonneuronal Cells Make the Human Brain an Isometrically Scaled-Up Primate Brain," *J Comp Neurology* 513, no. 5 (April 2009):532–37.

Bailey CH and Kandel ER. "Synaptic Remodeling, Synaptic Growth and the Storage of Long-Term Memory in Aplysia," *Prog Brain Res* 169 (2008):179–98.

Bamford DH et al. "What Does Structure Tell Us about Virus Evolution?" *Curr Opin Struct Biol* 15, no. 6 (Dec. 2005):655–63.

Bassler BL and Losick R. "Bacterially Speaking," *Cell* 125 (April 21, 2006):237–46.

Bateman A and Fonagy P. *Mentalization-Based Treatment for Borderline Personality Disorder* (Oxford, UK: Oxford University Press, 2006).

Biddle, WE. Hypnosis in the Psychoses (Springfield, IL: Charles C Thomas, 1967).

———. "Images, the Objects Psychiatrists Treat" *Archives of General Psychiatry* 9, no. 5 (1963):464–70.

———. Integration of Religion and Psychiatry (New York: Macmillan, 1955).

Bird CD and Emery JN. "Rooks Use Stones to Raise the Water Level to Reach a Floating Worm," *Curr Biol* 19, no. 16 (Aug. 6, 2009):1410–14.

Bloom JD and Arnold FH. "In the Light of Directed Evolution: Pathways of Adaptive Protein Evolution" *PNAS* 106 (June 16, 2009):9995–10000.

Bower B. "Crows Use Sticks, Stones to Show Skills at Manipulating Tools in Lab," *Science News*, Aug. 29, 2009.

Bowlby R. "The Trouble with Attachment Theory." From an address at UCLA March 9–10, 2002.

Burt A and Trivers R. *Genes in Conflict* (Cambridge, MA: Harvard University Press, 2006).

Caporale L. *Darwin in the Genome: Molecular Strategies in Biological Evolution* (New York: McGraw-Hill, 2003).

Collins F. *The Language of God* (New York: Free Press, 2006).

Carroll SB. *The Making of the Fittest: DNA and the Ultimate Forensic Record of Evolution* (New York: WW Norton, 2006).

Castelvecchi D. "Biowarfare: Engineered Virus Can Invade Bacterial Film," *Science News*, June 20, 2007, p. 404.

————. "Live Another Day: African Insect Survives Drought in Glassy State," *Science News*, March 29, 2008.

————. "Love Code: A Twist of Light Only Mantis Shrimp Can See," *Science News*, March 22, 2008.

Cavalier-Smith T. "Predation and Eukaryote Cell Origins: A Coevolutionary Perspective," *Int J Biochem Cell Biol* 41, no. 2 (Feb. 2009):307–22.

Chivian D et al. "Environmental Genomics Reveals a Single Species Ecosystem Deep within Earth," *Science* 322, no. 5899 (Oct. 10, 2008):275–78.

Clark D and Russell L. *Molecular Biology Made Simple and Fun* (St. Louis, MO: Cache River Press, 2005).

Colling RG. *Random Designer: Created from Chaos to Connect with the Creator* (Bourbonnnais, IL: Browning Press, 2004).

Collins F. *The Language of God* (New York: Free Press, 2006).

Coyne JA. *Why Evolution Is True* (New York: Penguin Books Worldwide, 2009).

Cunningham A. "Taken for a Spin: Scientists Look to Spiders for the Goods on Silk," *Science News*, April 14, 2007, p. 231.

Davidov Y and Jurkevitch E. "Predation between Prokaryotes and the Origin of Eukaryotes," *Bioessays* 31, no. 7 (July 2009):748–57.

Dawkins R. *The Extended Phenotype* (New York: Oxford Univ. Press, 1982).

Dietrich LEP et al. "Redox-Active Antibiotics Control Gene Expression and Community Behavior in Divergent Bacteria,"*Science* 321, no. 5893 (Aug. 29, 2008):1203–06.

Denes AS et al. "Molecular Architecture of Annelid Nerve Cord Supports Common Origin of Nervous System Centralizationin Bilateria," *Cell* 129 (April 20, 2007):277.

Dere E et al. "The Case for Episodic Memory in Animals," *Neurosci Biobehav Rev* 30, no. 8(2006):1206–24. Epub 2006 Oct 31.

Dougherty MJ and Arnold FH. "Directed Evolution: New Parts and Optimized Function," *Curr Opin Biotechnol* 20, no. 4 (Aug. 2009):486–91.

Ehrman B. *God's Problem: How the Bible Fails to Answer Our Most Important Question—Why We Suffer* (New York: HarperCollins, 2008).

Eisenberg J. *A Collector's Guide to Seashells of the World* (New York: McGraw-Hill, 1981).

Encounters at the End of the World. A Werner Herzog Film. Discovery Films. Image Entertainment, 20525 Nordhoff Street, Suite 200, Chatsworth, CA 91311.

Evans PD et al. "Microcephalin, a Gene Regulating Brain Size, Continues to Evolve Adaptively in Humans," *Science* 309, no. 5741 (Sept. 9, 2005):1717–20.

Falk D. *Coming to Peace with Science: Bridging the Worlds between Faith and Biology* (Madison, WI: InterVarsity Press, 2004).

Fernald RD. "Evolving Eyes," *Int J Dev Biol* 48 (2004):701–705.

Feschotte C. "The Contribution of Transposable Elements to the Evolution of Regulatory Networks," *Nat Rev Genet* 9, no. 5 (May 2008):397–405.

Forterre P. "The Origin of Viruses and Their Possible Roles in Major Evolutionary Transitions," *Virus Res* 117, no. 1 (April 2006):5–16.

Fowler TB and Kuebler D. *The Evolution Controversy: A Survey of Competing Theories* (Grand Rapids, MI: Baker Academic, 2007).

Freeland SJ and Hurst LD. "The Genetic Code Is One in a Million," *J Mol Evol* 47, no. 3 (Sept. 1998):238–48.

Freeland SJ, Knight RD, and Landweber LF. "Measuring Adaptation within the Genetic Code," *Trends in Biochemical Science* 25, no. 2 (Feb. 2000):44–45.

Freeland SJ et al. "Early Fixation of an Optimal Genetic Code," *Mol Biol Evol* 17, no. 4 (2000):511–18.

Gage R. "Neuronal Plasticity and Neuronal Diversity." Plenary address at the World Congress of Psychiatric Genetics, San Diego, November 2009.

Gao Y et al. "Early Maternal and Paternal Bonding, Childhood Physical Abuse and Adult Psychopathic Personality," *Psychol Med* 40, no. 6 (June 2010): 1007–16.

Gehring WJ. "New Perspectives on Eye Development and the Evolution of Eyes and Photoreceptors," *J Heredity* 96, no. 3 (2005):171–84.

Gerstein M and Zheng D. "The Real Life of Pseudogenes," *Scientific American*, Aug. 2006, 48–55.

Gibbons A. "Breakthrough of the Year: *Ardipithecus ramidus*," Science 326 (Dec. 18, 2009):1598.

Girard A and Hannon GJ. "Conserved Themes in Small-RNA-Mediated Transposon Control," *Trends Cell Biol* 18, no. 3 (March 2008):136–48.

Glanzman DL. "New Tricks for an Old Slug: The Critical Role of Postsynaptic Mechanisms in Learning and Memory in *Aplysia*," Prog Brain Res 169 (2008):277–92.

Goldsmith E. "Intelligence Is Universal in Life," *Riv Bio.* 93, no. 3 (Sept.–Dec. 2000):399–411.

Gordon C and Rendsburg G. *The Bible and the Ancient Near East* (New York: WW Norton 1997).

Harold F. *The Way of the Cell: Molecules, Organisms, and the Order of Life* (London: Oxford University Press, 2001).

Harrison PM and Gerstein M. "Studying Genomes Through the Aeons: Protein Families, Pseudogenes and Proteomic Evolution," *J Mol Evol* 318, no. 5 (May 17, 2002):1155–74.

Hedges DJ and Deininger PL. "Inviting Instability: Transposable Elements, Double-Strand Breaks, and the Maintenance of Genome Integrity, *Mutat Res* 616, nos. 1–2 (March 1, 2007):46–59.

Hesse E and Main M. "Disorganized Infant, Child, and Adult Attachment: Collapse in Behavioral and Attentional Strategies," *J Amer Psychoanalytic Assn* 48, No. 4 (2000):1097–1127.

Iturriaga G, Suárez R, and Nova-Franco B. "Trehalose Metabolism: From Osmoprotection to Signaling," *Int J Mol Sci* 10 (2009):3793–3810.

Jablonka E and Lamb M. *Evolution in Four Dimensions: Genetic, Epigenetic, Behavioral, and Symbolic Variation in the History of Life* (Cambridge, MA: MIT Press, 2005).

Jablonka E and Lamb MJ. "Précis of Evolution in Four Dimensions," *Behav Brain Sci.* 30, no. 4 (Aug. 2007):353–65.

Jiang Y et al. "Epigenetics in the Nervous System," *J Neurosci* 28, no. 46 (Nov. 12, 2008):11753–59.

Johnson LT. *The Apostle Paul* (Chantilly, VA: The Teaching Company, 2001).

Johnston W. *Mystical Theology: The Science of Love* (Maryknoll, NY: Orbis, 1995).

Kandel E. *In Search of Memory: The Emergence of a New Science of Mind* (New York: WW Norton, 2006).

Kauffman S. *Reinventing the Sacred: A New View of Science, Reason, and Religion* (New York: Basic Books, 2008), pp. 192-93.

Kendler KS, Thornton LM, Silman SE, and Kessler RC. "Sexual Orientation in a U.S. National Sample of Twin and Nontwin Sibling Pairs," *Am J Psychiatry* 157 (2000):1843–46.

Kirschner MW and Gerhart JC. *The Plausibility of Life* (New Haven, CT: Yale University Press, 2005).

Koch C and Greenfield S. "How Does Consciousness Happen?" *Scientific American*, Oct. 2007, pp. 76–83.

Koonin EV. "The Biological Big Bang Model for the Major Transitions in Evolution," *Biol Direct* 20, no. 1 (2007):21.

Kornfield J. *A Path with Heart: A Guide through the Perils and Promises of Spiritual Life* (New York: Bantam, 1993).

Kwon DN et al. "Identification of Putative Endogenous Retroviruses Actively Transcribed in the Brain," *Virus Genes* 36, no. 3 (June 2008):439–47.

Lake JA. "Evidence for an Early Prokaryotic Endosymbiosis," *Nature* 460, no. 7258 (Aug. 20, 2009):967–71.

Lapierre D. *The City of Joy* (New York: Warner Books, 1985).

Lieberman DE and Hall BK. "The Evolutionary Developmental Biology of Tinkering: An Introduction to the Challenge," *Novartis Found Symp* 284 (2007):1–19.

Lobdell W. *Losing My Religion: How I Lost My Faith Reporting on Religion in America and Found Unexpected Peace* (New York: HarperCollins, 2009).

Lynch M. "The Frailty of Adaptive Hypotheses for the Origins or Organismal Complexity," *PNAS* 104 (May 15, 2007):8597–8604.

Main M. "The Organized Categories of Infant, Child, and Adult Attachment: Flexible versus Inflexible Attention under Attachment-Related Stress," *J Am Psychoanal Assoc* 48, no. 4 (December 2000):1055–96.

Manning B. *A Glimpse of Jesus: The Stranger to Self-Hatred* (New York: Harper Collins, 2004).

Margulis L. "The Conscious Cell," *Ann NY Acad Sci* 929 (April 2001):55–70.

Margulis L et al. "Community Living Long Before Man: Fossil and Living Microbial Mats and Early Life," *Sci Total Environ* 56 (1986):379–97.

Margulis L and Sagan D. *What Is Life?* (Berkeley and Los Angeles: Univ. of Calif. Press, 1995).

Martinez-Romero E. "Coevolution in Rhizobium-Legume Symbiosis?" *DNA Cell Biol* 28, no. 8 (Aug. 2009):361–70.

Masterson JF. *The Narcissistic and Borderline Disorders: An Integrated Developmental Approach* (New York: Brunner/Mazel, 1981).

Maugh T II. "Fossils Shed Light on Human Lineage," *Los Angeles Times,* Aug. 9, 2007.

Maxmen A. "Animal Origins: Genome Reveals Early Complexity," *Science News,* Feb. 16, 2008, pp. 99–100.

McKenzie JL. *Dictionary of the Bible* (Milwaukee, WI: Bruce Publishing, 1965).

Mekel-Bobrov N et al. "Ongoing Adaptive Evolution of ASPM, a Brain Size Determinant in *Homo sapiens,*" Science 309, no. 5741 (Sept. 9, 2005):1720–22.

Menninger K. *Man against Himself* (San Diego, CA: Harcourt Brace Jovanovich, 1985).

Milius S. "Pothole Pals: Ants Pave Roads for Fellow Raiders," *Science News,* June 2, 2007.

Milius S. "Slave Ants Rebel," *Science News,* Sept. 13, 2008, p. 6.

Miller A. *For Your Own Good: Hidden Cruelty in Child-Rearing and the Roots of Violence* (New York: Farrar, Straus & Giroux, 1983).

Miller KR. *Only a Theory: Evolution and the Battle for America's Soul* (New York: Viking Press, 2008).

Moltmann J. *The Crucified God: The Cross of Christ as the Foundation and Criticism of Christian Theology* (New York: HarperCollins, 1991).

Morris SC. *Life's Solution: Inevitable Humans in a Lonely Universe* (Cambridge, UK: Cambridge Univ. Press, 2003).

Moyes D, Griffiths DJ, and Venables PJ. "Insertional Polymorphisms: A New Lease of Life for Endogenous Retroviruses in Human Disease," *Trends in Genetics* 23, no. 7 (2007):326–33.

Muotri AR et al. "The Necessary Junk: New Functions for Transposable Elements," *Hum Mol Gen* 16 (2007):R159–R167.

Nadell CD et al. "The Evolution of Quorum Sensing in Bacterial Biofilms," *PLoS Biol* 6, no. 1 (January 2008):e14.

"The Origins of Immunity?" *Science News,* August 25, 2007.

Pallen MJ and Gophna U. "Bacterial Flagella and Type III Secretion: Case Studies in the Evolution of Complexity," *Genome Dyn* 3 (2007):30–47.

Palmer D. *Prehistoric Past Revealed: The Four Billion Year History of Life on Earth* Berkeley and Los Angeles: University of California Press, 2003).

Papachristoforou A et al. "Smothered to Death: Hornets Asphyxiated by Honeybees," *Curr Biol* 17, no. 18 (Sept. 18, 2007):R795–96.

Parker WR and St Johns E. *Prayer Can Change Your Life* (New York: Prentice Hall Press, 1957).

Patton P. "One World, Many Minds," *Sci Am Mind*, Dec. 2008/Jan. 2009, pp. 72–77.

Penenberg AL. "Amazon Taps Its Inner Apple," *Fast Company*, July/August 2009.

Perkins S. "Microbes Thrive in Seafloor Rock: Diversity and Abundance Surprise Research Teams," *Science News* (June 21, 2008).

Persico, J. *Eleventh Month, Eleventh Day, Eleventh Hour: Armistice Day, 1918* (New York: Random House, 2005), p. 392.

Peterson E. *The Message* (Colorado Springs, CO: NavPress, 2002).

Phillips B and Shine R. "When Dinner Is Dangerous: Toxic Frogs Elicit Species-Specific Responses from a Generalist Snake Predator," *Am Nat* 170, no. 6 (Dec. 2007):936–42.

Pillard RC and Bailey JM. "Human Sexual Orientation Has a Heritable Component," *Hum Biol* 70, no. 2 (April1998):347–65.

Powell S and Franks NR. "How a Few Help All: Living Pothole Plugs Speed Prey Delivery in the Army Ant *Eciton burchellii*," *Animal Behavior* 73, no.6 (June 2007).

Prabhakar S et al. "Human-Specific Gain of Function in a Developmental Enhancer," *Science* 321, no. 5894 (Sept. 5, 2008):1346–50.

Prior H, Schwarz A, and Gunturkun O. "Mirror-Induced Behavior in the Magpie (Pica pica): Evidence of Self-Recognition," *PLoS Biol* 6, no. 8 (Aug. 19, 2008):e202.

Prochaska JO, Norcross J, and DiClemente C. *Changing for Good* (New York: Avon Books, 1994).

Putnam NH et al. "Sea Anemone Genome Reveals Ancestral Eumetazoan Gene Repertoire and Genomic Organization," *Science* 317, no. 5834 (July 6, 2007):86–94.

Quina AS, Buschbeck M, and Di Croce L. "Chromatin Structure and Epigenetics," *Biochem Pharmacol* 72, no. 11 (Nov. 30, 2006):1563–69.

Rahman Q. "The Neurodevelopment of Human Sexual Orientation," *Neurosci Biobehav* Rev 299, no. 7 (2005):1057–66.

Reed DL et al. "Genetic Analysis of Lice Suggests Direct Contact between Modern and Archaic Humans," *PLoS Biol* 2, no. 11 (Oct. 5, 2004).

Reik T. *Listening with the Third Ear* (New York: Farrar & Straus, 1949).

Robinson D. *Consciousness and Mental Life* (New York: Columbia University Press, 2008).

Roces F. "Individual Complexity and Self-Organization in Foraging by Leaf-Cutting Ants," *Biol Bull* 202, no. 3 (June 2002):306–13.

Roughgarden J. *Evolution and Christian Faith* (Washington, DC: Island Press, 2006).

———. *Evolution's Rainbow* (Berkeley: Univ. of Calif. Press, 2004, 2009).

———. *The Genial Gene* (Berkeley: Univ. of Calif. Press, 2009).

Roussel EG et al. "Extending the Sub-Sea-Floor Biosphere," *Science* 320, no. 5870 (May 23, 2008):1046.

Ruprecht K et al. "Endogenous Retroviruses and Cancer," *Cell Col Life Sci* 65 (2008):3366–82.

Ryan F. *Darwin's Blind Spot* (Boston, New York: Houghton Mifflin, 2002).

Saey TH. "Bacteria Make Molecular Snorkels for Surviving in Crowded Spaces," *Science News*, January 17, 2009, p. 8.

Saey TH. "Epigenetics: From Islands to the Shores: Tissue-Specific DNA Tagging Found in Unexpected Regions," *Science News*, February 14, 2009.

Saey TH. "Gold Mine Houses Community of One," *Science News*, November 8, 2008, p. 20.

Sahagun L. "Crashing Grunion's Beach Party: Researchers Collect Eggs, Sperm in an Effort to Establish a Stable Captive Population," *Los Angeles Times*, April 15, 2008, p. B1.

Sakai H et al. "Frequent Emergence and Functional Resurrection of Processed Pseudogenes in the Human and Mouse Genomes," *Gene* 389, no. 2 (March 15, 2007):196–203.

Sakurai M et al. "Vitrification Is Essential for Anhydrobiosis in an African Chiromomid, *Polypedilum vanderplanki*," PNAS 105 no. 13 (April 1, 2008):5093–98.

Sanders L. "Nonstop Godwit Flights," *Science News*, Nov. 22, 2008.

Sanders L. "Slime Mold as Master Engineer," *Science News*, Feb. 13, 2010.

Santelli CM et al. "Abundance and Diversity of Microbial Life in Ocean Crust," *Nature* 453, no. 7195 (May 29, 2008):653–56.

Scheme of Influenza A Virus Replication, "Influenza A Virus," Wikimedia Commons.

Schrödinger E. *What Is Life? The Physical Aspect of the Living Cell; with "Mind and Matter," and "Autobiographical Sketches"* (Cambridge, UK: Cambridge University Press, 1967).

Schwartz J and Begley S. *The Mind and the Brain* (New York: ReganBooks, 2002).

Shapiro, JA. "A 21st Century View of Evolution: Genome System Architecture, Repetitive DNA, and Natural Genetic Engineering," *Gene* 345 (2005):91–100.

Shapiro, JA. "Bacteria Are Small But Not Stupid: Cognition, Natural Genetic Engineering and Socio-Bacteriology," *Stud Hist Philos Biol Biomed Sci* 38, no. 4 (Dec. 2007):807–19. Epub 2007 Nov 19.

Siepka SM et al. "Genetics and Neurobiology of Circadian Clocks in Mammals," *Cold Spring Harb Symp Quant Biol* 72 (2007):251–59.

Sompayrac L. *How Pathogenic Viruses Work* (Sudbury, MA: Jones & Bartlett, 2002).

Sompayrac L. *How the Immune System Works* (Malden, MA: Blackwell, 2003).

Spencer N. *Darwin and God* (London: Society for Promoting Christian Knowledge, 2009).

Sullivan JC, Reitzel, AM, and Finnerty JC. "A High Percentage of Introns in Human Genes Were Present Early in Animal Evolution: Evidence from the Basal Metazoan *Nematostella vectensis*," *Genome Inform* 17 no. 1 (2006):219–29.

Tattersall I. "How Did Modern Human Cognition Evolve?" *In* H. Cohen and B. Stemmer (eds), *Consciousness and Cognition: Fragments of Mind and Brain* (San Diego, CA: Elsevier, 2007).

Telford MJ. "A single origin of the central nervous system?" *Cell* 129, no. 2 (April 20, 2007):237–39.

Tero A et al. "Rules for Biologically Inspired Adaptive Network Design," *Science* 327, no. 5964 (Jan. 22, 2010):439–42.

Trewavas A. "Aspects of Plant Intelligence." *In* S. C. Morris (ed), *The Deep Structure of Biology: Is Convergence Sufficiently Ubiquitous to Give a Directional Signal?* (West Conshohocken, PA: Templeton, Press 2008).

Valentine J et al. "Fossils, Molecules and Embryos: New Perspectives on the Cambrian Explosion," *Development* 126 (1999):851–59.

Van Schaik CP and Kappeler PM. "Infanticide Risk and the Evolution of Male-Female Association in Primates," *Proc R Soc Lond B* 264 (1997): 1687–94.

Volff JN. "Turning Junk into Gold: Domestication of Transposable Elements and the Creation of New Genes in Eukaryotes," *Bioessays* 28 (Sept. 2006):913–22.

Wagner GP, Pavlicev M, and Cheverud JM. "The Road to Modularity" *Nat Rev Genet* 8, no. 12 (Dec. 2007):921–31.

What Is Life? Retrieved January 2009, from http://en.wikipedia.org/wiki/What_Is_Life%3F/.

Wilkins AS. "Genetic Networks as Transmitting and Amplifying Devices for Natural Genetic Tinkering," *Novartis Found Symp* 284 (2007):71–86.

Wright B. "A Biochemical Mechanism for Nonrandom Mutations and Evolution,"
    J. Bacteriology 182, no. 11 (June 2000):2993–3001.

Zhu H et al. "Chasing Migration Genes: A Brain Expressed Sequence Tag
    Resource for Summer and Migratory Monarch Butterflies (Danaus
    plexippus)," *PLoS ONE* 3, no. 1 (Jan. 9, 2008):e1345.

Zhu H et al. "Defining Behavioral and Molecular Differences between Summer
    and Migratory Monarch Butterflies," *BMC Biol* 7 (March 31, 2009):14.

INDEX